Necessity, Volition, and Love

One of the most influential of contemporary philosophers, Harry G. Frankfurt has made major contributions to the philosophy of action, moral psychology, and the study of Descartes.

This collection of essays complements a successful earlier collection published by Cambridge University Press, *The Importance of What We Care About*. Some of the essays develop lines of thought found in the earlier volume. They deal in general with foundational metaphysical and epistemological issues concerning Descartes, moral philosophy, and philosophical anthropology. Some bear upon topics in political philosophy and religion.

A hallmark of Frankfurt's work is his crisp and incisive style, which means that these essays should appeal to a wide range of philosophers as well as to readers in neighboring disciplines who have philosophical interests.

Harry G. Frankfurt is a professor of philosophy at Princeton University.

Necessity, Volition, and Love

HARRY G. FRANKFURT

CAMBRIDGE
UNIVERSITY PRESS

PUBLISHED BY THE PRESS SYNDICATE OF THE UNIVERSITY OF CAMBRIDGE
The Pitt Building, Trumpington Street, Cambridge CB2 1RP, United Kingdom

CAMBRIDGE UNIVERSITY PRESS
The Edinburgh Building, Cambridge CB2 2RU, UK   http://www.cup.cam.ac.uk
40 West 20th Street, New York, NY 10011-4211, USA   http://www.cup.org
10 Stamford Road, Oakleigh, Melbourne 3166, Australia

First published 1999

Typeset in Garamond 3, 10/12 pt, MagnaType™ 3.52 [AG]

*A catalog record for this book is available from
the British Library.*

Library of Congress Cataloging-in-Publication Data
Frankfurt, Harry G. (date)
Necessity, volition, and love / Harry G. Frankfurt.
p.   cm.
Includes bibliographical references.
ISBN 0-521-63299-4. – ISBN 0-521-63395-8 (pbk.)
1. Philosophy.   I. Title.
B29.F6924   1999
110 – dc21   98-8081
CIP

ISBN 0 521 63299 4 hardback
ISBN 0 521 63395 8 paperback

Transferred to digital printing 2003

for Joan

Contents

Preface

The specific focus of my philosophical undertakings shifted during the period in which the essays collected here were written. For a number of years, my work was guided by an intense concern with certain metaphysical and epistemological issues in the philosophy of Descartes. This was followed by a similarly concentrated preoccupation with various interrelated topics in moral philosophy and with what I suppose may plausibly be construed as philosophical anthropology. Descartes has something to say about these topics, but that was not what led me to them; indeed, I never took much interest in those aspects of his thought. My attention was shifted adventitiously, by factors unrelated to the trajectory of my Cartesian studies.

I was first led to study Descartes's thought mainly (if I remember correctly) by a hopeful curiosity about what his professedly uncompromising dedication to methodological skepticism might actually be worth. Early in the *Discourse on Method,* he says that the impetus of his thinking "was always my most earnest desire to learn to distinguish the true from the false in order to see clearly into my own actions and proceed with confidence in this life." That was my most earnest desire too. Moreover, I was inclined by nature to the very sorts of doubt and self-doubt that Descartes proposed to employ constructively against themselves. His reputation as a "rationalist," his lucid style, and the fact that his books are short made him even more appealing. My sustained efforts to recapture the vitality of his thought, and to track its intricacies and its depths, taught me more about philosophy than I have learned in any other way.

For all his insistence upon the primacy of *reason,* Descartes – at least as I understand him – identifies success in inquiry as a matter of encountering irresistible constraints upon the *will*. The requirements of reason are not finally satisfied, nor are its claims decisively vindicated, by the inherent features of rationally endorsed truths. Identifying those features can settle our questions for us only in virtue of a fact about ourselves. The indispensable source and warrant of our confidence in reason, and in the contingent and eternal truths that it enables us to establish, lie in the circumstance that we are – when our attention is properly disciplined – literally incapable of withholding our assent from what we see to have no logically coherent alternative. Descartes's theory of knowledge is grounded in his recognition that we simply cannot help believing what we clearly and distinctly perceive. For him, the mode of necessity that is most fundamental to the enterprise of reason is not logical but volitional – a necessitation of the will.

The significance of volitional necessity in our lives is by no means confined, of course, to its role in cognition. It is manifestly pertinent as well to our attitudes, to our choices, and to our actions. So far as these are concerned, many people have believed that constraining the will of the agent impairs, and at the limit may be altogether incompatible with, his freedom. In my opinion, this is far from being the case. The grip of volitional necessity may provide, in certain matters, an essential condition of freedom; indeed, it may actually be in itself liberating. A number of my essays are devoted to exploring ways in which volitional necessities of one sort or another facilitate, or are essential to, an autonomy that they might be thought to diminish or to preclude.

I have become dissatisfied in recent years with what strikes me as the excessively pan-moralistic approach that many philosophers take to issues concerning practical normativity. For most people, the relevance of their moral obligations as legitimately binding constraints or as proper determinants of choice and conduct is quite limited. What morality has to say concerning how to live and what to do is important, but its importance is often exaggerated; and in any case there are other important things to be said as well. I think that philosophers need to pay more attention to issues belonging to a domain that is partially occupied by certain types of religious thought – issues that have to do with what people are to care about, with their commitments to ideals, and with the protean role in our lives of the various modes of love. These personal issues – to which some of the later essays in this volume are devoted – are generally more pertinent to our most urgent normative perplexities, and it seems to me that they are in considerably more need of conceptual illumination, than the problems concerning obligation and virtue that compose much of the standard repertoire of contemporary moral philosophy.

In most of my work, I have tried to stay closely in touch with problems and with lines of thought that I can recognize and appreciate not only as a professional philosopher but also – and particularly – as a human being trying to cope in a modestly systematic manner with the ordinary difficulties of a thoughtful life. It is sometimes claimed that the analytic philosophy in which I was educated, and to whose ethos and canons of intellectual style I still endeavor more or less to adhere, possesses certain new and especially powerful tools and techniques, which allegedly enable it to achieve an invaluable penetration and rigor but which inevitably also distance it from the uninitiated. I have no idea what these remarkable tools and techniques are supposed to be, and I am pretty sure that I do not possess them.

It is true that serious work on the problems of human life and thought, although it begins in common sense, must necessarily enter into painstakingly detailed investigations of a variety of unfamiliar puzzles and complexities. The results of these investigations could not be easy to comprehend unless they were shallow;

and how would that be worthwhile? On the other hand, the results do not have to be arcane; and I cannot imagine what special tools and techniques they might be thought to require. Surely one need not have been trained in any very distinctive philosophical tradition or skill in order to be able to think clearly, to reason carefully, and to keep one's eye on the ball.

Sources

The essays in this book previously appeared elsewhere in the order in which they are presented here.

1   *Philosophical Review* 73 (1964). Copyright 1964 Cornell University. Reprinted by permission of the publisher.
2   Ibid. 75 (1966).
3   Ibid. 86 (1977).
4   A. Donagan, A. N. Perovich, Jr., and M. V. Wedin, eds. *Human Nature and Natural Knowledge* (Dordrecht: D. Reidel, 1986), pp. 47–61. Reprinted with kind permission from Kluwer Academic Publishers.
5   Originally published in French as "Création continuée, inertie ontologique et discontinuité temporelle" in *Revue de Métaphysique et de Morale,* no. 4 (1987); first published in English in Georges Moyal, ed., *René Descartes: Critical Assessments,* vol. 3. (London: Routledge, 1991).
6   *Philosophical Topics* 17 (1989).
7   *Iyyun, the Jerusalem Philosophical Quarterly* 41 (1992), pp. 3–19.
8   Presidential address delivered in December 1991 to the Eastern Division APA, in *Proceedings and Addresses of the American Philosophical Association* 66.3 (1992).
9   G. C. Noam and T. Wren, eds., *The Moral Self* (Cambridge, Mass.: MIT Press, 1993), pp. 16–27.
10 Eleonore Stump, ed., *Reasoned Faith* (Ithaca, N.Y.: Cornell University Press, 1993), pp. 128–41. Used by permission of the publisher, Cornell University Press.
11 H. F. Fulda and R.-P. Horstmann, eds., *Vernunftbegriffe in der Moderne: Stuttgarter Hegel-Kongress 1993* (Stuttgart: Klett-Cotta, 1994).
12 *Ethics* 104 (1994). Published by the University of Chicago Press.
13 *Social Research* 64 (1997).
14 Delivered as the Kant Lectures at Stanford University, 1997. Previously unpublished.

I

The Logic of Omnipotence

George Mavrodes has recently presented an analysis designed to show that, despite some appearances to the contrary, a certain well-known puzzle actually raises no serious difficulties in the notion of divine omnipotence.[1] The puzzle suggests a test of God's power – can He create a stone too heavy for Him to lift? – which, it seems, cannot fail to reveal that His power is limited. For He must, it would appear, either show His limitations by being unable to create such a stone or by being unable to lift it once He had created it.

In dealing with this puzzle, Mavrodes points out that it involves the setting of a task whose description is self-contradictory – the task of creating a stone too heavy for an omnipotent being to lift. He calls such tasks "pseudo-tasks" and he says of them: "Such pseudo-tasks, not falling within the realm of possibility, are not objects of power at all. Hence the fact that they cannot be performed implies no limit on the power of God, and hence no defect in the doctrine of omnipotence."[2] Thus his way of dealing with the puzzle relies upon the principle that an omnipotent being need not be supposed capable of performing tasks whose descriptions are self-contradictory.

Now this principle is one that Mavrodes apparently regards as self-evident, since he offers no support for it whatever except some references which indicate that it was also accepted by Saint Thomas Aquinas. I do not wish to suggest that the principle is false. Indeed, for all I know it may even be self-evident. But it happens to be a principle which has been rejected by some important philosophers.[3]

1 George Mavrodes, "Some Puzzles Concerning Omnipotence," *Philosophical Review*, LXXII (1963), 221–223.
2 *Ibid.*, p. 223.
3 Descartes, for instance, who in fact thought it blasphemous to maintain that God can do only what can be described in a logically coherent way: "The truths of mathematics . . . were established by God and entirely depend on Him, as much as do all the rest of His creatures. Actually, it would be to speak of God as a Jupiter or Saturn and to subject Him to the Styx and to the Fates, to say that these truths are independent of Him. . . . You will be told that if God established these truths He would be able to change them, as a king does his laws; to which it is necessary to reply that this is correct. . . . In general we can be quite certain that God can do whatever we are able to understand, but not that He cannot do what we are unable to understand. For it would be presumptuous to think that our imagination extends as far as His power" (letter to Mersenne, 15 April 1630). "God was as free to make it false that all the radii of a circle are equal as to refrain from creating the world" (letter to Mersenne, 27 May 1630). "I would not even dare to say that God cannot arrange that a mountain should exist without a valley, or that one and two should not make three; but I only say that He has given me a mind of such a nature that I cannot conceive a mountain without a valley or

Accordingly, it might be preferable to have an analysis of the puzzle in question that does not require the use of this principle. And in fact, such an analysis is easy to provide.

Suppose, then, that God's omnipotence enables Him to do even what is logically impossible and that He actually creates a stone too heavy for Him to lift. The critic of the notion of divine omnipotence is quite mistaken if he thinks that this supposition plays into his hands. What the critic wishes to claim, of course, is that when God has created a stone which He cannot lift He is then faced with a task beyond His ability and is therefore seen to be limited in power. But this claim is not justified.

For why should God not be able to perform the task in question? To be sure, it is a task – the task of lifting a stone which He cannot lift – whose description is self-contradictory. But if God is supposed capable of performing one task whose description is self-contradictory – that of creating the problematic stone in the first place – why should He not be supposed capable of performing another – that of lifting the stone? After all, is there any greater trick in performing two logically impossible tasks than there is in performing one?

If an omnipotent being can do what is logically impossible, then he cannot only create situations which he cannot handle but also, since he is not bound by the limits of consistency, he can handle situations which he cannot handle.

a sum of one and two which would not be three, and so on, and that such things imply contradictions in my conception" (letter to Arnauld, 29 July 1648). "As for the difficulty in conceiving how it was a matter of freedom and indifference to God to make it true that the three angles of a triangle should equal two right angles, or generally that contradictions should not be able to be together, one can easily remove it by considering that the power of God can have no limits. . . . God cannot have been determined to make it true that contradictions cannot be together, and consequently He could have done the contrary" (letter to Mesland, 2 May 1644).

Descartes's Discussion of His Existence in the Second Meditation

The epidemic doubt that Descartes generates in the First Meditation is arrested early in the Second, when he finds in his own existence a belief apparently immune to even the most virulent skepticism. There are versions of this discovery in many of Descartes's works, but it is the *Meditations* which provides his most mature and fully developed account of it. Moreover, some of his most important statements elsewhere concerning the belief that he exists refer to the discussion in the Second Meditation. My aim here is to understand what he says in that discussion.

I

A novel and provocative interpretation of Descartes's views concerning his existence has recently been proposed by Jaakko Hintikka.[1] According to Hintikka, Descartes's assertion of his existence in *cogito ergo sum* is best understood as performatory in character rather than as primarily a matter of inference. Although I find Hintikka's approach fresh and interesting, it is difficult for me to evaluate his analysis of the *cogito* because I cannot make good sense out of the logical apparatus which he brings to bear in the course of developing his interpretation. Let me illustrate this difficulty by considering what he says about construing the *cogito* as an inference.

While he naturally places most emphasis on his original notion that *cogito ergo sum* has a performatory aspect, Hintikka does not deny that *sum* may also be regarded as inferred:

There is no incompatibility whatsoever between saying that *cogito ergo sum* is a performance and that it is an inference. There is no need for one to deny, even if one should claim that the *Cogito* is essentially performative, that in it *sum* is inferred from . . . *cogito,* provided that the sole basis of this inference is the fact that the denial of the corresponding implication "if I think, then I exist" – namely, "I think, but I do not exist" – is existentially inconsistent (self-defeating).[2]

Hintikka defines existential inconsistency as follows:

1 "*Cogito Ergo Sum:* Inference or Performance?," *Philosophical Review,* LXXI (1962), 3–32; and "Cogito Ergo Sum as an Inference and a Performance," *Philosophical Review,* LXXII (1963), 487–496. I will refer to these articles as "*H-1*" and "*H-2,*" respectively.
2 *H-2,* p. 489.

p is existentially inconsistent for the person referred to by *a* to utter *if and only if* . . . "*p*; and *a* exists" is inconsistent (in the ordinary sense of the word).[3]

Now to begin with, this definition of existential inconsistency is defective and surely does not adequately capture the notion which Hintikka wishes to define. For, according to his definition, *p* will automatically be existentially inconsistent for *a* (or, for that matter, for anyone) to utter whenever *p* is itself inconsistent. If *p* is inconsistent, any conjunction in which it is a term will, of course, be inconsistent, including "*p*; and *a* exists." And since an inconsistent statement entails *any* statement, a person who utters an inconsistent *p* will be making a statement which entails that he himself does not exist — the "awkwardness" which Hintikka says is characteristic of existentially inconsistent utterances. To be sure, this defect in Hintikka's definition is not serious. It can readily be eliminated by making explicit the condition that an existentially inconsistent statement or sentence must not be self-contradictory or false for logical reasons alone.

There is, however, a more interesting difficulty in what Hintikka says about *cogito ergo sum* as an inference. His point is that the basis of the inference from *cogito* to *sum* is the existential inconsistency of "I think, but I do not exist." This statement is existentially inconsistent because its conjunction with "I exist" is self-contradictory. But the trouble here is that *any* conjunction in which "I do not exist" is a term will be existentially inconsistent, since it will be inconsistent with "I exist." For instance, the statement "Johnson is a Democrat, but I do not exist" is existentially inconsistent (self-defeating). Now this statement is the denial of "If Johnson is a Democrat, then I exist." Hintikka seems committed to claiming that "I exist" can be inferred from "Johnson is a Democrat": the same basis of inference is available here as in the case of the inference, which Hintikka endorses, from *cogito* to *sum*. That is, the denial of the corresponding implication is existentially inconsistent. Perhaps "I exist" *can* (in some funny sense) be inferred from "Johnson is a Democrat," but such an "inference" would seem to be rather vacuous. Although Hintikka concedes that the *cogito* is an inference, then, his concession does not seem to amount to much and it is hard for me to understand what he has in mind.

Instead of focusing my attention, in what follows, on Hintikka's interpretation, I propose to develop my own account of Descartes's views by examining his text directly. In the course of doing so, however, I shall call attention to various important respects in which Hintikka misreads the key passage in the Second Meditation. Moreover, I shall argue that he fundamentally misconceives Descartes's purpose in discussing his existence. My interpretation of Descartes and my criticisms of Hintikka do not prejudice the question of whether the statement *sum* is performatory. They do indicate, however, that *sum* has an important characteristic which is not brought out by characterizing it as performatory. Hintikka's emphasis on performatoriness is, in my opinion, not so much erroneous as inade-

---

3 *H*-1, p. 11.

quate. It is far from my mind to deny the value of some of Hintikka's insights. But he does not tell the whole story and, because of his logical and textual errors, he does not even tell his part of the story well.

II

Descartes begins the Second Meditation with a brief review of the skeptical position to which he has so far been led. Then he asks a new question: "I myself, am I not at least something?" In thinking of himself, he is struck by the possibility that he has come across a belief which is not rendered uncertain by the First Meditation's arguments. This belief is formulated only in the vaguest way: "I am something," or *sum*. But without first seeking to make it more precise or explicit, Descartes undertakes to confront it with the grounds for doubt which he has already developed in his examination of sensory beliefs.

His discussion of *sum* proceeds in four steps, following the question with which it begins:

I myself, am I not at least something? (a) But I have already denied that I had either senses or a body. Yet I hesitate, for what follows from that? Am I so dependent on body and senses that I cannot exist without them? (b) But I persuaded myself that there was nothing at all in the world – that there was no heaven, no earth, no minds, nor any bodies. Did I not, then, also persuade myself that I was nothing? Certainly not. I doubtless did exist if I persuaded myself of something or if I merely thought of something. (c) But there is some sort of very powerful and cunning deceiver, who employs all his ingenuity to deceive me about everything. Then there is no doubt that I exist, if he deceives me; and though he deceive me as much as he likes, he can never bring it about that I am nothing as long as I think that I am something. (d) Hence, after having thought about it thoroughly and carefully examined everything, we must come to the settled conclusion that this proposition: *I am, I exist,* is necessarily true each time that I pronounce it or that I conceive it in my mind.[4]

This passage is clearly related to the dictum *cogito ergo sum;* indeed, Hintikka describes it as "Descartes's formulation of the *cogito* in the Second Meditation."[5] It is worth noticing at the start, however, that the passage consists of a number of different statements, *none* of which is the *cogito*. The statement *I think, therefore I am* simply does not occur in the passage at all; nor does any exactly equivalent statement. In fact, so far as I know, the *cogito* as such does not appear anywhere in the *Meditations*.

In the course of his discussion, Descartes does make a statement which closely resembles the *cogito*. This statement occurs in his argument's second step, along the

4   Charles Adam and Paul Tannery (eds.), *Œuvres de Descartes* (Paris, 1957), VII, 24–25 (Latin); IX, 19 (French), hereafter cited as "*AT*"; Elizabeth Haldane and G. R. T. Ross (eds.), *The Philosophical Works of Descartes* (New York, 1955), I, 150, hereafter cited as "*HR*." I have made some changes in the *HR* translation. In general, I will cite only the easily accessible *HR*, rather than *AT*. I will give no citations for quotations from the familiar and readily perused First and Second Meditations.
5   *H-2*, p. 490.

way to the conclusion, when he affirms that his having thought of something renders his existence certain. It seems clear to me, for reasons I shall give below, that in this step and elsewhere Descartes regards his existence as something inferred. The purpose of the inference, however, is not to prove that *sum* is true. One indication of this is that Descartes's argument does not terminate with the affirmation of his existence in (b); it proceeds until another conclusion is reached in its final step. Analysis of this conclusion reveals that Descartes's concern is not to decide whether or not he exists, or to offer a proof of *sum*, but to establish that his existence is in a rather unusual sense certain or indubitable. To clarify the significance of his conclusion concerning his existence, and to illuminate the intent of his inquiry, I shall follow the dialectical development of his views through the four steps of his discussion.

The first ground for doubt with which Descartes confronts *sum* is the supposition, arrived at in the First Meditation, that he has neither senses nor a body. Interestingly enough, the confrontation is inconclusive; Descartes does not know what to make of the logical relation between *sum* and this supposition:

(a) But I have already denied that I had either senses or a body. Yet I hesitate, for what follows from that? Am I so dependent on body and senses that I cannot exist without them?

It is unclear to him what his supposition implies, if anything, as to his existence. He hesitates; he cannot decide whether the nonexistence of his senses and body constitutes a reasonable basis for doubting that he is "something."

Descartes's puzzlement is readily intelligible, for his conception of his own nature at this stage is vague to the point of vacuity. Questions about existence require, in general, some nonvacuous description of what it is whose existence is being questioned. Since Descartes thinks of himself only as a "something," he is understandably unable to discern the logical relation between the proposition that he exists and the supposition that he has no body or senses. He cannot cope with the question of whether *sum* is undermined by this supposition, for coping with it requires a fuller understanding of his own nature than he is currently able to command.[6]

It is noteworthy, therefore, that in the next step of his discussion Descartes copes in quite a direct and decisive manner with a question which seems to be of an essentially similar kind. In (b), he recalls having been persuaded in the First

6 Some of the difficulties in comprehending Descartes's discussion of *sum*, and his subsequent analysis of his nature, derive from the fact that his discussion must contribute as much to developing an understanding of "I" as to determining the acceptability of *sum*. Descartes cannot deal with the belief that he exists in isolation from the question of *what* he is. It is to be expected, then, that the views which he subsequently develops about his nature will be foreshadowed in the course of his examination of *sum*. The legitimacy of the way in which he handles this matter is a problem of very great interest. I shall make no attempt to deal with it here, however, even though I recognize that limiting the scope of my essay in this way may interfere with a thoroughly satisfactory elucidation of the passage (a)–(d).

Meditation that there are no real things at all, either of a physical or of a mental character. When he asks whether reaching this conclusion was tantamount to being persuaded of his own nonexistence, he answers with no hesitation whatever: "Certainly not. I doubtless did exist if I persuaded myself of something or if I merely thought of something." Now this answer is the closest thing to *cogito ergo sum* in his entire discussion. Without altering its significance in any substantial way, it may in fact be rewritten as "I thought, therefore I existed," which differs from the classical formula only in tense.

Curiously, Hintikka mistranslates the final statement in (b), rendering it in the present tense instead of in the past tense that both the Latin and French texts plainly require.[7] Without wishing to speculate concerning the origins of Hintikka's error, I may suggest that "I thought, therefore I existed" does not fit nearly so well as "I think, therefore I am" with the notion that Descartes's affirmation of his existence is of performatory rather than simply of inferential character. Descartes's use of the past tense makes it much more natural to understand him as concerned with an ordinary inference than with a self-verifying thought-act or performance. There is another matter which may be mentioned in passing. In supporting his interpretation, Hintikka places considerable emphasis on the claim that Descartes derives the belief in his existence from a specific thought. This claim is important to Hintikka, but it is quite mistaken. In (b), Descartes makes a point of saying that the belief that he existed can be derived from the mere fact that he was thinking of *something* – that is, of *anything at all*.[8]

Because of its resemblance to the *cogito*, there is a special interest in clarifying Descartes's final statement in (b) and its role in his examination of the belief that he exists. We must begin by asking what accounts for his ability to grasp so straightforwardly the relation between his existence and the supposition recalled in (b), when he is unable to decide in (a) how a belief in his existence is related to the supposition which he considers there. The critical difference between the two steps must lie in the suppositions with which he confronts *sum*, but exactly what is the relevant difference between them?

III

The supposition which Descartes considers in (a) has to do with the nonexistence of various things, whereas in (b) he attends to the fact that he was persuaded or thought of something. Thus, there is a conspicuous difference in the content of the suppositions which figure in his first two steps. This difference, however, does not account for Descartes's ability to cope readily in the second step with a matter beyond his grasp in the first. After all, why should it be easier for him to discern

7 Cf. *H-2*, p. 490.
8 Cf. esp. *H-1*, pp. 16–18. It is true that Descartes does refer to particular thoughts later in his discussion. I shall consider the significance of these references below.

the logical relation between *sum* and a statement about his thinking (or mind) than between *sum* and a statement about his body?

To be sure, he decides later in the *Meditations* that mind is essential to him while body is logically irrelevant to his existence. This doctrine would be relevant to the problem at hand if Descartes drew a conclusion about his existence in (b) but maintained in (a) that no such conclusion is warranted; for that could be explained by the different logical relationships between himself and his mind on the one hand, and himself and his body on the other. In fact, however, he does not claim in (a) that his supposition does not entail *sum.* On the contrary, he is at a loss in (a) to understand the relation between the two beliefs.

It is not because he starts from body rather than from mind that Descartes cannot, in (a), see either that a conclusion about his existence is warranted or that it is not warranted. When he passes in (b) from "I persuaded myself of something" to "I existed," the nature of the transition is no different than if he had derived "I exist" from "I have a body"; the one transition is no more problematical than the other. In each case, the mere fact of predication suffices and the content of the predication plays no essential role. The transitions are straightforward inferences of the form "$B(a)$ implies (Ex) $(x = a)$."[9]

Thus, the critical difference between (a) and (b) is formal rather than substantive. Descartes's denial that he has a body or senses is not a predication, such as "I have the property of being bodiless and without senses." If it were, his hesitation would be unaccountable; for "I exist" follows as directly from this statement as "I existed" does from "I thought of something." His supposition in (a) is equivalent to "If there are bodies and I do exist, then no body is related to me in such a way as to be mine." In making this statement, he ascribes no property to himself and therefore in no way commits himself to an affirmation of his own existence.

At this stage of his inquiry, in any case, Descartes has not yet developed his doctrine concerning the logical connections between himself on the one hand and his mind and body on the other. He no more knows whether he can exist without a mind than whether he can exist without a body, and it would be inappropriate to invoke his metaphysical theory of the self to explain his hesitation in (a) or his lack of hesitation in (b). The only considerations upon which he relies for his conclusion in (b) are formal, and they have nothing particularly to do with minds or with bodies.

This is confirmed in his reply to a remark by Gassendi. Gassendi attempts to denigrate the special interest of the *cogito* by claiming that Descartes might just as well have inferred his existence from some activity other than thinking, "since our natural light informs us that whatever acts also exists."[10] Although he rejects this suggestion, Descartes accepts the logical point. He insists that there is a vital

9   Cf. *H-1*, p. 6.
10   HR, II, 137.

difference between the *cogito* and such an inference as "I walk, hence I exist"; but he locates this difference in the premises of the two inferences rather than in their logical structures, which he concedes to be the same. The peculiarity of the *cogito*, he maintains, lies in the fact that "there is none of my activities of which I am wholly certain (in the sense of having metaphysical certitude, which alone is involved here) save thinking alone."[11] Deriving *sum* from *cogito* is superior to deriving it from *ambulo*, but only because *ambulo* does not enjoy the metaphysical certitude which characterizes *cogito*.[12]

Two further pieces of evidence bearing on the character of the derivation in (b) may be mentioned briefly. Descartes is explicitly concerned with inference in (a), where he asks what "follows" from the supposition he considers there. It is most plausible to read (b) as continuing the pattern of inquiry in (a) and, accordingly, to understand the second step as similarly concerned with what follows from the supposition with which it begins. Moreover, near the end of the Second Meditation, Descartes says: "it follows . . . clearly that I am or that I myself exist from the fact that I see [this piece of wax]." This too suggests that he regards his existence as something which is inferred.

Now in his *Reply to the Second Set of Objections,* Descartes asserts:

He who says, "I think, hence I am or exist," does not deduce existence from thought by a syllogism but, by a simple act of mental vision, recognises it as if it were a thing that is known *per se.* This is evident from the fact that if it were syllogistically deduced, the major premise, *that everything that thinks is, or exists,* would have to be known previously; but yet that has rather been learned from the experience of the individual – that unless he exists he cannot think. For our mind is so constituted by nature that general propositions are formed out of the knowledge of particulars.[13]

Hintikka takes this passage as evidence that Descartes does not regard *sum* as inferred, but it is a mistake to do so. In the passage, Descartes denies that the *cogito* involves a syllogism, but not that it involves inference altogether. He despised the syllogism, which he thought to be worthless in inquiry, but he did not have similar contempt for inference in general. Thus, the term "inference" can surely not be substituted for "syllogism" in the passage's first sentence. Nor is Hintikka's substitution justified when he reads that sentence as expressing a claim by Descartes that in the *cogito* "he does not logically (syllogistically) deduce *sum* from *cogito*."[14] Descartes is interested only in maintaining that the *cogito* is not an enthymeme with a suppressed major premise. He does not deny that it is a logical inference of the immediate variety. Indeed, the specificity of his concern with the syllogistic model even suggests that he does have immediate inference in mind.

11   *Ibid.,* p. 207.
12   It seems to me, nonetheless, that Descartes's reply to Gassendi misrepresents the uniqueness of the *cogito.* Cf. my discussion of the point in Sec. IX below.
13   *HR,* II, 38.
14   *H-1,* p. 4.

It is true, as Hintikka points out, that Descartes says that existence, rather than the *cogito* as a whole, is recognized "by a simple act of mental vision . . . as if it were a thing that is known per se." But Hintikka is wrong to regard this as "very good evidence" that Descartes finds *sum* self-evident.[15] Hintikka wishes to construe Descartes's simple act of mental vision as one by which the self-evidence of *sum* is intuitively grasped. But then why does Descartes say that he recognizes existence only *as if* it were a thing known per se? If *sum* were intuited as self-evident, it *would* be known per se and not just *as if*. On the other hand, Descartes's qualified statement is not incompatible with the view that *sum* is inferred and that the inference involved is immediate and so unproblematical that it is almost as if *sum* were known per se. The act of mental vision might then be one by which *sum* is inferred from *cogito*. What Descartes says here, however, seems too vague to be relied upon as very good evidence for anything.

Hintikka's "gravest objection" against the view that Descartes infers *sum* is that using an inference of the form "$B(a)$ implies (Ex) $(x = a)$" begs the question:

> We in fact decided that the sentence "I exist" is true when we decided that the sentence "I think" is of the form "$B(a)$." That we were then able to infer "(Ex) $(x = a)$" from "$B(a)$" is undoubtedly true, but completely beside the point.[16]

In my opinion, Hintikka is right about this: Descartes's inference does presuppose *sum*. I disagree, however, with Hintikka's claim that this is a good reason for denying that Descartes infers *sum*. First of all, there is a good deal of textual evidence that Descartes supposes himself to be inferring *sum*, and no good textual evidence that he does not.[17] At the worst, then, it would be necessary to concede that Descartes is guilty of a blunder. But second, as I will explain below, Descartes is not trying to prove that *sum* is true. To charge that his inference is a *petitio principii* misses the point, therefore, since the question with which he is concerned (which is not the question of *sum*'s truth) is not begged in it.

IV

Although the premise from which Descartes derives his existence in (b) is "I thought of something," he acknowledges in his exchange with Gassendi that any other premise of the form "$B(a)$" yields a similar conclusion. The special interest of

---

15 *H-2*, p. 492; also *H-1*, p. 4.

16 *H-1*, p. 8.

17 Since he maintains that Descartes was no more than dimly aware of the performatory character of his assertion, it is easy for Hintikka to cope with statements in which Descartes indicates plainly that he regards *sum* as inferred. He needs only to suggest that these statements come from the dark side of Descartes's imperfect and confused understanding of his own insight. This would be fair enough, if there were good reason to suppose that there is in fact another side. But in citing passages to support his claim that performatoriness plays a role in Descartes's assertion of *sum*, Hintikka misreads the text. Additional evidence to support this claim will be presented below.

inferences from thought to existence must reside, then, in the peculiar character of their premises rather than in their logical structures. Now the explanation of this character which Descartes gives to Gassendi – in terms of the "metaphysical certitude" of *cogito* – is misleading. It does not do justice to the unique logical status of *sum*, and it obscures the radical import of the conclusion about his existence which Descartes reaches in (d). In order to develop a more adequate appreciation of the matter, I shall first explicate what Descartes does in the final two steps of his argument. Then I shall consider the significance of his conclusion and attempt to formulate the insight concerning the indubitability of *sum* in which his discussion culminates.

Of the grounds for doubt developed in the First Meditation, the strongest and the most inclusive is the supposition that there is a demon of great power who is bent on deception. Following his statement in (b) that he existed, Descartes confronts his belief with this demon:

(c) But there is some sort of very powerful and cunning deceiver, who employs all his ingenuity to deceive me about everything. Then there is no doubt that I exist, if he deceives me; and though he deceive me as much as he likes, he can never bring it about that I am nothing as long as I think that I am something.

In this step of his inquiry, Descartes recalls his notion that there is a demon trying to deceive him, and then makes two further statements: (i) "there is no doubt that I exist, if he deceives me," and (ii) "though he deceive me as much as he likes, he can never bring it about that I am nothing as long as I think that I am something."

Descartes does not describe some specific manner in which the demon might try to deceive him and then show that such an effort would be bound to fail. Rather, he reduces to absurdity the hypothesis that he can be deceived in believing that he exists. To be deceived, one must believe or think something erroneously; and (i) asserts that if he believes or thinks something erroneously then he exists. In the special case of the belief that he exists, Descartes would be deceived only if he believed *sum* while *sum* is false – that is, while he is nonexistent; and (ii) asserts that the occurrence of this situation is logically impossible. Since he cannot be deceived without existing, not even an omnipotent demon can arrange for Descartes to believe erroneously that he exists.

What Descartes says in (c) lends itself readily to formulation as the following *reductio ad absurdum*:

I am deceived in thinking that I exist.
If I am deceived about anything, then I exist.
Hence, if I am deceived in thinking that I exist, then I do exist.
Therefore I do exist.
If I do exist, then I am not deceived in thinking that I exist.
Therefore, I am not deceived in thinking that I exist.

It seems clear that this argument fairly represents Descartes's intention in (c). The argument shows that he cannot reasonably doubt *sum*, by showing that there is a contradiction in supposing that *sum* is falsely believed.[18]

Descartes's discussion concludes with a characterization of *sum*. Since his discussion begins with the question of whether he exists, it might have been expected to end with an answer to this question; that is, with an assertion or denial of *sum* or, perhaps, with an assertion or denial that *sum* is certain. Instead, however, the final outcome of the discussion is a characterization of *sum* as "necessarily true each time that I pronounce it or that I conceive it in my mind."

Just what is Descartes saying about *sum* here? It is apparent that he is not calling it a necessary truth in the familiar logical sense. In this sense, a proposition is necessarily true if its denial is self-contradictory; but the denial of *sum* is not a formal contradiction. Moreover, logical properties do not come and go. Hence, if what Descartes had in mind were necessary truth in the logical sense, it would be absurd for him to specify, as he does, the times when *sum* is necessarily true.

Descartes's conclusion *can* appropriately be formulated as an ascription of logically necessary truth to a certain proposition, but that proposition is not *sum*. It is the proposition that *sum* is true whenever he pronounces or conceives it. His conclusion is, in other words, that it is logically impossible for him to pronounce or to conceive *sum* without *sum* being true. This conclusion in no way denies, of course, that *sum* is logically contingent. When Descartes describes *sum* as necessarily true on certain occasions, he does not mean that on those occasions it possesses the logical property of necessary truth. He means that it is a logically necessary truth that *sum* is true on those occasions.[19]

V

It will be easier to appreciate the role of this statement in Descartes's inquiry if care is taken to distinguish it from several other statements which are similar to it. In

18 It may be noted that (c) involves a shift in tense. Descartes infers in (b) that he existed at the time, during the first of his meditations, when he persuaded himself that there is no heaven, no earth, etc. But the demon is not invoked to threaten this belief; in (c), Descartes does not refer to "I existed" but to "I exist." The explanation of this shift is fairly simple and has little philosophical significance. Descartes's use of the past tense in (b) arises out of the narrative mode of his discourse in the *Meditations*, which recounts what transpired during a series of meditations taking place on successive days. Early in the second of these meditations, it occurs to him that what happened yesterday entails that he existed then. But he is not especially interested in his existence at any particular time, and when he shifts to the present tense in (c), he is best understood as concerned with developing a generalized or tenseless account of the belief that he exists. His affirmation in (b) concerning his past existence is due merely to the literary or pedagogical strategy which he adopts in the *Meditations*, it seems to me, and reflects no analytical necessities of his inquiry.

19 The following statement from *Principles of Philosophy* tends to confirm this way of understanding Descartes's conclusion: "We cannot conceive that we who doubt . . . are not; for there is a *contradiction* in conceiving that what thinks does not exist at the same time that it thinks" (Pt. I, sec. vii; *HR*, I, 221; emphasis added).

the first place, then, his conclusion is not that *sum* is true whenever he is thinking, or that his thinking entails his existing. Despite the fact that the *cogito* does not occur in the Second Meditation, readers may feel a strong inclination to suppose that Descartes's examination of the question of his existence *must* culminate, regardless of the language used, in his most famous insight. But his conclusion does not concern thinking in general as the *cogito* does. It concerns pronouncing *sum* or conceiving it. Thus, his conclusion cannot be regarded as equivalent to *cogito ergo sum*.

Second, since pronouncing a proposition or conceiving it in one's mind are not the same as asserting or believing it, Descartes's conclusion is not that *sum* is necessarily true whenever it is believed. No doubt Descartes realized that *sum* cannot be believed falsely, but this is not his conclusion. What he evidently has in mind is, rather, that *sum* is necessarily true whenever it is *considered* — that it is logically impossible for *sum* to be so much as formulated or entertained without being true. A proposition may be formulated in words ("pronounced") or it may be formulated merely in thought ("conceived in my mind"). Descartes's point is that *sum* cannot be formulated at all unless it is true; and that it is true, accordingly, whenever it is considered.

Hintikka misses this point. Indeed, his interpretation relies quite heavily on a serious misreading of (d). In line with his thesis that *cogito ergo sum* is performatory, he claims that the function of the term *cogito* is

to express the performatory character of Descartes's insight; it refers to the "performance" (to the act of thinking) through which the sentence "I exist" may be said to verify itself. . . . [This act is] an attempt to think in the sense of making myself believe . . . that I do not exist.[20]

This is not the only thought-act through which, according to Hintikka, *sum* may verify itself: "The performance through which an existentially self-verifying sentence verifies itself may also be an act uttering it."[21] In support of this, Hintikka points out that Descartes speaks in (d) of uttering *sum*.

Actually, Descartes refers to neither of the thought-acts which Hintikka describes. It has already been pointed out that in (b), where an analogue of *cogito ergo sum* occurs, Descartes asserts that his existence is assured by the fact that he was thinking of *anything;* and in fact, what he was actually thinking of was not his own existence or nonexistence at all, but the nonexistence of heaven and earth. Although Hintikka's account of the thought-act which produces the indubitability of *sum* is apparently at odds with what Descartes says in (b), it may appear to fit quite well with the statement in (d) that *sum* is "necessarily true each time that I pronounce it or that I conceive it in my mind." This statement does seem at first glance to support Hintikka's claim that the indubitability of *sum* arises when *sum* is

20 *H-1*, p. 17.
21 *Ibid.*

13

"expressly uttered or otherwise professed."[22] A closer examination reveals an important discrepancy, however.

Hintikka's "uttering" may appear to be about the same as Descartes's "pronouncing." But when Hintikka speaks of uttering *sum* he means "uttering to make a statement" or, as he himself puts it, "uttering the sentence assertively."[23] Now to pronounce *sum* is not to utter it assertively, or to make any statement; at most, it is to formulate the statement in words. The discrepancy becomes more apparent when Hintikka goes on to speak of "professing" *sum*, while Descartes goes on to speak of "conceiving" it in his mind; for professing and conceiving are quite different. To profess *sum* involves asserting that one exists, or thinking that one exists; to conceive *sum*, on the other hand, is more like "entertaining" the proposition that one exists, "formulating it in one's mind," or, perhaps, considering it. It does not involve the making of an assertion, and Hintikka distorts the text when he says that Descartes is concerned in (d) with asserting or professing *sum*.

The thought-acts to which Descartes refers in (b) and in (d), then, are not the thought-acts required by Hintikka's interpretation. In neither place is there any reference to the thought-acts with which Hintikka supposes Descartes to be concerned. Moreover, Descartes indicates in these places a concern with *other* thought-acts which find no place in Hintikka's interpretation. Thus, Descartes's text not only provides no support for Hintikka's thesis, but is actually inconsistent with it.

There is a third statement from which Descartes's conclusion must be distinguished. When he asserts that *sum* cannot be considered without being true, Descartes is not claiming that whoever considers *sum* inevitably believes it. That is, he is not claiming that *sum* is indubitable in the sense that it can never be doubted by anyone. This point needs to be made because Descartes does hold that there are some propositions which are incapable of being considered without being believed, and it is important to notice that *sum* is not among those which he characterizes in this way. Two relevant passages read as follows:

Of [the clear perceptions of the intellect] there are some so evident and at the same time so simple, that . . . we never doubt about believing them true: e.g., that I, while I think, exist; that what is once done cannot be undone, and other similar truths. . . . For we cannot doubt them unless we think of them; but we cannot think of them without at the same time believing them to be true. . . . Hence we can never doubt them without at the same time believing them to be true; i.e., we can never doubt them.[24]

When we apprehend that it is impossible that anything can be formed of nothing, the proposition *ex nihilo nihil fit* . . . is a common notion or axiom. Of the same nature are the following: "It is impossible that the same thing can be and not be at the same time," and that "what has been done cannot be undone," "that he who thinks must exist while he

22 *H*-1, p. 15.
23 *Ibid.*
24 *HR*, II, 42.

thinks," and very many other propositions . . . which . . . we cannot fail to recognise . . . when the occasion presents itself for us to do so, and if we have no prejudices to blind us.[25]

The characteristic with which Descartes is concerned in these passages is not the one that he ascribes to *sum* in (d). In (d), he says that *sum* cannot be considered without being true, while in the quoted passages he speaks of what cannot be considered without being believed.

It is apparent that what Descartes has in mind in the quoted passages are logically necessary statements. His inclusion of "I, while I think, exist" among these statements confirms that the connection between his thinking and his existing is one which he regards as simply a case of an elementary logical entailment. The passages do not refer to *sum* at all. They refer to propositions which do not affirm existence but merely relate it to thinking: "I, while I think, exist" and "He who thinks must exist while he thinks." In (d), on the other hand, what is at issue is a categorical statement: "I exist."

It is clearly one thing for a proposition to be true and another thing altogether for its truth to be apparent to someone who is considering it. What Descartes says about *sum* in (d) is far from being tantamount to the claim that *sum* is known to be true by whoever considers it. So far as (d) goes, it is quite possible for *sum* to be considered without being believed and, a fortiori, without being known to be true.

This does not interfere with understanding Descartes's conclusion in (d) as being that *sum* is in an important sense indubitable. Although (d) does not assert that *sum* is indubitable in the descriptive sense of the term, according to which what is indubitable is what cannot in fact be doubted by anyone, there are other senses of indubitability as well. In particular, there are normative senses, according to which what is indubitable is what there is no reason to doubt or what there can be no reason to doubt. Descartes's intention in (d) is, as a matter of fact, to assert the indubitability of *sum* in a normative sense. This sense of indubitability must now be elucidated.

VI

It must be recognized that when Descartes opens his discussion with a question about *sum*, he is not actually proposing an inquiry about a single statement but about the members of an indefinitely large class of statements. There is a temporal reference implicit in *sum* – "I exist now" – which differs on each occasion that *sum* is asserted or considered. Now it is not his existence at any particular time with which Descartes is concerned. In setting out to test the belief that he exists against the doubts generated in the First Meditation, it is not any particular statement – "I exist at time $t1$" – whose indubitability preoccupies him.

25 *Principles of Philosophy*, Pt. I, sec. xlix; *HR*, I, 238–239.

Indeed, it is quite obvious that no such statement can be altogether immune to doubt. At any given time, a person can readily doubt his own existence at some other time; there is always some time $t2$ at which a person may reasonably doubt his own existence at time $t1$, where $t2$ differs from $t1$. The question which interests Descartes is whether there can be a time at which he could not reasonably count on his own existence *at that time*. What he wants to know is whether there could ever be an occasion when it would be reasonable for him to refuse assent to the statement "I exist now."[26]

The peculiar certainty of *sum*, which Descartes seeks to establish, may be elucidated by contrasting it with the indubitability of various other types of statement. There are many logically contingent statements which, when they are true, may be known with certainty. Statements about the sensory content of experience, for instance, are widely supposed to be of this sort. Thus, a person who feels a pain may reasonably regard his belief that a pain is occurring as entirely beyond his doubt. But suppose that a person does not feel pain. Then it may be quite reasonable for him to doubt that a pain is occurring; moreover, he can be certain that he himself is feeling no pain. The statement that a pain is occurring is one which may be beyond a person's doubt on some occasions but dubitable on others. And a person's statement that he himself feels pain is one which he may at certain times properly regard as indubitable, while at other times he may know quite well that it is false.

The situation is similar with regard to empirical statements. Although a person may sometimes have evidence for an empirical statement which leaves no room for doubt, it may be reasonable for him to doubt the statement at other times when this evidence is not available to him. Moreover, if the statement were in fact false, it might be quite possible for him to have conclusive evidence of its falsity or at least to have evidence sufficient to justify reasonable doubt concerning its truth.

Finally, there are statements which are rendered true by the mere act of making them, such as "I am making a statement." Because of their self-confirming character, such statements cannot be made falsely. Nonetheless, there are occasions when they can reasonably be doubted or when they can be known to be false. When I am not making a statement, I may know that I am not. Moreover, there may be circumstances in which I am simply not sure whether what I am doing constitutes making a statement, and in those circumstances I can reasonably doubt whether I am doing so. The same holds, of course, for more straightforward and commonplace performatives, such as "I hereby promise to do such and such." When I am not promising, I may be well aware that I am not; and in certain circumstances I may have a reasonable doubt as to whether what I am doing really constitutes the making of a promise.

Statements of the sorts just considered may be beyond doubt under certain conditions, but there are also conditions under which they may reasonably be

---

26 His reason for being interested in this question will be considered below.

doubted or known to be false. Everything depends upon the evidence currently available or upon what is currently happening. A person's own existence, on the other hand, is something which he can never have good reason to doubt. As Descartes says in (d), it is logically impossible for there to be an occasion on which a person considers the statement *sum* and on which the statement is false. The indubitability of *sum* thereby differs from that which a statement may enjoy at certain times and not at others.

VII

Sum is not altogether unique in this respect. There are many statements concerning which it is contradictory to suppose that someone considers them while they are false or that someone believes them falsely. Indeed, all logically necessary truths have this characteristic. Although logically necessary statements resemble *sum* in this, however, they differ from it in other important ways. For one thing, they are entirely formal in content and involve no assertion of existence; on the other hand, *sum* is a synthetic and logically contingent statement which does assert the existence of something. This renders it of greater relevance to Descartes's inquiry.[27]

There is another difference as well, which is closely related to the first. Though it is contradictory to suppose that a person entertains or believes either *sum* or a logically necessary statement while it is false, the source of the contradiction is not the same in the two cases. In the latter case, it is due to the fact that the denial of a logically necessary statement is self-contradictory. This means that recognizing the indubitability of such a statement involves recognizing that the statement is true. In the case of *sum*, however, the situation is otherwise. When Descartes recognizes that there is a contradiction in supposing that he entertains or believes *sum* while it is false, this is by no means tantamount to his knowing that *sum* is true.

For the indubitability of *sum* is not a function of its logical status or of its truth, but of its relation to the supposition that it is entertained or believed. Thus, Descartes's conclusion in (d) does not entail his existence, nor does he need to know that *sum* is true in order to be able to affirm this conclusion. This becomes fully apparent if the point made in (d) is applied to some person other than himself. Descartes's conclusion is quite general in import and readily permits such applications. For instance, it justifies the assertion: "It is necessarily the case that the statement *I exist* is true whenever Caesar pronounces or conceives it." Someone who recognizes the correctness of this assertion clearly does not commit himself to regarding *Caesar exists* as true.

27 That Descartes's inquiry is devoted to finding indubitable assertions of existence is clear from numerous statements. In the *Conversation with Burman*, while describing the enterprise undertaken in the First Meditation, he says: "*Il s'agit principalement d'une chose existante: savoir, si elle est*" (*op. cit.*, p. 5). And in the passage from *Principles of Philosophy* which is quoted above in Sec. IV, he makes it clear that his demand for certainty is not satisfied merely by certainties "which of themselves give us no knowledge of anything that exists."

Descartes's discussion is not intended to prove that *sum* is true, in the sense of deriving it validly from premises which have been securely established. It is easy to be misled about this, for a variety of reasons. The discussion begins, after all, with what is apparently a question about the truth of *sum*. Moreover, immediately following the end of his discussion Descartes says: "But I do not yet know clearly enough *what* I am, I who am certain *that* I am," and this suggests strongly that he regards *sum* as having been proven. Finally, Descartes is patently concerned with establishing that *sum* is indubitable, and it is very natural to suppose that this must be tantamount to a concern with proving that *sum* is true. Against these considerations, however, is the plain fact that the final conclusion of Descartes's discussion in (d) involves no commitment to the truth of *sum,* as well as the fact that *sum* is never categorically asserted in the course of his discussion.

It seems to me that Descartes is no more interested in the fact that he exists than he is interested in the facts which he considers in the First Meditation – for instance, that he is seated by a fire, wearing a dressing gown, and so on. Even if he had started out by taking these facts for granted, instead of by suspending judgment about them, the course of his inquiry would hardly have been affected. For his fundamental concern is not with the empirical question of what the facts are but with the epistemological and metaphysical question of how to attain certainty. His primary interest in the various facts he discusses is not an interest in whether or not they are truly facts but in whether it is reasonable to be entirely certain of them. Similarly, when he considers the belief in his own existence, his aim is not to establish its truth value but to reveal its indubitability. To be sure, his conclusion justifies him in asserting *sum*. The justification does not consist in a proof of *sum,* however. It consists in a proof that *sum* can never reasonably be doubted.

VIII

Descartes tries to show that *sum* is indubitable in the sense that he never runs any risk in believing it. His point is not that he has or that he could have conclusive grounds for asserting *sum;* that point, as has been observed, could correctly be made about numerous statements. What he seeks to establish is that whenever he raises the question of his existence – that is, whenever he considers *sum* – it must *always* be reasonable for him to assert that he exists; he need *never* be in doubt about his existence.

Now why is it this particular sort of indubitability which Descartes finds so essential to his enterprise? An important clue to the answer can be found in the opening sentence of the First Meditation, where he announces that his intention is "to build anew from the foundations" in order "to establish something *firm and constant* in the sciences."[28] Scientific beliefs cannot be relied upon to be firm and

28 Emphasis supplied.

constant if there is any chance that their foundations will turn out to need revision. As he proceeds to develop a system of science, accordingly, Descartes requires a foundation which *can never* be subject to doubt. He must have statements for which reasonable grounds for doubt are logically impossible. Otherwise, there will always be a lingering concern that grounds for doubting or rejecting them will one day be discovered and that the structure they support will totter in consequence.

But this in itself does not account for Descartes's refusal to settle for anything less than the kind of indubitability which characterizes *sum.* When a person has a pain he can be quite certain of the belief that he has one, without fear that subsequent evidence will require it to be rejected or held in doubt. Why is such a belief unsuitable to serve as a foundation for science? The reason is that a person cannot always be certain that he has a pain, for sometimes he does not have one. The certainty of beliefs concerning the content of consciousness is, as it were, contingent upon the occurrence of those contents. But the certainty of *sum* is not contingent in this way, since a person can never be aware that he does not exist.

The certainty of *sum* is, so to speak, ubiquitous and inescapable; it has a kind of *generality.*[29] The certainty which may be enjoyed by statements of other sorts lacks this characteristic. Their certainty may not be available when it is needed since, unlike *sum,* such statements are detachable from the facts which confirm them. But *sum* is entailed by the mere fact that it is being considered; hence, it is not detachable from what confirms it. The certainty of *sum* is always current, and there can never be an occasion when a person need admit doubts concerning it.[30]

One of Descartes's doctrines may at first sight seem very difficult to reconcile with what he says about *sum* in the Second Meditation. This is the doctrine that no one can be really certain of anything until he knows that God exists. Since Descartes does not arrive at a knowledge of God's existence until the Third Meditation, how can he properly regard *sum* as indubitable in the Second? In his *Reply to the Second Set of Objections,* Descartes indicates how this difficulty is to be resolved. There he explains:

When I said that we could know nothing with certainty unless we were first aware that God existed, I announced in express terms that I referred *only* to the science apprehending such

29 Because of its generality or inescapability, *sum* may be regarded as a kind of necessary statement, despite its logical contingency. It may not be improper, indeed, to regard it as a synthetic necessary statement.

30 There is another point which may be mentioned, though its relevance is a matter of speculation. Descartes is working toward the establishment of a foundation for scientific thinking, and there is an obvious advantage in providing a foundation which is sharable or transferable from one scientific thinker to another. If the foundation consisted of statements about the content of consciousness, it would differ from one scientist to the next; for one man's experience is not that of another. If it consists of statements like *sum,* however, each scientist can begin from a similar point. *Everyone* can be certain of his own existence, but different men can be certain only of the different contents of their own particular consciousness. Descartes never says anything which shows that he has this point in mind, however, which is why I say that its relevance is a matter of speculation.

conclusions as can recur in memory without attending further to the proofs which led me to make them.[31]

No one can proceed very far in science if he must keep before his mind at all times evidence that confirms the various statements which he has already established and upon the basis of which he seeks to develop additional knowledge. As his work continues, he must be able to rely upon what he has concluded in the past without having to be constantly aware of the proofs which guarantee his conclusions. But if he is not aware of their proofs, how can he be confident of the acceptability of statements previously established?

Clearly, he must count on the recollection that the statements were once satisfactorily proven. Now Descartes's contention is that this recollection is not sufficient unless it is known that God exists; no one can be really certain of a statement which he remembers having once proven unless he knows that God exists.[32] As Descartes makes clear in the passage just quoted, however, it is not necessary to know that God exists in order to be certain of a statement for which one has conclusive evidence immediately before him.

The need for God's guarantee arises only with regard to statements which are detachable from what confirms them. If there can be an occasion on which a statement may be considered without conclusive grounds for it being available, then there can be an occasion on which the statement may reasonably be doubted unless God's existence is known. But *sum* is not a statement of this kind. It is not detachable from evidence which confirms it. A conclusive ground for it is currently available whenever it is considered, since the ground consists simply in the fact that it is being considered.

This ubiquity or generality of *sum*'s certainty accounts for the fact that Descartes's discussion of his existence reaches its conclusion without a categorical affirmation of *sum* being made. The purpose of his discussion is to show that he can count on *sum* whenever he needs it, rather than to affirm it as a current truth.

IX

What Descartes says in his reply to Gassendi about *ambulo ergo sum* is somewhat misleading, for it tends to obscure the character of the indubitability which *sum* enjoys. One point upon which the case for this indubitability rests is that Descartes's existence is entailed by his considering *sum*. This entailment is taken entirely for granted in the discussion. Descartes never analyzes it or subjects it to doubt; he treats it as palpably self-evident and unexceptionable. It is a "clear perception of the intellect" – that is, a logical truth. Like other logical truths, such

31 *HR*, II, 38; emphasis supplied.
32 For an interpretation and analysis of God's role in validating such recollections, cf. my essays entitled "Memory and the Cartesian Circle," *Philosophical Review*, LXXI (1962); and, particularly, "Descartes' Validation of Reason," *American Philosophical Quarterly*, 2 (1965).

as "what is once done cannot be undone," it is "so evident and at the same time so simple" that it cannot be doubted.[33]

But it is also a logical truth that *sum* follows from *ambulo*. That Descartes's existence is entailed by his walking is no less evident to him than that it is entailed by his thinking. Each entailment is an equally clear-cut instance of "$B(a)$ entails $(Ex) (x = a)$." Descartes would be unable to accept *sum* as indubitable, however, if he knew only that it is entailed by *ambulo*. For the question of whether *sum* is true can arise when *ambulo* is not true, and on such an occasion Descartes would have no ground for affirming his existence.

Now the critical point here is not that *ambulo* is a physical-object statement and therefore one which the skeptical arguments of the First Meditation render uncertain. Even if Descartes could be certain about whether or not he is walking, an awareness that his existence is entailed by his walking would still not enable him to regard *sum* as indubitable in the relevant sense. For it might be false that he is walking on some occasion when he considers his own existence. And then it would be reasonable for him to doubt his existence, if he knew only that *sum* is entailed by *ambulo*.

In his reply to Gassendi, Descartes locates the essential difference between *cogito ergo sum* and *ambulo ergo sum* in the "metaphysical certitude" of *cogito*. This suggests that the advantage of deriving *sum* from *cogito* rather than from *ambulo* lies in the fact that *cogito* is immune to the doubts which still beset statements about the physical world, such as *ambulo*. Indeed, Descartes explains that the reason he regards *ambulo ergo sum* as unsatisfactory is that "the motion of the body sometimes does not exist, as in dreams, when nevertheless I appear to walk."[34] Thus he describes the superiority of *cogito ergo sum* as due to the fact that he can be certain of *cogito*, whereas the dream argument undermines the certainty of *ambulo*.

It seems to me, however, that Descartes misrepresents his own case here. The relevant difference between *cogito* and *ambulo* is not, as he says, that he can be certain of the former but not of the latter; it is that the former is inseparable from *sum* whereas the latter is not. In fact, if the account of the matter given to Gassendi were actually correct, there would be a serious gap in Descartes's discussion of his existence in the Second Meditation. For nowhere in that discussion does he either show or assert that *cogito* (or any similar statement) escapes the doubts raised in the First Meditation against statements concerning physical things. If the peculiar value of deriving *sum* from *cogito* actually consisted in the certitude of *cogito*,

---

33 It may seem that Descartes is not entitled to accept logical truths such as these without argument, since he has resolved to doubt everything. To explain his justification for accepting them, and to show that he does not beg any questions in doing so, is beyond the scope of this essay. Let it suffice here to make two points rather dogmatically. Descartes believes that such truths *cannot*, in fact, be doubted; hence, the question of whether they ought to be doubted does not arise. And he regards them as constitutive of rationality, so that accepting them does not beg the question to which his metaphysical enterprise is devoted: namely, how can a rational person achieve certainty?

34 *HR*, II, 207.

Descartes ought to establish or at least to claim that *cogito* is in fact a statement of which he can be certain. He does not, however, do so.

The third step of his discussion is the most plausible place to look for an argument establishing the premise from which *sum* can be inferred, but the certainty of such a premise is not considered there at all. In (c), Descartes first remarks that his existence is entailed by his being deceived; then he asserts that he cannot be deceived about his existence when he thinks that he exists. It is not relevant that he might have argued, if he had chosen, that he cannot be deceived about whether or not he is thinking. The fact is that he presents no such argument. He concerns himself in (c) only with showing that the demon's powers of deception cannot subvert his belief that he exists. Neither in this step nor elsewhere in his discussion does he make the point that *cogito* (or any similar statement) cannot be doubted.

X

Despite what Descartes says to Gassendi, the indubitability of *cogito* is not part of the case made in the Second Meditation for the indubitability of *sum*. The latter does not depend on Descartes's ability to maintain a premise like *cogito* even in the face of the possibilities that he is dreaming or that there is a demon out to deceive him. His discussion of his existence in the Second Meditation is not devoted to showing that he can *prove* that he exists by first becoming certain that he is thinking and then deducing his existence from this premise. Instead of showing that *sum* can be deduced from a premise which is certain in its own right, what Descartes points out is, in effect, that a premise from which *sum* can be elicited is an essential and inescapable element of every context in which the need for assurance concerning *sum* arises. The permanent availability of *sum* rests upon its derivability from a premise which is necessarily available whenever it is needed.

A puzzling feature of Descartes's inquiry is the variety of premises from which his existence is said to be inferable. In (b), the premise is that he *thought of something*. In (c), he says that he exists whenever he *believes that he exists*. In (d), he commits himself to the claim that he exists whenever he so much as *considers the belief that he exists*. Elsewhere in his writings, moreover, Descartes speaks of inferring his existence from the premise that *he is doubting something*.[35] What accounts for this variation?

Each of the inferences is, of course, equally legitimate. But they are not equally appropriate to Descartes's final purpose in his discussion. The most general of them is *cogito,* since it is entailed by all the others: doubting, being deceived, thinking that one exists, considering the belief that one exists – these are all cases of *thinking.* None of the other premises, then, has the same degree of ubiquity as *cogito,* since none of them is in turn entailed by it.

35 *The Search After Truth, HR,* I, 324. Cf. also *Principles of Philosophy,* Pt. I, sec. vii; *HR,* I, 221.

The premise to which Descartes refers in the conclusion of his discussion, however, has a degree of ubiquity which is cut to the measure of his need. There are times when a person can realize that he is neither doubting his existence nor thinking that he exists, and at such times *sum* cannot be derived from these premises. But while there may well be times when a person is not considering his own existence, it is clear that he is *ipso facto* doing so whenever he becomes interested in the question of whether *sum* can be asserted. Moreover, a person can never be aware that he is neither pronouncing *sum* nor conceiving it in his mind: to be aware of this would necessarily involve formulating *sum,* either in words or in thought, and would accordingly not be an awareness that *sum* was not being formulated. Even without claiming that he can be certain of whether he is thinking or of whether he is considering *sum,* therefore, Descartes can properly maintain that a premise entailing *sum* can never be lacking on an occasion when the reasonableness of asserting *sum* becomes a question.

3

Descartes on the Creation of the Eternal Truths

I

In a letter to Mersenne dated 15 April 1630, Descartes remarked that if it had not been for his metaphysical investigations – that is, his endeavors to know God and himself – he would never have discovered the foundations of physics. Without elaborating on this provocative statement concerning the connection between his philosophical and his scientific ideas, he goes on to say that he intends to defer publishing his metaphysics until he has completed a treatise on physics which he is currently writing, and has had an opportunity to observe how it is received.[1] Descartes tells Mersenne, however, that this treatise itself will include a certain amount of metaphysics:

In my treatise on physics I shall discuss a number of metaphysical topics and especially the following. The mathematical truths which you call eternal have been laid down by God and depend on Him entirely no less than the rest of His creatures. Indeed, to say that these truths are independent of God is to talk of Him as if He were Jupiter or Saturn and to subject Him to the Styx and the Fates. Please do not hesitate to assert and proclaim everywhere that it is God who has laid down these laws in nature just as a king lays down laws in his kingdom. There is no single one that we cannot understand if our mind turns to consider it. They are all inborn in our minds, just as a king would imprint his laws on the hearts of all his subjects if he had enough power to do so. The greatness of God, on the other hand, is something which we cannot comprehend even though we know it. But the very fact that we judge it incomprehensible makes us esteem it the more greatly; just as a king has more majesty when he is less familiarly known by his subjects, provided of course that they do not get the idea that they have no king – they must know him enough to be in no doubt about that. [K 11]

This is the earliest account we have of Descartes's remarkable doctrine that the eternal truths are created by God.

Despite his eagerness in 1630 to have Mersenne broadcast the doctrine freely, Descartes never included it in any of his scientific works; nor did he present it recognizably as an explicit part of the argument of any of his philosophical books.

---

1   It is uncertain what treatise this is, but perhaps Descartes is referring to the *Dioptrique*. Cf. his letter to Mersenne dated 25 November 1630, in Anthony Kenny, *Descartes: Philosophical Letters* (Oxford, 1970), pp. 18–19. Hereafter I shall refer to this book as "*K*".

He wrote about it only in various letters, and in his *Replies* to the *Fifth* and *Sixth Objections* against his *Meditations*. In none of those places did he explain its role in his philosophy, or the special pertinence he evidently believed it to have to his physics.

The doctrine presents a variety of difficulties, some of which it may well be impossible to resolve. It is problematic just what the doctrine is, what Descartes thought it implied, what motivated him to adopt it, how he would have met the rather plausible charge that it is incoherent, what his main arguments for it are, where those arguments and the doctrine itself fit into the general scheme of his reasoning, why he did not discuss the doctrine in his systematic accounts of his philosophy and his science, whether it actually does make a veiled appearance in some of those accounts, how it bears upon his attempt to validate reason, what its relation to his physics, and so on. There is very little agreement concerning these matters among commentators on Descartes's work.

Most commentators do agree, however, that the doctrine is extremely important. For instance, it is characterised by Alquié as "the foundation of Descartes's metaphysics," and by Gilson as "one of the most fecund among Descartes's metaphysical conceptions."[2] On the other hand, Koyré believes that it is destructive of Descartes's whole intellectual enterprise – consistent "neither with his physics, nor with his psychology, nor with his metaphysics, nor with his theory of knowledge." In Koyré's judgment, the only way to make sense of Descartes's thought is to suppose that his adherence to the doctrine was a temporary aberration, which he subsequently overcame.[3]

There is no good evidence to support Koyré's claim that Descartes substantially changed his mind about the creation of the external truths.[4] On the contrary, I think it is clear that he continued to maintain more or less his original view of the matter, as he described it to Mersenne in 1630, throughout the remainder of his life. I shall attempt to establish and to clarify the main elements of that view, and to consider some (but by no means all) of the problems of interpretation I have enumerated.

2 F. Alquié (ed.), *Descartes: Oeuvres Philosophiques*, vol. 1 (Paris, 1963), p. 208 fn.; E. Gilson, *La liberté chez Descartes et la théologie* (Paris, 1913), p. 14.
3 A. Koyré, *Essai sur l'idée de Dieu et les preuves de son existence chez Descartes* (Paris, 1922), pp. 19–21.
4 Koyré argues that the 1630 doctrine was "bien vite remplacée par une concept beaucoup plus hésitante et incertaine," citing in support a letter from Descartes to Mesland. He also cites two other letters, to Henry More (*K* 237–245) and to Clerselier (*K* 252–255), to show that Descartes ultimately abandoned the doctrine more or less completely. Now the letter to Mesland (*K* 146–152) is dated 2 May 1644. Not so *vite*, after all; and besides, this letter fails to support in any way Koyré's claim that Descartes had modified his views by the time he wrote it. The other two letters were written in 1649. The one to Clerselier has no evident bearing on the matter, while the one to More quite plainly confirms the view Koyré says it refutes. Koyré's argument is so unconvincing that it appears to be motivated less by a desire to follow the evidence than by desperation, engendered by his conviction that the 1630 doctrine makes both Descartes's philosophy and his science impossible.

II

What Descartes calls "eternal truths" are truths about essences. The Pythagorean theorem, for example, is (or purports to be) an eternal truth about what is essential to right triangularity.[5] Now to lay down the Pythagorean theorem is to make the essence "right triangularity" what it is, at least to the extent that this essence is defined by that theorem; in other words, it is to create a fact concerning what is essential to right triangles. Asserting that the eternal truths are laid down by God is tantamount, then, to saying that God is the creator of essences. And this is precisely Descartes's view: God is "no less the author of creatures' essence than He is of their existence," he observes, "and this essence is nothing other than the eternal truths" (to Mersenne, 27 May 1630, K 14).

In his initial formulation of his doctrine, the only eternal truths to which Descartes explicitly refers are mathematical propositions. The doctrine is not, however, limited to these. Descartes's examples indicate that there are physical, metaphysical, and moral essences within its scope, as well as mathematical ones. Indeed, so far as I can see, Descartes intends no essence of any kind to be outside the scope of his doctrine. But whether the intended application of the doctrine is in fact entirely unlimited is a controversial question, to which I shall return.

III

Descartes suggests that accepting his doctrine is the *only* way to avoid the conclusion that the eternal truths would be true even if God did not exist, a conclusion which plainly conflicts with the supposition of divine omnipotence.[6] But Aquinas and other scholastics *neither* share Descartes's belief that God creates essences; *nor* do they suppose that the eternal truths would be true if God did not exist, or that these truths are independent of God in anything like the way intimated by Descartes's analogy to the relation between Jupiter or Saturn and the Styx or the Fates.

Scholastic philosophers such as Suarez and Aquinas sometimes make use, in this connection, of a distinction between two types of essence – real and possible. A real essence is the essence of an existing individual; it is created by the creation of that individual, and it ceases to exist when that individual ceases to exist. A possible

5   The point of my parenthetical qualification will become apparent in due course.
6   In his letter of 15 April 1630, from which I have already quoted the pertinent passage, Descartes presents his claim that the eternal truths "have been laid down by God" as though the only alternative to it is the view that "these truths are independent of God." In his letter to Mersenne dated 6 May 1630 (K 14) Descartes warns that "we must not say that if God did not exist nonetheless these truths would be true," as though rejecting his doctrine would commit one to saying that.

essence is just a possibility, which does not, strictly speaking, exist at all. It has only "objective existence," which consists simply in its being an object of aware-ness – that is, of God's awareness that He might create an individual of the kind in question. Given this metaphysics, the eternal truths are truths about possible essences.

Now possible essences are not, according to scholasticism, creatures of God. Rather, they comprise the divine essence itself. One consequence of this assign-ment of possible essences to God's essence is that the necessity of the eternal truths can be derived directly from the necessity that God be what He is. Another consequence is that God's knowledge of possible essences is self-knowledge, which makes Him the exemplar of all His creatures. It is to Himself that He looks, in other words, for a guide in creating.

This theory clearly implies that there would be no eternal truths if God did not exist. Without maintaining that essences or eternal truths are *created* by God, then, scholasticism can readily construe them as dependent upon Him in the sense of being incapable of existing without Him. If possible essences comprise God's own essence, then, certainly, the eternal truths do not constitute – as the Styx and the Fates do with respect to Jupiter and Saturn – an *external* limitation to God's power.

Descartes appears to take it for granted that there are only two ways in which God might be related to possible essences and eternal truths. Either God creates them, in which case they depend upon Him no less than do created things generally; or He is dependent upon them, in which case He, like the gods of the classical pantheon, is limited by something other than Himself. But Descartes is surely aware that scholastic philosophy contemplates a third possibility, in which possible essences are *neither* creatures of God *nor* realities other than Him which limit His omnipotence. Descartes's contention that his doctrine *alone* avoids as-cribing an unacceptable independence to the eternal truths may well seem to be, then, a bit disingenuous.

What explains his attitude, I believe, is that he regards the scholastic alternative as simply untenable. Scholasticism envisages a distinction between God's knowing and His creating, or between the divine understanding and the divine will. It supposes that real essences, like all created things, depend upon a contingent act of God's will – that is, they exist only because He is their ultimate efficient cause. But it regards possible essences as objects only of God's understanding – that is, as depending just upon His awareness of possibilities. Since He does not create them, they are in no way dependent upon His will. Now Descartes categorically refuses to admit any distinction whatever between God's understanding and His will. "In God," he insists, "willing and knowing are a single thing, in such a way that by the very fact of willing something He knows it and it is only for this reason that such a thing is true" (to Mersenne, 6 May 1630, K 13–14).

Given that the divine understanding and the divine will are identical, God cannot merely contemplate *anything,* not even His own essence. His will cannot be guided by any antecedent knowledge of possible essences or eternal truths, which He does not create and upon which His creation is modelled. "For there is," Descartes explains,

no idea representing the good or the true – what must be believed, or what must be done or left undone – which we can suppose to have been an object of divine understanding before its nature had been constituted by the determination of God's will. I am not speaking here merely of temporal priority; I am saying that it was impossible for any idea of this sort to have preceded the determination of God's will even by priority of order or of nature of reasoned reflection, as they say in the Schools, in such a way that it would have moved God to choose one thing rather than another.[7]

The scholastic alternative to Descartes's doctrine understands possible essences to be dependent upon God's understanding but independent of His will. If God's understanding and His will are identical, no such alternative is available. This means that it cannot be correct to construe God's essence as providing the exemplar for creation, because doing so relies upon the incoherent assumption that God's knowing is prior to His willing. It also means that possible essences must be either creatures of God, as Descartes maintains, or independent of Him altogether. In my opinion, this is what accounts for Descartes's refusal to acknowledge that scholasticism can offer a viable alternative to his own doctrine.

IV

Identifying the divine understanding and the divine will leads Descartes to the view that God's freedom consists in absolute indifference. Since there *are* no truths prior to God's creation of them, His creative will cannot be determined or even moved by any considerations of value or of rationality whatever. "It is inadmissible," Descartes declares, "that God's will has not been indifferent from all eternity to everything that has been or ever will be done."[8] The divine will is, in other words, entirely arbitrary. There are no prior conditions of right or reason to which it must conform; indeed, there are none to which it might choose to conform. Here is how Descartes describes the situation:

7 *Sixth Replies,* HR II, p. 248: AT IX, p. 233. Descartes does not explain just why it is a mistake to distinguish God's understanding and His will. The following general line of argument would have been available to him, however, given his views on the relevant subjects: in humans, the understanding is a passive faculty; but since it is inadmissible to ascribe any passivity to God, the divine understanding must be construed as active; and this means supposing that, like the divine will, it necessarily has an effect upon its object. It is plausible to conjecture that Descartes came to this theory through his association, just prior to his move from Paris to Holland, with the Oratory of Cardinal Bérulle. The central feature of Bérulle's theology was its particular emphasis upon the unity and simplicity of God's nature.
8 Ibid.

It is not for having seen that it was better that the world be created in time rather than from eternity, that He willed to create it in time; and He did not will that the three angles of a triangle equal two right angles because He knew that it could not be otherwise, etc. On the contrary, it is because He willed to create the world in time that its having been created in time is better than if it had been created from eternity; and it is because He willed that the three angles of a triangle equal two right angles that it is now true that this is so and that it cannot be otherwise; and similarly for everything else.[9]

If God is to be compared to a king who lays down laws for his kingdom, He might be compared to a king who is utterly capricious and quite mad. These characterisations are not *entirely* apt, since they suggest an indifference to or a flouting of the canons of rationality, which cannot be ascribed to God's determination of those canons. In any event, on Descartes's account, God has no reasons whatsoever for His decrees and His choices are in no way submissive to any moral or rational constraints at all.

On Descartes's account of God's power and freedom, the eternal truths are no more ultimately necessary than truths concerning real essences are according to scholasticism. All essences, both real and possible, are equally creatures of God's indifferent will. There is no more reason for any essence to be than for it not to be, and no more reason for any to be what it is than to be otherwise. The eternal truths do not enjoy, as the scholastics maintain, an absolute necessity which derives from being rooted in the necessity of God Himself; for they are, in Descartes's view, "no more necessarily attached to His essence than other creatures are" (to Mersenne, 27 May 1630, *K* 15). God has established them merely "by the same kind of causality as He created all things, that is to say, as their efficient and total cause" (ibid., *K* 14). In short, the eternal truths are inherently as contingent as any other propositions.

This means that God was free in creating the world to do *anything,* whether or not its description is logically coherent. "Just as [God] was free not to create the world," Descartes explains, "so He was no less free to make it untrue that all the lines drawn from the center of a circle to its circumference are equal" (ibid., *K* 15). Descartes evidently thinks that God could have omitted creating the essence "circularity" entirely. In that case there would be *no* eternal truths about circles: every proposition about a circle would have the status now enjoyed by the proposition that the diameter of the circle on a certain blackboard is one foot. Descartes also evidently thinks that God, while creating the essence "circularity," could have made it different from what we conceive it to be. In that case there would be eternal truths about circles, but they would differ from – and perhaps be the negations of – the propositions that are necessarily true of circularity as we now understand it.

9   Ibid.

V

There is a rather obvious difficulty in the very attempt to formulate this doctrine. What can it mean, after all, to assert that God *could have* made it false that the radii of a circle are equal? This assertion seems to entail that it is logically possible that the radii of a circle be unequal. But logical possibility consists in the absence of contradiction, and Descartes knows as well as anyone that a contradiction results from negating the proposition that all the radii of a circle are equal. In any event, he commits himself quite openly to the claim that God could have made contradictory propositions true: "God cannot have been determined to make it true that contradictories cannot be true together, and therefore . . . He could have done the opposite" (to Mesland, 2 May 1644, *K* 151).

What is troublesome in this claim that God could have made contradictions true is, of course, understanding the "could." The assertion that some state of affairs can be brought about ordinarily entails that the state of affairs is logically possible. Descartes's statement that God could have made contradictions true seems to entail, accordingly, the logical possibility of the logically impossible. This appears to make very little sense, which is why Geach (among others) characterizes Descartes's doctrine concerning the creation of the eternal truths as "incoherent."[10]

Descartes is aware that his doctrine involves a difficulty of this sort. Instead of being disturbed by it, however, he transforms the difficulty into a thesis – the superficially plausible, or at least unsurprising, thesis that God, being infinite, is unintelligible to a finite mind. "It is . . . useless to ask how God could have . . . made two times four not equal eight, etc.," he writes, "for I freely admit that we cannot understand this."[11] We should not *expect* to comprehend God's infinite power, Descartes contends, and it would therefore be misguided to try to make sense of the dependence upon the divine will of essences and eternal truths. In other words, it is a mistake to *seek* a logically coherent explication of the assertion that God could have made self-contradictory propositions true.

The viability of this position, within the context of Descartes's philosophy, depends upon the value of the distinction he draws between knowing that an infinitely powerful God exists and understanding Him. "It is possible," Descartes maintains, "to know that God is infinite and all-powerful although our soul, being finite, cannot comprehend or conceive Him" (to Mersenne, 27 May 1630, *K* 15). Now a person's assertion that there is something he cannot understand is often entirely comprehensible, and there may be quite good evidence that it is true. In the present instance, however, the assertion is peculiar and problematical. That

---

10 P. Geach, "Omnipotence," *Philosophy* (1973), p. 10.
11 *Sixth Replies, HR* II, p. 251; *AT* IX, p. 236.

there is a deity with infinite power is supposed by Descartes to entail the possibility of what is logically impossible. But if it must entail this, then the assertion that God has infinite (and hence unintelligible) power seems itself unintelligible. For it appears that no coherent meaning can be assigned to the notion of an infinitely powerful being as Descartes employs it – that is, to the notion of a being for whom the logically impossible is possible. And if this is so, then it is no more possible for us to know or to believe that God *has* infinite power than it is, according to Descartes, for us to understand that power. If we cannot understand "infinite power," we also cannot understand, and hence cannot believe or know, the proposition that God's power is infinite.

VI

Descartes has a reply to objections of this type. Its details are somewhat uncertain, however, and I shall attempt only to sketch it rather broadly.

Descartes regards the scope of human understanding as strictly limited within boundaries defined by the set of logically necessary propositions. The negations of these propositions – that is, self-contradictions – are unintelligible to us; we cannot conceive their truth. But this inability to conceive the truth of a contradiction is, Descartes suggests, merely a contingent characteristic of our minds. It is by an indifferent act of God's will that "He has given me such a mind that I cannot conceive . . . an aggregate of one and two which is not three" (to Arnauld, 29 July 1648, *K* 236). That our minds cannot conceive such things signifies nothing beyond itself, however, except that God has freely chosen to create us like that.

God might just as well have given us minds of a different sort. If He had done so, some of the propositions we now find inconceivable would have been conceivable by us; and some of the propositions we are now able to conceive would have been inconceivable. From our recognition that we are unable to conceive some state of affairs because its description is self-contradictory, accordingly, we are not entitled to conclude that it was impossible for God to have brought about that state of affairs.

The propositions we find to be necessary – like the Pythagorean theorem – need not be truths at all. The inconceivability of their falsity, which we demonstrate by the use of innate principles of reason, is not inherent in them. It is properly to be understood only as relative to the character of our minds. We cannot escape this character, of course, but we *can* realize that God might have made it different from what it is. Since God is not constrained by the boundaries within which He has enclosed our minds, the theoretical limits of human reason must be recognised as *limitations* by which we are bound, rather than as guides to the actual limits of possibility. They are imposed upon us arbitrarily by God's free creation. So we cannot presume that what we determine to be logically necessary coincides with the ultimate conditions of reality or of truth. The necessities human reason discovers by analysis and demonstration are just necessities of its own contingent nature. In coming to know them, it does not necessarily discover the nature of the world as it is in itself, or as it appears to God.

This line of thought, which contributes to the explication of Descartes's claim that God's power is beyond our comprehension, requires that we be able to conceive ourselves as having been created with minds different from the ones we have. That is, it requires that we be able to conceive ourselves as finding certain propositions conceivable – namely, self-contradictions – which we presently find inconceivable. The question of whether Descartes's position concerning divine omnipotence is coherent thus comes down to whether this requirement can be satisfied or whether it too is unintelligible. Descartes does not discuss the matter directly. However, he does hold certain opinions which bear upon it and which may enable him to explain how it is possible to conceive that the inconceivable might be conceivable.

There is, first of all, his claim that clear and distinct perception determines the will. When a person perceives something clearly and distinctly, Descartes maintains, he cannot help assenting to it: "our mind is of such a nature," he says, "that it cannot refuse to assent to what it apprehends clearly" (to Regius, 24 May 1640, K 73). Second, there is his general conviction that our knowledge of principles, including the principles of logic, derives ultimately from knowledge of their instances. These two opinions provide materials from which it might be possible to construct a theory according to which what is conceivable or inconceivable, what we identify as necessary or as impossible, depends in the end upon the occurrence of certain experiences – our experiences of an inability to refuse assent.

Given such a theory, the possibility that contradictions might be true, or that we can conceive ourselves judging that a proposition is true even while we recognize that the proposition is self-contradictory, could be supplied with a meaningful explication. The explication would refer to the possibility that the experiences from which our conceptions and ascriptions of necessity and impossibility derive might occur under circumstances other than those under which they now occur. When we now attentively consider the proposition that one and two make three, having first discriminated and analyzed its terms, we cannot help assenting to it; and that is ultimately why we regard the proposition as necessary. But this experience of a compulsion to assent might not occur under these conditions; and it might instead occur when we consider, in the same way, the negation of the proposition that one and two make three. In that case we would, on Descartes's account, construe the proposition that one and two make three as inconceivable; and the general logical and mathematical principles we adopted would reflect that experience. It is along these lines, I suggest, that a coherent substance can be provided for Descartes's assertion that our inability to understand God's infinite power is due just to a contingent characteristic of our minds, namely, the fact that

32

we have the experience of necessity under certain conditions rather than under others.[12]

VII

I want now to consider the important contention that Descartes substantially qualifies his claim that God's freedom is unconstrained by the principle of contradiction. Some commentators argue that Descartes recognizes a class of necessary truths that are not created at all, and that he acknowledges that God could not have made the negations of those propositions true. This is an extremely fundamental point in the interpretation of Descartes's theory of knowledge. If it is correct that his doctrine concerning the creation of eternal truths is less than universal in its scope, then Descartes does not commit himself to the view that God's power is entirely unintelligible to us. Instead he believes that divine omnipotence has certain limits, which coincide with an identifiable proper subset of the set of contradictory propositions. And he thinks that human reason is therefore capable of determining autonomously the inherent nature of at least some aspects of reality — namely, those with regard to which the range of God's power is coextensive with the range of what we understand as logical possibilities. If this interpretation of Descartes's doctrine is *not* correct — and in my judgment it is not — then that doctrine commits him to certain quite radical views, which I shall identify in due course.

Gueroult is among those who maintain that there are contradictions which Descartes's God cannot transcend. In particular, Gueroult asserts that, in Descartes's opinion, God can do nothing which would negate His own omnipotence:

God's omnipotence, which by definition implies that nothing is impossible for Him, establishes by the same token a superior order of impossibility — to wit, whatever could be only by the negation of this omnipotence itself. There are then, in spite of everything, impossibilities for God: they are those things that would limit His omnipotence or His being (being and power being the same). In short, God excludes non-being. It follows from this that whatever involves non-being is an absolute impossibility. Thus it is absolutely impossible that God should not exist, that He should be a deceiver, that He might bring it about that what is or was should not be . . . , that He might be unable to do what we

---

12   Neither I nor (to my knowledge) others have explored Descartes's views concerning the foundations of logic thoroughly enough to make it clear whether or not a saving construction of this kind can in fact be accomplished with the materials he makes available. It is worth noticing, incidentally, the apparent similarity between Descartes's views on this subject and those of Wittgenstein. Both seem to locate the ultimate ground of our logical and mathematical knowledge in some sort of experience of necessity. Anthony Kenny has pointed out to me in conversation that, as a consequence of this, Descartes and Wittgenstein (alone among philosophers) make an emphatic distinction between our grounds for accepting very elementary logical or mathematical propositions and our grounds for accepting more complicated ones.

33

conceive to be possible, that He might tolerate atoms, that He might create a vacuum . . . His infinite omnipotence thus creates for God a whole class of absolute impossibilities.[13]

On this account, Descartes regards God's freedom as unlimited by the constraints of logic only with respect to essences other than His own, which is comprised by omnipotence. The divine essence itself, Gueroult maintains, is uncreated. Hence it constitutes a locus of uncreated truths. The necessity of *these* truths is not an artifact of God's indifferent will, but is entirely unconditioned.

The pertinent texts do not, in my opinion, support this account of Descartes's doctrine. On the contrary, I believe they show that Descartes is unwilling to admit any limitation or qualification of God's power whatever. Consider the following, from a passage Gueroult himself cites in evidence for his interpretation:

I agree that there are contradictions which are so evident, that we cannot put them before our minds, without judging them entirely impossible, like the one which you suggest: that God might have made creatures independent of Him. But if we would know the immensity of His power we should not put these thoughts before our minds. [To Mesland, 2 May 1644, K 151]

God would not be omnipotent if any creature were independent of Him. Gueroult must therefore ascribe to Descartes the view that it is an *absolute impossibility* for God to have made creatures independent of Himself. But Descartes does not, in the quoted passage, say that it is absolutely impossible for God to have made creatures independent of Himself. He says only that we cannot think of God's making independent creatures without *judging* it entirely impossible that He should do so. And the unmistakable import of Descartes's remarks is that this judgment is *misleading*.

The proposition that God might have made independent creatures is, Descartes admits, so evidently a contradiction that we cannot consider it at all without believing it to be necessarily false. But our compulsion to believe it false whenever we consider it is something Descartes plainly regards as *endangering* a proper appreciation on our part of divine omnipotence. That is the only possible explanation of his recommendation that those who wish to know God's power rightly should avoid considering the proposition in question. If Descartes thought that a belief in the falsity of this proposition were warranted, he would obviously have no reason to warn us – as he does – against getting into a situation in which we are unable to avoid believing that it is false.

Descartes regards the impossibility of self-contradictory propositions only as a function of the particular character human reason happens to have, rather than as providing us in any way with a measure of God's power. Thus he issues the following entirely unqualified caution:

13   Martial Gueroult, *Descartes selon l'ordre des raisons* II, pp. 26–29.

I do not think that we should ever say of anything that it cannot be brought about by God. For since everything involved in truth and goodness depends on His omnipotence, I would not dare to say that God cannot make a mountain without a valley, or that one and two should not be three. I merely say that He has given me such a mind that I cannot conceive a mountain without a valley, or an aggregate of one and two which is not three, and that such things involve a contradiction in my conception. I think the same should be said of a space which is wholly void, or of an extended piece of nothing or of a limited universe. [To Arnauld, 29 July 1648, K 236–237]

Here Descartes speaks of one of the very propositions which, according to Gueroult, he construes not only as contradictions but as absolute impossibilities: namely, that God might create a vacuum. Far from characterizing it as absolutely impossible, however, Descartes limits himself to acknowledging that the proposition is a contradiction. He explicitly renounces the assertion that God cannot make the proposition true. Despite Gueroult's claim to the contrary, Descartes declares that he "would not dare to say" that God cannot make a space that is wholly void.

Gueroult uses the following text, in which Descartes says that it is inconceivable that God should undermine His own omnipotence, to support his interpretation:

It involves a contradiction that there should be any atoms which are conceived as extended and also indivisible. Though God might make them such that they could not be divided by any creature, we certainly cannot conceive Him able to deprive Himself of the power of dividing them. . . . [To More, 5 Feb. 1649, K 241]

Taken by itself, this text may indeed appear to support Gueroult's claims. The appearance, however, is deceptive. The passage to which the text belongs is devoted only to setting forth what is required by a *rational* – that is, a logically coherent or intelligible – conception of God's power. But Descartes has already made it clear that, since God is infinite, we can give no intelligible account of His power. Given that God's power is not constrained by considerations of rationality, it is not reasonable to think that God actually is as our need for intelligibility and coherence requires us to conceive Him. Thus the text must not be understood as defining a limit within which God is really confined, but only as defining a limit to our ability to conceive Him. Our minds are of such a nature, to be sure, that "we cannot conceive Him able to deprive Himself of the power of dividing" atoms. According to Descartes, nonetheless, this does not mean that God actually is unable to deprive Himself of that power.

This way of reading the text is not speculative or tendentious. It is *required*, it seems to me, by what Descartes says straightforwardly just before the sentences I have quoted:

For my part, I know that my intellect is finite and God's power is infinite, and so I set no bounds to it; I consider only what I can conceive and what I cannot conceive, and I take great pains that my judgment should accord with my understanding. And so I boldly assert that

35

God can do everything which I conceive to be possible, but I am not so bold as to deny that He can do whatever conflicts with my understanding – I merely say that it involves a contradiction.

Here Descartes openly reaffirms, quite unequivocally, his doctrine that God's power is unlimited by the principle of contradiction. And he acknowledges that a person may be justified in asserting that a proposition is self-contradictory without being justified in asserting that it is false.

VIII

Inevitably, Descartes's conceptions of inquiry and of knowledge are shaped by his recognition that there is a decisive and ineradicable uncertainty concerning the relation between the class of judgments required by rational considerations and the class of judgments that correctly describe the inherent nature of reality. In view of God's freedom from rational constraints, it cannot be assumed that the member-ship of the first class coincides with the membership of the second. Descartes must accordingly forswear the hope of penetrating, *through* the limits of rationality set by the character of the human mind, to an unconditioned apprehension of how things are. As he conceives it, the aim of inquiry is just to arrive at beliefs which it would be irrational for us to doubt because the assumption that they are false involves us in contradiction. But we cannot be so bold as to claim that rational inquiry leads us to the truth as God has created it. God's truths may be inaccessible to us, for we cannot establish that reason is a suitable instrument for discovering them. On the other hand, there is no need for us to be concerned about our inability to discover what is absolutely true. For any absolute truth that conflicts with the beliefs reason requires us to adopt is *ipso facto* self-contradictory and unintelligible to us. We could not make use of it even if we were somehow able to identify it as absolutely true.

The possible discrepancy between rationally warranted belief and absolute truth does not, therefore, preclude our confident reliance upon the former. In fact, Descartes says, "it would be entirely contrary to reason to doubt what we under-stand very well because of something else which we do not understand and which we see no need to understand.[14] We can reasonably be satisfied with the products

---

14 *Sixth Replies, HR* II, p. 251; *AT* IX, p. 236. This statement echoes a passage which has not heretofore been associated with Descartes's doctrine concerning the eternal truths:

> What is it to us if someone should perhaps imagine that the very thing of whose truth we have been so firmly persuaded appears false to God or to an angel and that as a consequence it is false speaking absolutely? What do we care about this absolute falsity, since we by no means believe in it or even have the least suspicion of it? For we are supposing a persuasion so firm that it can in no way be removed – a persuasion, therefore, that is exactly the same as the most perfect certainty. [*Second Replies, HR* II, p. 41; *AT* VII, p. 145]

There is some controversy over how this passage is to be understood. In my own view, it suggests

of reason without making the absurd attempt to supersede them, by nonrational means, for the sake of beliefs which would in any case be incomprehensible to us.

IX

But what about Descartes's famous proof that God is not a deceiver, and that therefore no rationally warranted belief – that is, no belief based upon clear and distinct perception – can be false? Does this proof not enable him to eliminate the uncertainty his doctrine concerning the eternal truths arouses with respect to the absolute authority of reason? That doctrine implies, after all, only that God *could* have made truths of self-contradictory propositions; it does not imply that God has actually done so. So the necessities of human reason *might* in fact coincide with God's truths. And if these do coincide, then human reason *is* competent to determine the inherent nature of things. For the character of our minds would be harmonious, albeit contingently so, with the actual principles of God's creation. According to the standard interpretation of Descartes's theory of knowledge, this coincidence or harmony between the principles of human reason and the eternal truths God has created is precisely what Descartes intends his proof that God is not a deceiver to establish.

In my view, the standard interpretation is untenable. First of all, I believe that the most satisfactory way to meet the familiar charge that Descartes's reasoning is circular requires a construction of his argument to and from God's veracity which makes it impossible to conclude that what is perceived clearly and distinctly is true "absolutely speaking."[15] Second, and more pertinent in the present context, the standard interpretation fails to take sufficient account of the radical implications of Descartes's conception of divine omnipotence.

The proof that God is not a deceiver, like any rational demonstration, can establish for Descartes nothing more than that its conclusion is required by the principles of human reason. The proof is designed to show that the notion of a deceiving God is logically incoherent and hence unintelligible, as other demonstrations offered by Descartes are designed to show that the notions of a vacuum or of an indivisible atom are incoherent and unintelligible. But the proposition that God is a deceiver, however offensive to human reason it may be, cannot be regarded by Descartes as any more an absolute impossibility than the propositions – which on his account are equally unintelligible – that God can create a wholly void space or that He can create an atom He cannot divide. In the one case as in the others, Descartes can permit himself to say merely that the proposition involves a con-

that Descartes recognizes the possibility of a discrepancy between what is absolutely certain and what is absolutely true, and that he is indifferent to the possibility that the outcome of successful rational inquiry may be a belief that is false "speaking absolutely." This way of reading the passage receives some confirmation, I believe, from the parallel text – the "echo" – quoted above.

15   Cf. H. G. Frankfurt, *Demons, Dreamers and Madmen: The Defense of Reason in Descartes's Meditations* (Indianapolis: Bobbs-Merrill, 1970), especially Chapter 15.

tradition, and that we are consequently unable to believe it when we attend to its logical incoherence. He is not so bold as to deny that God could have made any of these contradictory propositions true.

The inquiry to which Descartes devotes his *Meditations* is an exploration by reason of its own limits or necessities. Its goal is, and can only be, to determine what it is reasonable for us to believe – that is, what it would be irrational for us to doubt – and not what is true in the eyes of God or of the angels. Thus Descartes intends his proofs that God exists to establish just that it is irrational to deny the existence of God, and that it is therefore irrational to doubt the reliability of reason.

These proofs necessarily leave open the question of whether their conclusions are true "speaking absolutely" or in God's eyes. That is, they leave open the unintelligible possibility that God knows that He does not exist. This is perhaps the ultimate paradox that my interpretation entails. But it is no more paradoxical, though it is more bizarre, than Descartes's refusal to reject, despite his recognition of its logical incoherence, the proposition that God might have made creatures independent of Himself. This too is a proposition which, according to Descartes, we cannot help judging to be entirely impossible whenever we think of it. With respect to the first proposition, Descartes's recommendation can only be the one he actually makes when he discusses the second: it is better not to think of such things.[16]

X

Scholasticism supposes that human reason and divine understanding, while they differ greatly in power, share a common nature which is specified by logic; and that, since God's understanding guides His will, the principles of logic define the limits of what is possible for God as well as the limits of what is intelligible to us. On this account the universe must be inherently comprehensible, for God could not have made it otherwise. There are mysteries, to be sure, which we cannot understand and which only faith enables us to grasp at all. But these mysteries are understood by God, and He understands them in accordance with the *same* principles of rationality that govern our own thinking. Thus their incoherence is merely apparent – notwithstanding that it is an appearance we are unable to overcome – since all truth is necessarily rational.

16 Despite his repeated and unequivocal professions of Roman Catholicism, and the fact that there is substantial evidence of his piety, Descartes's religious convictions have always aroused the most dire suspicions. He has been mistrusted on this score, in fact, by practically everyone. The Catholics accused him of being a Protestant, the Protestants thought he was an atheist, and the atheists have tended to suspect that he was a hypocrite. I shall not consider here what light is shed on these matters, or how they are made additionally obscure, by Descartes's doctrine concerning the eternal truths.

Descartes's vision, on the other hand, is that the world may be inherently absurd. He disrupts the harmonious connection which the scholastics envisage between human reason and divine understanding, by denying that rationality is in any way essential to God. In place of reason, he sees at the source of the universe sheer unconstrained will or power. This introduces the possibility that the divine is not only remote from us but utterly alien. Reality may not be rational. There may be a discontinuity *in principle* between what we can understand and what God knows. Rationality may be nothing more than a conveniently collective form of lunacy, which enables those who suffer from it to communicate with each other, but which isolates them all equally from what is ultimately real.

According to Koyré, Descartes cannot have persisted very long in the belief that God creates the eternal truths, because that belief implies the impossibility of science altogether; it means that "the clearest reasons could in no way guarantee either the truth or the existence of anything."[17] Now Koyré is in a way right about this. Descartes's doctrine *does* imply that science is impossible, *if* science is construed naively as an attempt to discover the truth "speaking absolutely." What Koyré fails to appreciate, however, is that Descartes understands all rational inquiry as an attempt to determine only what beliefs are warranted by the principles of human reason. In this limited enterprise, reason is called upon to satisfy no criteria except its own. Since science makes no claim to apprehend the absolute truth, but only to decide what it is irrational for us to deny or what reason requires us to believe, the clearest reasons are exactly and definitively adequate to their purpose.

XI

What Descartes proposes to accomplish by invoking just this possibility that the world is not inherently rational is the liberation of human reason from a destructive anxiety about its own adequacy and its entitlement to independence. The liberation of reason is to be advanced in two ways. First, the assertion that the eternal truths do not belong to God's essence removes a serious impediment to our confidence that we can understand them fully. For it means that a claim to understand them fully is not to be understood, as it must be on scholastic assumptions, as a preposterous boast to possess perfect knowledge of God's essence.[18] Second, and more important, the assertion that reality as it is in itself may be in principle unintelligible to us exempts reason from having to regard itself as a competitor of transrational modes of access to truth.

My speculation is that Descartes's interest in the latter consequence of his doctrine concerning the eternal truths derives from a preoccupation with issues

---

17   Koyré, op. cit., p. 19.
18   Cf. E. Bréhier, "The Creation of the Eternal Truths in Descartes's System," in W. Doney, *Descartes: A Collection of Critical Essays* (New York: Doubleday, 1967).

which were raised urgently in the leading intellectual controversy of his time — that between Galileo and the Church over the status of heliocentrism. I am not referring to the scientific issue in that dispute, which was whether the sun or the earth is at the center of the solar system, but to the philosophical question at the bottom of the whole conflict: namely, whether science can unequivocally apprehend reality or whether one must rely in the last analysis upon extrascientific considerations in order to determine the inherent nature of things.

The Church claimed that there are logically consistent alternatives to Galileo's heliocentrism which account, no less completely than his theory does, for all the empirical data. It insisted that science cannot conclusively justify a preference for one of these alternatives over another. Since each is consistent with itself and with the facts, God might, for all we know, have made any one of them true. We can discover which of the alternatives God has actually chosen only because we possess a Book in which He reveals what He has done.

Galileo conceded that there are coherent alternatives to his theory which also save all the appearances. However, he maintained that it is reasonable to select heliocentrism in preference to them on the basis of such considerations as simplicity; and he insisted that a theory whose selection is warranted on these grounds is true in the sense of explaining how the world really is. To this the Church retorted, quite plausibly I think, that there is no sufficient reason to assume that God is bound by considerations, like simplicity, which happen to appeal to the human mind.

Descartes was convinced that the superiority of heliocentrism does not lie merely in pragmatic advantages like simplicity. He believed that the heliocentric account of the solar system is derivable by demonstrative reasoning from self-evident first principles,[19] and that no account which conflicts with it can similarly be proven. In this he differs from Galileo, whose approach to physics he con-

---

19 In a letter to Mersenne dated "end of November 1633," Descartes refers to the news that Galileo has been condemned by the Church, and says: "I cannot imagine that he, who is Italian and who is even (as I understand) well-liked by the Pope, would have been treated as a criminal for anything except for having sought to establish the movement of the earth. I know that [this doctrine] had been censured previously by various Cardinals, but I thought I had heard that it continued to be taught publicly, even in Rome. And I confess that *if it is false, then all the foundations of my philosophy are false, for it is plainly demonstrable by them*" (F. Alquié, *op. cit.*, pp. 487–488; my translation; emphasis added). In another letter to Mersenne, dated April 1634, Descartes says: "Doubtless you know that . . . [Galileo's] views about the movement of the earth were condemned as heretical. I must tell you that all the things I explained in my treatise [i.e., *Le Monde*], which included the doctrine of the movement of the earth, were so interdependent that it is enough to discover that one of them is false to know that all the arguments I was using are unsound. Though *I thought they were based on very certain and evident proofs,* I would not wish, for anything in the world, to maintain them against the authority of the Church" (*K* 25–26, emphasis added). Given that Descartes thought heliocentrism true, his belief in its demonstrability appears to follow from his assertion that "I do not accept or desire any other principle in Physics than in Geometry or abstract Mathematics, because all the phenomena of nature may be explained by their means, and sure demonstration can be given of them" (*Principles of Philosophy* II, LXIV).

demned as excessively empirical. Now if heliocentrism is demonstrable then revelation must be self-contradictory, and therefore unintelligible, insofar as it conflicts with the heliocentric account. This does not mean, according to Descartes, that geocentrism is false "speaking absolutely." God might have made that contradiction true. But it does mean that the geocentric hypothesis cannot be considered to be in competition with heliocentrism for the endorsement of *reason*.

Descartes's response to the controversy between the Church and Galileo is to accept the claims of neither entirely, but to allow to each what he thinks each must be most anxious to salvage from the dispute. He concedes to the Church that revelation provides superior access to the inherent nature of reality. Reason cannot disturb the truths of faith, since it cannot with any legitimate authority claim to have a purchase on the ultimate object of those truths – to wit, the creative power and will of God. By denying that it is a proper aim of reason to discover absolute truth, however, he frees reason from the need to acknowledge any dependence upon what is revealed to faith. Thus he agrees with Galileo that science is rightfully autonomous, while renouncing Galileo's claim that science takes precedence over revelation as a description of the inherent nature of things.

Scholasticism is committed, by its assumption that all reality is rational, to construing any conflict between reason and faith as in fact a conflict between a shallower and a deeper insight into what *reason* permits or requires us to believe. Descartes's doctrine, on the other hand, renders human reason and divine revelation discontinuous. His account seals the one off from the other by assigning a different objective to each. Thus there is no competition, and no possibility of conflict, between them. Revelation is ontologically more profound than reason, since it alone enables us to share the perspective of God. But this perspective is blinding, and therein lies the irrelevance of revelation to the rational interests of men. For its part, reason can do no more than to submit to its own necessities, without knowing whether these reflect anything beyond a merely adventitious contingency. But just in this lies a warrant for the epistemological confidence which the program of rationalism requires.

4

Two Motivations for Rationalism:
Descartes and Spinoza

I

This essay deals with certain relatively neglected features of the theories of knowledge of Descartes and Spinoza. My aim is not to criticize or to evaluate the views of these philosophers, but to bring out certain parallels and contrasts in the motives which guided their epistemological preoccupations. In the case of Descartes, the pertinent materials appear almost exclusively in his letters. Even though they hardly figure at all in his systematic philosophical and scientific writings, they are highly theoretical and unmistakably germane to his central doctrines. With respect to Spinoza, the situation is somewhat the reverse. While the considerations in question appear in one of his major philosophical treatises, they are of a quite concrete and indeed personal nature. It is customary to classify both Descartes and Spinoza as rationalists, although the differences between them are far from peripheral or insignificant. So far as concerns the underlying motivations of their inquiries, the divergence between them is particularly sharp and unequivocal.

What they did share was an ambition to construct a body of philosophical and scientific knowledge grounded in absolutely certain fundamental principles. Neither was willing to assent to any proposition whose acceptability could not be thoroughly guaranteed by a rigorous demonstration from these principles. Nothing is more characteristic of Descartes and Spinoza than the importance ascribed to *order* and to unshakable conviction: that is, to starting with the most indubitable beliefs, and to proceeding by carefully planned and fully justified steps to develop an unequivocally reliable understanding of everything within the scope of human intelligence.

My primary interest here is, with respect both to Descartes and to Spinoza, in the *other* side of their uncompromising demands for rationality and logical order. I want to call attention to the particular way in which each of them was fundamentally preoccupied with *disorder,* and how for each of them his commitment to reason was conceived as the solution to a disturbing problem concerning irrationality. I shall delineate the disorder which Descartes contemplated, identify the quite different source of Spinoza's compelling need for order, and suggest how the philosophical position of each man resolved or allayed the pre-theoretical concern – with a sort of chaos – by which his craving for the rationalist ideal was mobilized.

II

Descartes begins his effort to understand the world with the rather discouraging concession that, for all he knows or can hope to prove, the world he wishes to understand may be totally and inherently unintelligible to a rational creature. The concept of unintelligibility pertinent here is a severely logical one. What troubles Descartes is that the canons of rational discourse or thought – in other words, the fundamental principles and standards of logic – may not coincide at all with the structure of reality. His anxiety is that the inconceivable may be actual, that what is logically impossible (what has a self-contradictory description) may nonetheless be a fact, that propositions which are internally incoherent may nevertheless be true.

This appears not to be a very promising starting-point for an inquiry devoted to discovering how a comprehensive knowledge of the natural world can be deduced with unshakable certainty from self-evident first principles. It is a commonplace that human reason is, even at its best, disappointingly limited in power and scope. But Descartes's initial lack of confidence in rationality is of a far more radical and inhibiting sort. It derives from a belief that the possession of reason may actually be an insurmountable *obstacle* to the acquisition of any genuine knowledge at all: our rationality may be not merely too little of a good thing but in fact a crippling defect, sufficient to guarantee the failure of any inquiry into how things really are.

Descartes's anxiety concerning the authority of reason has its source in his distinctive view that the so-called eternal truths are created by God and that God's power is therefore in no way constrained by them.[1] Eternal truths are propositions concerning the essences or essential natures of things. They specify characteristics which a thing necessarily has just in virtue of being of a certain type – as, for instance, the Pythagorean Theorem specifies a characteristic which any right triangle will inescapably possess. Truths or facts of this kind can be established entirely on the basis of logical or conceptual considerations; and, by the same token, denying any of them produces a contradiction. But Descartes insists nonetheless that their truth is wholly subject to God's will. The alternative, he claims, is that the eternal truths are *independent* of God. This alternative would fatally compromise divine omnipotence: for if the eternal truths are independent of God, then what God can do is limited by truths or facts over which He has no control.

The orthodox view has always been that God is truly and sufficiently omnipotent as long as He can do anything *conceivable*. Since it is not conceivable that a self-contradictory proposition should be true, most philosophers and theologians have felt that acknowledging that He cannot make contradictions true implies no defect in His power. Descartes does not really provide any substantial argument for his claim that God's power is unconditioned by the laws of logic or, to put the same

---

[1] The following discussion draws heavily on Frankfurt (1977).

point in another way, that God is not necessarily rational. Perhaps this is because he construes the claim as serving only a heuristic purpose, rather than as a doctrine to whose truth he definitively commits himself. Descartes's general philosophical project is to consider how (if at all) a reasonable person can attain absolutely certain knowledge of the natural world. In order to carry out this project in the most convincing way, he begins by supposing that the conditions under which he must proceed are as unfavorable as can be imagined. He approaches his problem, in other words, by considering the worst possible case. Let me elaborate his assumption concerning divine omnipotence and explain just how unfavorable to the prospects for knowledge it really is.

Descartes's way of construing divine omnipotence means that when God creates things He is not limited by any antecedent knowledge of what they must be like, how it would be best for them to be, or whether they need or ought to exist at all. The standards of what must be and of what should be are themselves creatures of God; so God is free to create or to alter them entirely as He likes, in any way whatever. His creative will cannot be determined or even influenced by any antecedent considerations of value or of rationality, because there *are* no truths before He creates them. Thus the divine will is entirely arbitrary. Here is how Descartes describes the situation:

> He did not will that the three angles of a triangle equal two right angles because He knew that it could not be otherwise. On the contrary, it is because He willed that the three angles of a triangle equal two right angles that it is now true that this is so and that it cannot be otherwise; and similarly for everything else.[2]

In Descartes's view, then, God has no reasons for His decrees. His choices are submissive to no moral or rational constraints at all.

Descartes quite openly embraces the remarkable implication that a proposition might be true even if it is self-contradictory: "God cannot have been required to make it true that contradictories cannot be true together, and therefore . . . He could have done the opposite."[3] One can see, of course, what Descartes has in mind. After all, if God is all-powerful then nothing can *require* Him to do anything; so there is nothing that He *must* do or that He *cannot* do. On the other hand, it is not so easy to see what sort of rationalistic program can possibly be feasible if the world which is to be explained has no rational explanation. The eternal truths are the very foundation and substance of rationality. Yet on Descartes's account they are inherently as contingent and in need of explanation (which they cannot be given) as any other proposition.

The principles of logic delineate the boundaries of what it is possible for us to understand, but Descartes maintains that it is only a psychological fact that they

---

2 Descartes (1897–1910), vol. IX, p. 233; Descartes (1972), vol. II, p. 248 (sixth "Replies to Objections").
3 Descartes (1897–1910), vol. IV, p. 118; Descartes (1970), p. 151 (letter to Mesland, 2 May, 1644).

do so. Propositions that violate logic – that is, self-contradictions – are unintelligible to us; we simply cannot conceive their truth. But our inability to conceive the truth of a contradiction is merely a contingent characteristic of our minds. God simply happened to make us that way: "He has given me such a mind," Descartes says, "that I cannot conceive . . . an aggregate of one and two which is not three."[4] This is just a fact about *me*, about what I can and cannot do, and not about the inherent relationship of one and two. My inability to conceive something, Descartes holds, signifies nothing beyond itself except that God freely chose to create me like that. It does not signify that He might not have created me with a mind of another sort, or that the world outside of me must conform to the characteristics of my intelligence.

We cannot legitimately presume that the world is subject to the necessities of logic and reason. We only know that, as it happens, *we* cannot conceive a world that does not conform to them. Here is what Descartes says:

I do not think we should ever say of anything that it cannot be brought about by God. For since everything involved in truth and goodness depends on His omnipotence, I would not dare to say that God cannot make a mountain without a valley, or that one and two should not make three. I merely say that He has given me such a mind that I cannot conceive of one and two which is not three, and that such things involve a contradiction in my conception.[5]

The upshot is that we cannot arrive at any certainty concerning how things are by relying upon the standards of rationality set by the human mind. In other words, we cannot dare to assume that rational inquiry leads to the truth as God created it. That truth may be inaccessible to us, because reason may not be a suitable instrument for discovering it.

On the other hand, however, there is no need for us to be concerned about our inability to discover what is absolutely true. Since any absolute truth that conflicts with the beliefs reason requires us to adopt is *ipso facto* self-contradictory and unintelligible to us, we could not make use of it even if we were somehow able to identify it as absolutely true. The possibility of a discrepancy between rationally warranted belief and absolute truth therefore does not prevent Descartes from relying confidently upon reason. In fact, he says, "it would be entirely contrary to reason to doubt what we understand very well because of something else which we do not understand and which we see no need to understand."[6] We can reasonably be satisfied with the products of reason, since no *comprehensible* truth – no truth comprehensible by us – can conflict with them. Descartes's account leads him, then, to a conception of rational inquiry as an exploration by reason of its own limits and necessities, whose goal is to determine what it is reasonable for us to

4 Descartes (1897–1910), vol. V, p. 224; Descartes (1970), p. 236 (letter to Arnauld, 29 July, 1648).
5 Descartes (1897–1910), vol. V, pp. 223–224; Descartes (1970), pp. 236–237 (letter to Arnauld, 29 July 1648).
6 Descartes (1897–1910), vol. IX, p. 236; Descartes (1972), vol. II, p. 251 (sixth "Replies to Objections").

believe, or what it would be irrational for us to doubt, rather than what is true in the absolute sense of grasping the inherent nature of things as they are in themselves and as they appear to the eyes of God.

This way of understanding the point of rational inquiry liberates reason from the uncertain and dangerous competition in which, during the early seventeenth century, it found itself engaged with religious faith. By acknowledging that reality may be in itself unintelligible, Descartes concedes that reason cannot claim authoritative access to the inherent nature of things. In order to know how God made the world, we must rely upon whatever truth divine revelation provides; for rational methods of inquiry are incommensurate with the range of alternatives available to God in creation. By the same token, however, Descartes frees reason from the need to acknowledge any dependence upon what is revealed to faith because he denies that it is the proper aim of reason to discover absolute truth. Thus science becomes autonomous, albeit at the cost of renouncing any claim to precedence over revelation as a description of the inherent nature of things. By assigning different objectives to reason and to revelation, Descartes seals them off from each other and eliminates the possibility of competition or conflict between them.

In more personal terms, the movement of Descartes's thought constitutes a withdrawal from a universe whose unconstrained and unintelligible power might well have seemed uninviting into the secure coherence and familiarity of his own mind. Contemplating the omnipotence of God, Descartes recognizes that there may be an irreconcilable discontinuity between his own needs and capacities and the objective character of the universe. So he proceeds to find within himself, in his own rational faculty, the stability and intelligibility which he requires and which he cannot be confident of finding in a world created without concern for his requirements and tastes. The possibility that the real is inescapably alien to him becomes irrelevant, as he undertakes to be satisfied with the rational whether or not it coincides with the real.

Descartes sacrifices the grandiose ambition to become intellectually the master and possessor of the world, in other words, and resolves to content himself with the opportunity to develop and to complete his own thought. He turns away from the world, which he cannot presume to be even tolerably congenial to his intelligence, and seeks only to become harmoniously attuned to the regularities and standards of his own nature. As I hope to make apparent, the movement of Spinoza's thought is just the opposite of this.

III

Spinoza's *Ethics* is written in a forbiddingly austere and impersonal way, in the form of a geometric treatise set out with definitions, axioms, postulates, theorems, corollaries, lemmas, and scholia, linked together by elaborate and often obscure trains of deductive argumentation. Unlike Descartes's *Discourse on Method* or *Meditations,* it is not an engaging piece of work. It gives the impression that Spinoza wishes to expunge from his writing every trace of his own individuality and personality, in order that the universal voice of reason – which is, presumably, identical in all men, in quality if not in quantity – should be more plainly heard and recognized as such.

In his excellent book on Spinoza, Stuart Hampshire accepts this impression. "Spinoza thought it right," he suggests, "that a philosopher should remain impassively concealed behind his philosophy." Perhaps Spinoza did actually think that. But Hampshire goes on to declare further that Spinoza has, in fact, "effectively concealed himself behind his work."[7] It may well be that Spinoza attempted to do this, and that his attempt to do it accounts for the peculiar style and form of his writings, but the concealment is by no means entirely complete. For one thing, the very attempt at concealment, and the devices employed in it, are themselves revealing. The degree of austerity and rigidity which Spinoza attempted to impose upon the expression of his thought strongly conveys that he may have felt an especially powerful tendency in the contrary direction.

But there is another source of insight into Spinoza's more intimate and personal characteristics, which does not depend upon supposing that people who present themselves in exaggerated or extreme ways are striving to conceal characteristics which they consider to require special restraint or cosmetic treatment. The first few pages of one of Spinoza's more important philosophical books – his *Treatise on the Improvement of the Understanding* – are quasi-autobiographical. They do not tell us about Spinoza's inner life in unqualified or explicit terms. Nonetheless, reading them attentively does bring to light far more of what motivated Spinoza's philosophical work – how he was quite personally involved in his philosophical project – than Hampshire's characterization of his selflessness might lead us to expect.

The opening section of the *Treatise* (its first 16 or 17 paragraphs) has been regarded by many readers as one of the most inspiring pieces of writing in our philosophical literature. One commentator speaks of the "sweep and grandeur of the thoughts it embodies" and declares that it "undoubtedly merits the universal admiration it has received."[8] My own opinion of it is somewhat less enthusiastic. I find its "grandeur" a trifle conventional and its moral stance perhaps even somewhat banal. But it is certainly an interesting text, if not for the novelty or the inherent value of its ideas then for the rather surprising illumination of Spinoza's intimate psychic processes and concerns which it provides.

7   Hampshire (1951), pp. 234–235.
8   Joachim (1958), pp. 14–15.

Here is the paragraph with which the *Treatise* begins:

After experience had taught me that all the usual surroundings of social life are vain and futile; seeing that none of the objects of my fears contained in themselves anything either good or bad, except insofar as the mind is affected by them, I finally resolved to inquire whether there might be some real good having power to communicate itself, which would affect the mind singly, to the exclusion of all else: whether in fact there might be anything of which the discovery and attainment would enable me to enjoy continuous, supreme and unending happiness.[9]

In the early parts of his *Discourse on Method,* Descartes had complained of how empty and unsatisfying he had found the science and other learning to which his early education had been devoted. Spinoza starts by expressing a more general complaint against the vanity and futility, not merely of education and of standard learning, but of *all* the usual surroundings of social life. And the goal to whose pursuit he commits himself is correspondingly general and uncompromising: not merely a reliable and productive method of scientific inquiry, but nothing less than the secret of "continuous, supreme and unending happiness."

This is extremely ambitious. It makes Spinoza's project rather unreal, a bit preposterous, and perhaps somewhat intimidating. In any case, it is notable that Spinoza makes a close link between the improvement of the understanding or intellect – which is, after all, the primary theme of the *Treatise* – and the attainment of happiness, which is the subject to which he first turns. Of course, it is natural enough to suppose that increasing our capacity for reliable knowledge would facilitate the improvement of our lives. But Spinoza connects perfecting our rational capacities and perfecting our lives in a particularly intimate way.

After stating the goal to which his *Treatise* is to be devoted, Spinoza explains that he cannot conduct his proposed inquiry effectively without abandoning, or at least substantially modifying, the customary preoccupations of life. Most people, he says, assume that the highest goods are money and material things, fame, and sensual pleasure; and they devote themselves to pursuing these. But he has found in his own experience that pursuing them is too absorbing and too distracting. Since it does not permit a serious and fruitful effort to discover the nature of what is ultimately valuable, he must turn away from it.

It is quite commonplace for moralists to warn people against supposing that sensual pleasure, fame, and money are genuine or unequivocal goods. It is worth looking in some detail, however, at the particular critique of these attractions that Spinoza offers. Of sensual pleasure he says this: "By sensual pleasure the mind is enthralled to the extent of quiescence, as if the supreme good were actually attained, so that it is quite incapable of thinking of any other object; when such pleasure has been gratified it is followed by extreme melancholy, whereby the

9 Spinoza (1913), vol. I, p. 3; Spinoza (1951), vol. II, p. 3.

mind, though not enthralled, is disturbed and dulled."[10] Spinoza is clearly not talking about the sort of physical pleasure one gets from a brisk walk in the country. That is not the sort of activity which enthralls us to the point of quiescence or whose appeal drives out all thoughts of other things. Nor is it common, or even understandable, that an activity of that sort should be followed by melancholy, much less by "extreme melancholy." A bit further on Spinoza asserts that sensual pleasure is followed not merely by melancholy but by *repentance*. This only confirms the strong impression that, whether or not he is clear about this himself, Spinoza is describing sexual pleasure, which he evidently finds extremely enticing but which he also finds to be mixed characteristically with unpleasant experiences of depression and guilt.

Spinoza's initial point about money and fame is a somewhat different one. It is that there is no limit to how much of those things people who care about them desire; indeed, the more people have of them the more they tend to want. The pursuit of sensual pleasure is limited by our susceptibility to fatigue or to the exhaustion of our capacity for engaging in, or for enjoying, whatever activity is in question. But no limitation of this kind is inherent in the pursuit of money or the pursuit of fame, which are by nature endless and uncompleteable and which will continue as long as they are not limited by something outside themselves – some goal which defines how much money or how much fame is enough. Spinoza finds that these goods cannot of themselves bring satisfaction, because there is no particular amount of them which is naturally or inherently satisfying. Moreover, pursuing either of them is inevitably competitive and leads inescapably to undesirable experiences, such as those of envy, hatred, fear, and disappointment. People who are committed to the pursuit of conventional goods, Spinoza warns, expose themselves to extremes of contradictory emotion. They swing from intense pleasure to feelings of melancholy and guilt; and their satisfactions are often mixed with frustration when they discover that attaining what they desire serves only to arouse a further desire for more than they already have.

As Spinoza elaborates these points, the quality and tone of his account undergo a conspicuous change. The conventional goods, he says, are not only unreliable and unsatisfying. They are actually *evil* and extremely *dangerous* to us; and anyone who devotes himself to them is "in a state of great peril." As he goes on, Spinoza seems to be more and more carried away. The peril to which he refers turns out to be not just a danger of moral corruption or of misery or of some sort of deterioration of the soul. He insists that it is literally a peril of *death*. And then it becomes not only a peril but even a *certainty* of death! Conventional goods *often* cause the deaths of those who possess them, Spinoza declares, and they *always* cause the deaths of those who are possessed by them. The context makes it unmistakably clear, by the way,

10   Spinoza (1913), vol. I, p. 3; Spinoza (1951), vol. II, p. 4.

that these references to death are not metaphorical. Spinoza's statements really are just as wild as they seem.[11]

Spinoza never completed the *Treatise on the Improvement of the Understanding*. He clearly had some notion of completing it, however, since he made a number of notes in the margin of his manuscript concerning changes to be made in a subsequent version which he never actually wrote. One of those notes occurs at the point where he makes the remarkable – indeed, incredible – claim that giving in to or allowing oneself to be possessed by desires for sensual pleasure, money, or fame brings certain death. His note to himself reads: "These considerations should be set forth more precisely."[12] Indeed! Evidently he became aware of the exaggeration into which he had permitted himself to be swept, caught himself up short in his marginal admonition to himself, and intended one day to give a more measured and less fantasy-ridden account of his subject.

As I read Spinoza's text, my impression is that he is expressing very considerable anxiety concerning urges and desires within himself which he recognizes as having no inherent limit and which he therefore fears he may be unable to control. His desires for sensual pleasure *are* self-limiting in a way, since satisfaction exhausts them. But they are difficult to resist, and they and their satisfactions are naturally linked in his experience to melancholy and to guilt. When he imagines himself giving in to the other desires with which he is concerned, his thought of doing so is closely associated in his mind with a fantasy of being severely punished and even, if the urges are permitted to career altogether out of control, of being killed.

In discussing the desires for money and fame, Spinoza attributes much of the unsatisfactory quality of these objects as ends in themselves to the fact that they are necessarily *scarce*. Since there cannot be enough of them to satisfy all possible desires, the satisfaction of one person's desires diminishes the chances of satisfaction for others. Those who desire money or fame are therefore inevitably in competition with others who are also ambitious to acquire them. It is the inevitability of competition which leads Spinoza to regard the value of attaining these goods as inextricably compromised by the evils of hatred, envy, fear of loss, and other disturbances of the mind.

The general impression given by Spinoza's examination of conventional goods as a whole is that he is concerned – only slightly beneath the surface and with so much intensity that it bubbles up at times into more or less open view – about powerful sexual desires and competitive urges, by which he is strongly moved but which he believes he must control and limit because of intense feelings of guilt and fear of punishment which are closely associated with them in his mind. I think it very natural and plausible to identify these competitive and sexual urges, the anxiety that they will get out of control, and the exaggerated fear of punishment

---

11 Spinoza (1913), vol. I, p. 4; Spinoza (1951), vol. II, p. 4.
12 Spinoza (1913), vol. I, p. 4; Spinoza (1951), vol. II, p. 5.

which Spinoza associates with them, as comprising elements in an Oedipal syndrome. But I will not insist upon this characterization of his underlying preoccupation. It will suffice, for my purposes, to notice that he is concerned with desires which lead to trouble because they do not naturally limit themselves, because they bring those who give in to them into conflict with others, and because for a variety of reasons they entail an array of undesirable disturbances of the mind.

What is the cure for all this? How are we to avoid these disturbances of the mind, which obstruct and interrupt the sustained serenity and joy which Spinoza seeks? The secret, he declares, is to care deeply only for what is eternal and infinite – in other words, for what is neither transitory nor scarce. The enjoyment of something of that kind will be, he assures us, unmingled with any sadness; no contrary pain will be inherent in the pleasure it brings. Now, it is pretty clear that being eternal and infinite is not really enough. After all, the number six is eternal; and even if we add all the other positive integers, so that we get an object that is not only eternal but infinite as well, this hardly solves the problem of how to achieve perfect happiness.

Of course Spinoza has something more particular in mind, which comes out when he begins to describe the ideal condition of human life. Here is the paragraph in which his central claim emerges:

All things which come to pass, come to pass according to the eternal order and fixed laws of Nature. However, human weakness cannot attain to this order in its own thought, but meanwhile man conceives a human character much more stable than his own, and sees that there is no reason why he should not himself acquire such a character. . . . What that character is we shall show in due time, namely that it is the knowledge of the union existing between the mind and the whole of nature.[13]

It is clear enough what eternal and infinite object it is that Spinoza identifies in this passage as capable of playing a fundamental role in the achievement of human happiness. It is "the eternal order and fixed laws of Nature." But the observation Spinoza makes next is sometimes misunderstood. After referring to the eternal order and fixed laws of Nature, he observes that we are too weak to attain this order in our own thoughts. Now this has been construed by some readers as a lament over our inability to arrive at a totally comprehensive knowledge of Nature. That is how Joachim, for example, appears to read the passage. He evidently supposes that the human weakness to which Spinoza calls attention is an intellectual or scientific inadequacy; we are simply not intelligent enough to grasp the eternal order in all its details.[14]

Spinoza himself makes it rather clear, however, that his attention is not focused primarily on our intellectual limitations. After alluding to human weakness and to

13 Spinoza (1913), vol. I, pp. 5–6; Spinoza (1951), vol. II, p. 6.
14 Joachim (1958), pp. 22–23.

the incapacity it entails, he declares that "man conceives a human character much more stable than his own," and that this conception of a more stable character provides the ideal goal toward which human endeavor must strive. The ideal is not formulated in terms of intelligence or of knowledge or of understanding, but as a matter of *stability*. In other words, what we conceive as the ideal character for ourselves is not one distinguished primarily by greater knowledge than we possess, but one which emulates the characteristics which Spinoza has just been ascribing to Nature – namely, order and fixity or, to use his word, stability. Our aim is to be rid of the disturbances which unbalance our condition, interrupt the evenness of our thoughts and feelings, and make us suffer passively the effects upon us of forces with which we do not identify and which we experience as alien to ourselves.

How does Spinoza imagine this stability can be achieved? There, of course, is where knowledge comes in. We achieve stability by understanding "the union existing between the mind and the whole of nature" – that is, by recognizing ourselves as products of forces which are generated systematically and in a lawful manner according to the fixed nature of the world, and by understanding that what goes on within us is by no means random or unintelligible but that it is (like everything else that happens) a necessary consequence of the fundamental substance and structure of the universe. The more we come to see the events of our own lives – and especially the events of our minds – as manifestations of an eternal and fixed order of natural law and natural necessity, the more intelligible they become to us and the less we are beset by emotions which breach and undermine the order of our nature and the stability of our existence. This reduces our sense that the power of the universe is alien to us and that we are merely passive with respect to it.

IV

Both Spinoza and Descartes are fundamentally preoccupied with what each takes to be – or fears may be – a crippling discrepancy between his own nature and the general nature of reality. The problem is in each case one of order and intelligibility. Descartes's concern is that the world around him may be literally a chaos, altogether lacking in any coherence or intelligible structure which he might grasp. Spinoza, on the other hand, is attentive primarily to the experience of disorder within himself, which represents an estrangement between himself and the rational stability of the order of Nature.

Descartes's response to the problem posed by his realization that he may not "belong" in the world – that his intellectual standards may not be satisfiable by the inherent nature of things – is to decide that he does not and need not care, because he can find sufficient satisfaction within the processes of his own thought without establishing that these processes reflect those of the world as it is in itself. Spinoza's solution to the problem posed by his inner disorder is to turn away from himself and to have his life ordered and structured through being embraced within the comprehensive rational order forming the intelligible structure of the world as a whole. Descartes seeks to escape the irrationality of the universe by discovering and cultivating an orderliness and coherence within his own mind. Spinoza attempts to escape the irrationality and violent disorder he finds within his own psychic experience by discovering and connecting himself to the coherence and necessity of the world outside himself.

This difference between Descartes and Spinoza reflects a different sort of confidence in the two men: the former believes in himself and is willing to rely upon his own inner resources and character without caring whether or not they can be validated by an authority external to themselves; on the other hand, the latter despairs of satisfying his own inner needs without turning for support to a source of strength and stability outside himself. Descartes substitutes the order within himself for the chaos in the world. Spinoza substitutes the order of the universe for the chaos within himself.

Each of the two philosophers wishes to avoid the implications of a fundamental conflict between his own nature and the nature of the world. But Descartes's notion is to achieve harmony by insisting that the world be describable (whatever its inherent nature) in terms congenial to the requirements of his own mind, while Spinoza's idea is to achieve the harmony for which he recognizes a need by submitting himself to an order which he gladly acknowledges to be superior to his own. On the one hand there is the rebel, who defies opposition to the satisfaction of his own requirements; on the other there is the mystic, who copes with conflict and opposition by denying himself and by seeking to be absorbed into the whole from which he finds himself separated. The rebel and the mystic share a desire to overcome the discrepancy between themselves and what is other than themselves, one by changing the world to suit himself and the other by merging himself into the external order.

I do not know what moral to draw from these comparisons and contrasts, or whether there is in fact any significant or useful moral to be drawn from them. No doubt the differences between Spinoza and Descartes reflect to some considerable extent the difference between two fundamentally divergent types of individual character structure. Not much serious work has been done to illuminate the relationships between individual character and psychic structure on the one hand and types of philosophical thought on the other. I believe that these relationships might prove to be very interesting, but I am uncertain whether they can reliably be pursued in satisfactory depth.

REFERENCES

Descartes, R. *Oeuvres*. Ed. C. Adam and P. Tannery. 11 vols. Paris: Cerf, 1897–1910.

Philosophical Letters. Trans. A. Kenny. Oxford: Clarendon Press, 1970.

Philosophical Works. Trans. E. Haldane and G. Ross. 2 vols. Cambridge: Cambridge University Press, 1972.

Frankfurt, H. "Descartes on the Creation of Eternal Truths." *Philosophical Review* 86 (1977): 36–57.

Hampshire, S. *Spinoza.* Harmondsworth: Penguin Books, 1951.

Joachim, H. *Spinoza's Tractatus de Intellectus Emendatione.* Oxford: Clarendon Press, 1958.

Spinoza, B. (1913). *Opera.* Ed. J. Van Vloten and J. P. N. Land. 3d ed. 4 vols. in 2. The Hague: Martinus Nijhoff, 1913.

Chief Works. Trans. R. Elwes. 2 vols. New York: Dover Publications, 1951.

5

Continuous Creation, Ontological Inertia, and the Discontinuity of Time

I

Descartes's doctrine that natural things cannot endure unless divine creation is continuous appears in each of his three major philosophical works. There are two brief allusions to it in the *Discourse on Method.* It plays a larger role in the *Third Meditation,* where it is developed as a step in Descartes's second argument for the existence of God. Evidently the doctrine did not become less significant in Descartes's thought as time went on. He presents it in the *Principles of Philosophy* (I, 21) as sufficient in itself to serve as a proof that God exists.

In Part IV of the *Discourse* (AT VI, 36), Descartes observes that if there are any finite minds or bodies in the world, "leur être devait dépendre de sa puissance, en telle sorte qu'elles ne pouvaient subsister sans lui un seul moment." This suggests that created things, besides owing to God their creation, owe to Him at each moment the continuation of their existence as well. They could no more endure without God than they could begin to exist without Him. Descartes does not make very explicit what he has in mind here. He leaves it unclear both why God's power is essential to the subsistence of things and how God's power accounts for their subsistence. The doctrine is introduced without argument and without explanation.

Later in the *Discourse,* during a discussion of how the world reached its present condition, Descartes says this:

... il est ... vraisemblable que, dès le commencement, Dieu l'a rendu tel qu'il devait être. Mais il est certain, et c'est une opinion communément reçue entre les théologiens, que l'action, par laquelle maintenant il le conserve, est toute la même que celle par laquelle il l'a créé. (AT VI, 45)

What is here said to depend upon God is not the continued existence of individual finite things, as in the earlier passage, but the preservation of the world. This apparent discrepancy is somewhat confusing. On the other hand, the later passage does partially illuminate another matter: it provides some clarification concerning how God enables things or the world to continue existing. He does this, Descartes explains, by performing an act that is "toute la même" as His act of original creation. Of course, this explanation is itself equivocal. Are we to understand that the act of preservation is *just like* the act of creation but *numerically distinct* from it –

55

that it is another act, though of the same kind as the first? Or are we to understand that it is *literally the same* act – in other words, that there is only a single act by which God both creates and preserves?

Descartes provides further clarification of his views concerning God's creative activity, and he introduces some additional complications, in the *Third Meditation*:

Car tout le temps de ma vie peut être divisé en une infinité de parties, chacune desquelles ne dépend en aucune façon des autres; et ainsi, de ce qu'un peu auparavant j'ai été, il ne s'ensuit pas que je doive maintenant être, si ce n'est qu'en ce moment quelque cause me produise et me crée, pour ainsi dire, derechef, c'est-à-dire me conserve. En effet c'est une chose bien claire et bien évidente (à tous ceux qui considéreront avec attention la nature du temps), qu'une substance, pour être conservée dans tous les moments qu'elle dure, a besoin du même pouvoir et de la même action, qui serait nécessaire pour la produire et la créer tout de nouveau, si elle n'était point encore. En sorte que la lumière naturelle nous fait voir clairement, que la conservation et la création ne diffèrent qu'au regard de notre façon de penser, et non point en effet. (AT IX, 39)

Here the focus is again upon individual finite things, rather than upon the world. With respect to a finite person, Descartes says, it follows from the nature of time that the existence of the person at one time does not entail the person's existence at any later time. In order for the person to continue existing for any period of time, at each moment some cause must, "pour ainsi dire," create it afresh. Things would not endure at all without the same exercise of power that was required to bring them into existence.

There is an even sharper formulation of Descartes's thesis in *Principles of Philosophy* (I, 21):

. . . la nature du temps ou de la durée de notre vie . . . étant telle que ses parties ne dépendent point les unes des autres et n'existent jamais ensemble, de ce que nous sommes maintenant, il ne s'ensuit pas nécessairement que nous soyons un moment après, si quelque cause, à savoir la même qui nous a produits, ne continue à nous produire, c'est-à-dire ne nous conserve. Et nous connaissons aisément qu'il n'y a point de force en nous par laquelle nous puissions subsister ou nous conserver un seul moment. (AT IX-II, 34)

In the *Third Meditation,* Descartes asserts that my existence can be preserved only if there is some cause that "me crée, pour ainsi dire derechef." In this passage from the *Principles* he says that, since we have no power to keep ourselves in existence, our continued existence depends upon our being continually reproduced "as it were" by the same cause that brought us into existence originally. How are we to understand this fresh creation, or this continual reproduction? What exactly does God do, how does He do it, and why is this activity on His part necessary?

II

Descartes's assertions concerning the need for continuous creation entail a particular way of understanding what may be referred to, with some plausibility, as "ontological inertia." According to the Cartesian account, the existence of finite things or of the world will cease unless it is continually sustained by an external force. Now it is evident that this principle of ontological inertia corresponds very closely to the principle of inertia with respect to motion ("kinetic inertia") that had been formulated by Aristotle and that was generally accepted by medieval and scholastic thinkers. The Aristotelian principle states that a moving body will continue to move only as long as it continues to be acted upon by a force that constitutes a source of motion; in other words, a body will immediately cease moving as soon as it fails to receive an additional or renewed impetus to motion.[1] Just as Descartes's principle stipulates that *existence* will continue only if it is sustained or conserved by a source of existence, so the Aristotelian principle stipulates that *motion* will cease unless it is sustained by a source of motion. There appears to be, then, a quite clear analogy between the Aristotelian way of understanding kinetic inertia and the understanding of ontological inertia by Descartes.

Aristotle's theory of motion was superseded in the seventeenth century by a different way of understanding kinetic inertia, according to which a moving body will continue moving unless some external force causes it to stop. This alternative to the Aristotelian account was to become a cornerstone of Newton's physics. It was first published by Gassendi in 1642 (*De Motu Impresso a Motore Translato*). However, the first person to articulate the new principle fully was in fact Descartes himself, who introduced it in *Le Monde* as follows:

Que chaque partie de la matière, en particulier, continue toujours d'être en un même état, pendant que le rencontre des autres ne la contraint point de le changer. C'est-à-dire que: si elle a quelque grosseur, elle ne deviendra jamais plus petite, sinon que les autres la divisent; si elle est ronde ou carrée, elle ne changera jamais cette figure sans que les autres l'y contraignent; si elle est arrêtée en quelque lieu, elle n'en partira jamais que les autres ne l'en chassent; et si elle a une fois commencé à se mouvoir, elle continuera toujours avec une égale force jusques à ce que les autres l'arrêtent ou la retardent. (AT XI, 38)

Although its publication was delayed, *Le Monde* was written several years before Gassendi's work. "Descartes can thus be claimed," Crombie asserts, "as the first to have given expression to the complete principle of inertia."[2] In *Principles of Philosophy* (II, 37), Descartes gives the principle a somewhat plainer formulation:

. . . que chaque chose en particulier continue d'être en même état autant qu'il se peut, et que jamais elle ne le change que par la rencontre des autres. . . . Si elle est en repos, elle ne commence point à se mouvoir de soi-même. Mais lorsqu'elle a commencé une fois de se mouvoir, nous n'avons aussi aucune raison de penser qu'elle doive jamais cesser de se mouvoir de même force, pendant qu'elle ne rencontre rien qui retarde ou qui arrête son mouvement. (AT IX-II, 84)

1   A. C. Crombie, *Medieval and Early Modern Science* (New York: Doubleday, 1959), pp. 64–5, n. 11.
2   Ibid.

Whether or not Descartes deserves credit for being the veritable originator of the modern principle of kinetic inertia, he was unquestionably an unequivocal advocate of adopting that principle in place of the account provided by Aristotle.

Now there is something about this that strikes me as rather puzzling. The problem it raises may perhaps be conveyed by the following mildly paradoxical question: why does Descartes remain an Aristotelian in the account he gives of *existence,* when he is so emphatically a Cartesian in his theory of *motion?* Evidently he adopts with respect to the former a conception of inertia which he deliberately and energetically rejects with respect to the latter. But why does he not say of existence, as he is so eager to say of motion, that it will continue unless some external force causes it to cease? Or why does he not say of motion, as he so insistently says of existence, that it will continue only if it is sustained by a continuous activity of renewal?

Descartes argues for his doctrine of continuous creation by observing that (a) "tout le temps de ma vie peut être divisé en une infinité de parties," (b) each part "ne dépend en aucune façon des autres," and (c) "de ce qu'un peu auparavant j'ai été, il ne s'ensuit pas que je doive maintenant être, si ce n'est qu'en ce moment quelque cause me produise et me crée, pour ainsi dire, derechef, c'est-à-dire me conserve." However, it is no less true of motion than it is of existence that a preceding stage does not of itself necessitate a later one. A movement is (a') divisible into as many parts as a lifespan; (b') each segment of a movement is completely independent of the others; and (c') it does not follow from the fact that a body was moving a little while ago that it must be moving now. So why is it not equally true that it will *not* be moving now unless some cause renews its motion — that is, preserves it — at this moment? In his doctrine of continuous creation, Descartes appears to insist upon a way of understanding inertia which he refuses to employ in his theory of motion. His conception of kinetic inertia is distinctively modern, yet his conception of ontological inertia is backward-looking. What account is to be given of this seemingly odd discrepancy in his views?

The explanation cannot lie in the importance of maintaining that existence is contingent and dependent. Treating existence in the same way as motion would no more jeopardize the dependency of existence, or the supposition that finite existence is a contingent matter, than Descartes's treatment of motion jeopardizes the contingency or dependency of motion. The non-Cartesian proposition that existence continues unless something forces it to cease is quite compatible with Descartes's observations that a temporal sequence can end at any point or that no moment of time necessitates a next moment. Nor does the proposition imply that finite existence is independent of God in any sense that conflicts with the presumption of divine omnipotence. Asserting that existence will continue unless God stops it does not entail that God lacks the power to stop it. A principle of ontological inertia analogous to Descartes's principle of kinetic inertia would simply state that existence continues until it is stopped by something external to itself. Whether in a particular instance anything external does actually stop it would be either a contingent matter or, if it were a matter of necessity, the necessity would derive from something other than the thing whose continued existence is at issue.

III

The underlying question, on which disagreement leads to the difference between the Aristotelian and the Cartesian conceptions of kinetic inertia, has to do with whether the motion of a moving body is to be considered a state or property of that body, or whether it is to be understood as a process which the body undergoes. If the motion is a state or a property of the moving body, then a continuation of the motion naturally means that this property of the body does not change or that the body remains in the same state as long as the motion continues. Construing motion as a property or state of a moving body means that the continuation of the body's motion implies no change of property or state. Now it is only to account for changes that reference to external forces must be made; when things do not change, but remain just as they were, no such explanation is required. Descartes and Newton understood uniform rectilinear motion as a condition that involves no change. Accordingly, they did not consider any force to be needed in order to maintain a body in that condition. On the other hand, Aristotle regarded motion as a process; that is, he regarded a moving body as undergoing change as long as it continues to move. He considered it necessary, accordingly, to provide an explanation for this change.[3]

Everything depends upon whether the continuation of a body's motion is understood as the continuation of a process of change, or whether it is understood as equivalent to remaining unchanged. As Crombie explains the matter:

The revolution in dynamics in the seventeenth century was brought about by the substitution of the concept . . . that uniform motion in a straight line is simply a state of a body and is equivalent to rest, for the Aristotelian conception of motion as a process of becoming which required for its maintenance continuous efficient causation.[4]

Although Descartes helped to bring about this revolution in dynamics, by proposing that motion be construed as a state of a body rather than as a process, his theory of continuous creation depends upon construing the continuation of existence in a manner similar to that in which the continuation of motion is construed by Aristotle. Thus, Descartes's theory appears to depend upon supposing that temporality or duration — that is, the continuation of existence — implies a process of becoming and not merely the persistence without change of a state or a property.

3 Ibid.
4 Op. cit., p. 135.

But how can this be so? If the passage of a body from one place to another does not imply any change of property or state, and hence does not as such require any causal explanation, why should the passage of time be thought to entail a change for which some cause must be found? The question seems even more difficult if we consider what Descartes believed concerning the relation between existence and duration – that is, concerning the relation between the fact that something exists and the fact that it continues to exist for some finite period of time. His view is that existence and duration are equivalent. There can be neither existence without duration, he maintains, nor duration or passage of time without something that exists. Thus there can be no such thing as existence for a durationless instant. If anything exists at all, then it exists long enough to permit the differentiation of earlier and later stages of its existence.

Gueroult attributes to Descartes the view that "exister et durer sont synonymes."[5] Whether Descartes actually considers them synonymous, he does consider them inseparable. There can be no passage of time, in his view, without existence. Thus he says: "Je crois qu'il implique contradiction de concevoir une durée entre la destruction du premier monde et la création du nouveau."[6] If nothing existed, there would be no duration whatever because there would be nothing to endure. As for the converse, Descartes says this:

Enfin, la distinction qui se fait par la pensée consiste en ce que nous distinguons quelquefois une substance de quelqu'un de ses attributs sans lequel néanmoins il n'est pas possible que nous en ayons une connaissance distincte. . . . Par exemple, à cause qu'il n'y point de substance qui ne cesse d'exister lorsqu'elle cesse de durer, la durée n'est distincte de la substance que par la pensée.[7]

This makes it clear that it is in Descartes's view impossible for there to be a substance that does not endure. In other words, Descartes believes that existence requires duration.

But if what exists is necessarily enduring, why should its existence need to be continuously renewed? Given that duration is entailed by existence, the continuation of existence would seem to be at least as much a property inherent in what exists as motion is a property inherent in what moves. And in that case, continuing to exist should no more require explanation in terms of an external force than continuing to move does. How are we to account, then, for Descartes's insistence that continuous creation by God is needed in order to conserve or to provide for the endurance of what exists?

It is obvious that the assertion that existence is impossible without duration does not entail that an existing thing must exist for any particular length of time.

5   All quotations from the work of Gueroult are from his *Descartes Selon l'Ordre des Raisons*, vol. I (Paris: Aubier, 1953), pp. 272–85.
6   Letter to More, 15 April 1649, in F. Alquié, *Descartes, Œuvres Philosophiques*, vol. III (Paris: Garnier, 1973), p. 909.
7   *Principes* I, 62; AT IX-II, 53.

The requirement that an existing thing must endure for some period is satisfied no matter how brief the duration of the period. Now this might suggest the following principle: whatever exists must have at least the minimum possible duration. Whatever the shortest possible length of time may be, in other words, nothing can exist without lasting at least that long. When God creates an existing thing, He must create it with a career no shorter than that; otherwise it can have no career, and hence cannot exist at all. What if the thing continues to exist for a longer period? It might be suggested that this happens when God's creative activity with respect to the thing continues, or when it is repeated, or when in some manner it extends beyond the activity by which God brought about the initial segment of the thing's existence. This line of thought might lead to a view of creation and of existence as pulsating: when God creates something, it necessarily endures for a minimum length of time – a pulse – and it continues to exist beyond that time if God produces additional creative pulses.

However, the notion of a minimum possible period of time is not acceptable to Descartes. He does not allow that there can be natural temporal units of irreducible brevity. We are incapable, to be sure, of discerning temporal periods of less than some finite duration. But this is a function of our limited capacities; it does not mean that periods of even lesser duration do not occur. For Descartes, time is infinitely divisible. Whatever the inadequacies of humans may be, God is aware that no temporal sequence is too short to include a sequence of even lesser extent. There are, in other words, no atoms of time. Descartes does speak of instants, which have no duration. But instants are not parts of time, out of which time is composed; they are limits or extremities. Just as a surface is the limit or extremity of a body, so an instant is a limit or terminus of a duration or period of time. Since a surface may be common to two bodies, it is plainly not a part of either. Similarly, an instant is not a part of the periods of time whose common boundary it marks.[8]

IV

It is important to recognize that with the supposition that any period of time whatever is divisible, there follows from the doctrine of continuous creation a consequence somewhat more radical than any that Descartes explicitly articulates. If every duration is divisible, then the proposition that the continued existence of an entity requires continuous divine creation entails that the original bringing into being of the entity also requires continuous creation. That is, God's continuous creative activity is required for the *initiation* of existence, and not only for conserving or prolonging it. In other words, *any* creation must be continuous creation.

8   J.-M. Beyssade, *La Philosophie Première de Descartes* (Paris: Flammarion, 1979), pp. 347–8.

The reason for this is that any existence whatever must be an existence that continues for some period of time. Now since there is no shortest period of time, and since everything that exists must exist for some period of time, it is inescapable that every existing thing might exist for a shorter period of time than it actually does. However brief its duration, it necessarily continues beyond what is indispensable for its existence; however short its career, it is longer than it needs to be. The premises of Descartes's argument concerning continuous creation are: (i) only divine creative activity can insure the existence of a thing whose continued existence is not necessary, and (ii) an existing thing can cease existing at any moment. Let us add to this the further provision: (iii) no period is a temporal atom but always includes a period of even shorter duration. Then the following conclusion is derivable: (iv) there can be no existing thing whose duration is so short that it does not require continuous creation. On Descartes's account, then, all creation entails continuous creation. For he insists that existence through any divisible period of time requires continuous creation throughout that time; and from this, together with the supposition that every period of time is divisible, it follows that there can be no existence at all without continuous creation. God cannot create anything without conserving it for some period of time by continuous creative activity.

But why is continuous creation on God's part needed at all? Why is it not possible for God to create an existing thing that has its own capacity to endure, without any further attention from Him? Motion is presumed by Descartes to continue without requiring any additional external impetus. Why, then, does he insist that existence cannot endure — which means that it is not possible at all — without a continuous direct exercise of divine power? Suppose it *were* possible for God to endow the things He creates with a power to endure. In that case no continuous conserving activity on His part would be needed to sustain them. Once He had created them, they would sustain their own existence by virtue of the power with which He had endowed them. So far as I can see, Descartes simply takes for granted with respect to these issues the view of Saint Thomas and other scholastics, according to which the possession by created things of a capacity to exist on their own would compromise divine omnipotence.

The point is not that having an inherent power to exist would make created things independent of God. After all, His power might still be greater than theirs, and sufficient to destroy them, so that their continued existence would depend upon His continued toleration even though it did not depend upon Him as its source. The point is, rather, that God is being; and therefore He cannot cause non-being. Aquinas says: "Not-being has no essential cause; for nothing is a cause except inasmuch as it is a being, and a being essentially as such is a cause of being. Therefore, God cannot cause a thing to tend to not-being. . . ."[9] God cannot cause

---

9 *Summa Theologica*, Question 104, art. 3, reply obj. 1.

anything to cease existing. Thus if the world had within itself a power to continue existing, God could not directly overcome that power. The world would be independent of Him, not because He would not be powerful enough to destroy it but because He could not use His power to destroy it. If we are to regard continuing existents as remaining dependent upon God throughout their durations, accordingly, we must not regard them as continuing to exist by virtue of a power that is inherent in them.

V

What does God's continuous creation conserve? It must be clear that it cannot be the existence of particular finite things as such. If it were, then those things would continue to exist as long as God's creative activity continued; and this means, of course, that they would continue to exist forever. What the divine creativity conserves can only be the *substance* or *being* of things. Individual finite things come into being through the acquisition by substance – especially material substance – of specific forms: for instance, a builder arranges construction materials so that they form a house. Now in principle a house might cease to exist in either of two ways. The materials of which it is made may come to be arranged differently; they may change their form, in other words, as happens when the house collapses into rubble. Or the materials of which the house is made – its substance or matter – may cease to exist entirely; they may be annihilated, or fall back from being into sheer nothingness. Needless to say, God does not prevent the former of these alternatives from occurring. Houses do, after all, collapse into rubble.[10] The second alternative is prevented by God's continuous creative activity, which conserves the substance of the house not only so long as the house exists but throughout the manifold transformations of form that any finite portion of matter undergoes.

This suggests that Descartes's account of the situation with respect to motion actually differs far less than may at first sight appear – and less than I have suggested – from his account of the situation with respect to existence. He supposes that God's continuous creative activity conserves material substance, which neither increases nor diminishes since God's act is always the same. But he recognizes that the forms and configurations of matter at any time depend upon the changing impacts of natural forces: particular material things do not change or pass out of existence except as a result of the action of these forces upon them. The same is true of motion. Descartes supposes that particular motions persist except

---

10 In the *Third Meditation*, to be sure, Descartes speaks of God as conserving the existence of a particular finite thing – namely, Descartes himself. But in the *Third Meditation*, Descartes does not yet think of himself as a composite being with both a body and a soul. He thinks of himself as a thinking thing – that is, a simple mental substance which has no parts, which is therefore not susceptible to rearrangement or dissolution, and which can cease to exist only if God destroys it.

insofar as natural forces affect them. He understands the total quantity of motion, however, to be constant. It is unaffected by natural forces, because it is sustained by the same divine creative activity by which matter is conserved. Perhaps, then, it is in the end misleading to use the term "ontological inertia" at all. It may well be that the concept of inertia pertains more properly to the forms or arrangements of being, rather than to being or existence itself. The forms and arrangements of what exists are, it would seem, the most genuine analogues of those aspects of motion – namely, direction, velocity, and distribution – to which the principle of kinetic inertia applies.

VI

Descartes's theory of continuous creation is regarded by many interpreters of his work as entailing what they refer to as "the discontinuity of time." Gilson is among these. He understands the assertion by Descartes that no moment of time depends upon the preceding moment as tantamount to a claim that time is "radicalement discontinu."[11] On Gilson's account, this claim concerning the discontinuity of time means that duration is not intrinsic to existence. The continuing existence of the world and of its contents is to be conceived as, strictly speaking, a matter of "discontinuous successive states." Each of these successive states of the world requires, according to this interpretation, specific and separate creation by God. Thus Gilson contrasts a universe in which time is continuous – "un univers doué d'une durée intrinsèque et d'une permanence réelle" – with "un univers d'états successifs discontinus tel que l'univers cartésien." In Descartes's view, as Gilson construes it, time does not flow on its own; nor do the changes that occur in natural objects occur by virtue of active powers that are inherent in nature. What happens in the natural world is not due to the efficient causality of immediately preceding natural events. Instead, all events are the direct outcomes of divine agency. Thus Gilson maintains that the idea of the discontinuity of time is closely related to the doctrine of occasionalism, which attributes all effective causation to God. It is also closely related, in Gilson's view, to Descartes's rejection of the metaphysics of substantial forms. For rejecting that theory meant that Descartes abandoned the only available account of change as a process that is to be understood in terms of forces inherent in nature.

Gueroult undertakes, in somewhat greater detail, the same approach to Descartes's theory of continuous creation. On his account, as on Gilson's, the discontinuity of time is entailed by Descartes's claim that all temporal instants are reciprocally independent. The commonsense conception of change is that there are enduring objects which, from time to time, undergo various alterations of their characteristics. Gueroult argues that from Descartes's claim that each instant is

11   E. Gilson, *René Descartes, Discours de la Méthode* (Paris: J. Vrin, 1947). All quotations from Gilson are from pp. 340–2 of this work.

independent of the others, it follows that this commonsense view of change is incorrect. The conception of change to which Gueroult believes Descartes is committed by his account of continuous creation is essentially cinematographic. In terms of this cinematographic conception, we must not suppose that there are in the world enduring things that undergo change. When change occurs, what happens is that the world ceases to exist and is replaced by another world in which things are somewhat different. Instead of enduring objects, we have an infinite succession of instantaneous worlds or world-states each of which is separate from and independent of the others. Continuity and duration are no more inherent in any of these successive worlds than motion is inherent in the still photographs whose succession provides the illusion of movement in a motion picture.

As Gueroult understands the matter, Descartes regards movement as having no intrinsic dynamic reality. Rather, "le mouvement est constitué par une infinité d'instants absolus où . . . il n'y a pas de mouvement." Thus, "le mouvement temporel de translation décrit par un corps qui se meut se résout en une répétition de créations d'univers. . . . Il n'y a pas transport du corps, mais celui-ci est créé ici, puis il est créé là." This is tantamount to the thesis of temporal discontinuity, as Gueroult understands it: "les diverses créations [d'univers] sont discontinues, puisque aucune d'elles n'est intrinsèquement liée à la précédente, puisqu'il n'y a pas passage, mais instauration répétition de créations libres. . . ." The point of the account is not merely, of course, that as a matter of fact created things do not happen to move. The point is that there is no possibility that a created thing should move. For movement takes time, and created things do not endure. The continued existence of the world is not constituted by the persistence in being of created things, which are capable of moving or of undergoing alteration of their characteristics during the period during which they persist. It is constituted by a sequence of world-states, each of which is instantaneous – i.e., without any duration at all.

In my judgment, the attribution of this doctrine to Descartes rests upon a misunderstanding or confusion. For Gueroult, as evidently for Gilson as well, the thesis that time is discontinuous is equivalent to the thesis that the parts of time are independent. Thus, in speaking of the parts of time Gueroult refers to "leur auto-suffisance intrinsèque, leur absolue indépendance réciproque qui constituent précisément leur discontinuité." On this interpretation, the successive states of the world are discontinuous precisely because "aucune d'elles n'est intrinsèquement liée à précédente" and because, accordingly, "il n'y a pas passage, mais . . . répétition de créations libres."

Now this is confusing. For the idea of a continuum, or of a continuous series, seems to have nothing at all to do with the characteristic upon which Gueroult focuses his attention and his argument. Whether a series is continuous is not essentially a matter of whether its elements are self-sufficient or whether they are dependent. Being continuous has to do with something else entirely. It has to do with whether the series is interrupted by gaps. A continuous series is not comprised of irreducible units or atoms, each of which would be separate from and external to all the others. It is a series that is infinitely divisible, and such that any finite segment of it is also infinitely divisible. There appears to be no close connection whatever between this idea of continuity and the idea of a series whose elements are generated in such a way that each successive element is dependent upon the preceding element in the series. Descartes does rather plainly maintain that time is not a series of the latter sort. But this hardly commits him to the view that time is not continuous.

The idea of continuity pertains to the *formal* characteristics of a series. The idea of independence that is pertinent here concerns the *substantive* relationships that may obtain among the elements of a series. Each successive element of a series might depend for its occurrence upon the preceding element of the series, even if the series were not continuous, infinitely divisible, or dense. On the other hand, a series might be altogether uninterrupted, with its elements flowing along in a wholly continuous way, even if no element of the series were dependent for its existence upon any other. Suppose that each atom in a sequence of indivisible atoms generates a next atom. We would then have a series that is discontinuous but in which each element depends for its existence upon the one before.

The discontinuity interpretation of Descartes's theory of continuous creation supposes that Descartes regards God's conservation of existence as consisting in the performance of a succession of creative acts. It entails that the act by which God conserves existence, and the act by which He creates it, are the *same* only in the sense that they are acts of the *same kind*. In another sense, the acts are quite different: their effects differ, not only with respect to the times at which their effects occur but also with respect to the qualitative features of the effects. Thus continuous creation involves, according to the discontinuity interpretation, the performance by God of numerous creative acts. These acts are the same in that all are creative, but they differ so far as concerns what they create. On this account, then, God creates both *repeatedly* and *variously*.

Now it is unquestionable that Descartes insists that the elements of a temporal succession are reciprocally independent. The type of independence he affirms is not substantive, however, but strictly formal. When he says that "de ce qu'un peu auparavant j'ai été, il ne s'ensuit pas que je doive maintenant être," he is making nothing more than a simple logical point: namely, that there is no contradiction in supposing that someone who existed a little while ago does not exist now. When he speaks of "la nature du temps ou de la durée de notre vie . . . étant telle que ses parties ne dépendent point les unes des autres," he means only that there is nothing in the concept of a temporal sequence that makes it impossible for the sequence to end at any point. There is no logical necessity, for any temporal series, that it continue past any given point. The continuation of existence is as much a logically contingent matter, in other words, as is its beginning.

If the discontinuity of time were equivalent just to this sort of independence, then it would manifestly be a contradiction to assert both that the parts of time are independent and that time is continuous. Thus it is easy to understand Gueroult's bewilderment at commentators who deny that Descartes construes time as discontinuous, for he believes that they make both of these assertions; he understands them as simultaneously acknowledging that for Descartes the parts of time are independent and as claiming that Descartes regards time as continuous. Gueroult complains: "Il semble bien difficile . . . de comprendre le *distinguo* établi ici entre, d'une part, la contingence, la séparation et l'indépendance réciproque des parties, et, d'autre part, la discontinuité, vu que celle-ci se définit précisément par ces trois caractères." It is much easier to understand the attempt to distinguish between discontinuity and the reciprocal independence of the parts of time, on the other hand, once one recognizes that the discontinuity thesis Gueroult and others attribute to Descartes is not in fact definable in terms of Descartes's claim that the parts of time are logically independent.

VII

The reason that commentators like Gueroult and Gilson interpret Descartes's doctrine of continuous creation as they do is, I believe, that they see his adoption of the doctrine as a consequence of his rejection of the medieval theory of substantial forms. The theory of substantial forms was an attempt to provide a metaphysical account of change. According to this account, the natural and normal changes undergone by a thing occur by virtue of the influence of the thing's substantial form, which guides its development and which explains the inherent process by which an enduring object passes from one state to another. The substantial form of an object determines what characteristics the object has during the successive segments of its continuing existence. Thus the object's various successive states manifest a natural order; the natural sequence of these states has an inner coherence, which consists in the progressive expression of a substantial form. On this account, natural change has an inherent direction, meaning, or goal. The various temporal segments of a thing's history are in these respects not at all independent. As in a process of growth, the character of each segment depends at least in part upon the character of the preceding. This dependency is not purely formal; it is a substantive relationship. The specific characteristics manifested by each temporal segment are pertinent, in ways that are determined by the thing's substantial form, to the characteristics that will be manifested in the next.

Now Descartes emphatically rejects the theory of substantial forms. Moreover, doing so is a fundamentally important aspect of his philosophical and scientific program. It is essential to recognize, however, that it is not from his rejection of this theory that he derives his theory of continuous creation. The reason he believes that creation must be continuous is not that there are no substantial forms to insure and to explain the conditioning of subsequent stages in the careers of natural objects by the characteristics of stages that precede. The reason for his adherence to the doctrine of continuous creation is the very same as that on the basis of which he supposes that original creation is indispensable: since the existence of the world is not self-caused, the world must be created by some agency external to it. Just as those things that are created must be created because they cannot (as God does) derive their existence from themselves, so they must be created continuously because they cannot derive the continuation of their existence from themselves either.

The validity of this simple point does not depend upon supposing that the theory of substantial forms is unacceptable. Even in a world pervasively shaped and guided by substantial forms, the point would be just as applicable and just as sound. After all, it is surely obvious that, regardless of whether there are substantial forms or not, Descartes's existence at one moment does not require his existence at the next. It is true that the theory of substantial forms implies that subsequent stages in the natural career of an object depend upon earlier stages. But this is not the sort of dependency that Descartes denies when constructing his argument for the necessity of continuous creation. Thus the type of continuity that he rejects, when he abandons the theory of substantial forms, is not the type of continuity to which the discontinuity insisted upon by Gueroult and Gilson is an alternative. Descartes's rejection of the theory of substantial forms does indeed commit him to a certain kind of discontinuity. But this does not mean that he is also committed to the kind of discontinuity that is entailed by a denial that time is continuous.

The theory of continuous creation is designed to explain the fact that created things continue to exist even though it is not possible to find in them anything that necessitates their continued existence. As for the question of whether their continued existence is continuous or discontinuous, it would appear that the theory of continuous creation leaves it open. Perhaps something can be made of the fact that Descartes, in speaking of the activity by which God preserves or conserves created things, invariably refers to it as "continuous." One might perhaps argue that there would be no point in saying that the conserving activity of God is a matter of *continuous* creation unless the existence of the created world is itself also continuous. If created temporal existence were *dis*continuous, why would continuous activity be required to conserve it? Similarly, it is difficult to understand in what way continuous creative activity by God could have as its product a discontinuous sequence. How could it be possible that the effect should in this respect fail to reflect its cause? If there are no interruptions in God's creative activity, what could account for interruptions in the product of that activity? Are we to suppose that God's agency misfires from time to time, so that at those times nothing is created by it?

The continued existence of created things requires continued creative activity on God's part because there is nothing intrinsic to the nature of temporal existence by which the continued existence of a temporal existent can be guaranteed. It would be somewhat inaccurate to say that the continued existence of a temporal thing is never *necessary;* rather, the point is that the continuation of its existence is not *self-caused.* Someone who considers it to be a necessary truth that God creates temporal things might well consider the existence of such things to be necessary but not self-caused. What Descartes wants to maintain concerning time is that the continued existence of temporal things, whether or not it is necessary, must be accounted for by something outside of them. No moment of their existence depends simply and sufficiently upon a preceding moment. The continuation or duration of a temporal object is not guaranteed by the inherent nature of that object. It can be guaranteed only by the power of God.

VIII

Descartes's abandonment of the theory of substantial forms, and of the substantive continuity for which it provides, raises the question of how he proposes to account for the natural changes undergone by created temporal things. The only response Descartes offers to this question is conveyed in the following rather succinct passage from Chapter VII of *Le Monde:*

Sachez donc, premièrement, que . . . je me sers de ce mot ["la Nature"] pour signifier la Matière même en tant que je la considère avec toutes les qualités que je lui ai attribuées comprises toutes ensemble, et sous cette condition que Dieu continue de la conserver en la même façon qu'il l'a créée. Car de cela seul qu'il continue ainsi de la conserver, il suit de nécessité qu'il doit y avoir plusieurs changements en ses parties, lesquels ne pouvant, ce me semble, être proprement attribués à l'action de Dieu, parce qu'elle ne change point, je les attribue à la Nature; et les règles suivant lesquelles se font ces changements, je les nomme les lois de la Nature.[12]

This passage makes it clear, I believe, that God is not directly or immediately the cause of change. In this respect Descartes agrees with the scholastics, whose theory of substantial forms also located the immediate source of natural change elsewhere than in divine activity.

God's active relation to temporal reality, as Descartes understands it, is straight-forwardly consistent with divine immutability. Although God creates contin-uously, there is no change or alteration in His creative act. The act by which He conserves created things does not differ from the act of creation either in character or in number. It is not another creative act of the same kind. Much less is it another creative act that has a different effect and that must therefore have a different character. It is the identical act. God's continuous creation involves no repetition or

12   AT XI, 36–7.

alteration of His activity. The very same act both creates and conserves what it creates.

Descartes objected against the theory of substantial forms that it makes no sense and explains nothing. It does not truly help us to understand how change occurs or what makes things happen. Whether Descartes provides a more helpful account of change is another matter. The laws of nature formulate, as he says, the rules by which natural changes take place. But these rules do not of themselves explain what makes natural changes occur in accordance with them. Thus Descartes needs to do something more, besides invoking the laws of nature, in order to illuminate the fact that nature conforms to its laws. Modern philosophy has for the most part forsaken this task, at least since Hume's annihilation of the notion of causality. Many post-Humean philosophers believe that they have something useful to say concerning the validity of inductive reasoning, or about the justification of our reliance upon what we identify as laws of nature. But what they have to say is merely epistemological. Even if we suppose that they are correct in what they assert, they contribute little to our understanding of what it is that accounts for the conformity of natural objects and events to those laws.

Descartes seems to have believed that it is possible to give "des démonstrations *a priori* de tout ce qui peut être produit" in the world.[13] It may be, then, that he regards the laws of nature as logically necessary. That would be a sufficient explanation of why the world conforms to them. In any event, his understanding of the role of God with respect to the course of nature is in certain respects quite clear. Since God is immutable, His activity never varies. Whatever natural changes occur must therefore be due to permanent and invariant characteristics of the created world. God creates that world, with the invariant characteristics that account for change, by a creative act which serves of itself to sustain the existence of what it creates.

13   *Le Monde,* chap. 7; AT XI, 47.

6

Concerning the Freedom
and Limits of the Will

I

What are we talking about when we talk about "the freedom of the will"? Neither in common speech nor in the special vocabulary of philosophers does the term "free will" have an unequivocal standard use. Nor is there, in our thinking about ourselves, any clear and specific function that the notion of free will is generally understood to serve. Just what aspect or possibility of experience is it supposed to grasp? What location in the schematism of our reflection does it address?

The notion is problematic, indeed, with respect to both of its elements. Not only is it as difficult in this context as it is in others to pin down the precise meaning of *freedom*. In addition, our idea of *the will* is itself rather vague. It is no wonder, then, that discussions of the freedom of the will tend to be murky and inconclusive.

Even people who recognize that they do not quite know what they are talking about, however, may be fully and (more or less) justifiably confident concerning what to say. That is the position in which Rogers Albritton confesses that he finds himself: "Free will is what we've got if the will is free, as of course it is. I don't know exactly what any of that means, but I don't know how to doubt that we've got free will, either. The will is free, whatever that means."[1] Moreover, Albritton is drawn to an additional thesis concerning the *extent* of the will's freedom. He identifies this thesis as one that was advanced by Descartes:

Descartes held that the will is perfectly free, "so free in its nature that it cannot be constrained." "Let everyone just go down deep into himself," he is reported to have said to Frans Burman, "and find out whether or not he has a perfect and absolute will, and whether he can conceive of anything which surpasses him in freedom of the will. I am sure that everyone will find that it is as I say." . . . I am inclined to agree with Descartes. (p. 239)

Albritton anticipates that understanding why he finds this doctrine so appealing would illuminate the meaning of his judgment that the will is free. So he undertakes "to discover something about what these expressions ["free will," etc.] . . .

---

1 "Freedom of Will and Freedom of Action," *Proceedings and Addresses of the American Philosophical Association* 59.2 (Nov. 1985): 243. Page references to this essay will henceforth be inserted within parentheses in the text.

mean" by considering "why . . . I am so strongly inclined to agree with Descartes's prima facie absurd estimate of *how* free the will is" (p. 243).

In the passages Albritton cites, the Cartesian estimate is conveyed by judgments such as these: the will is perfect, the will is absolute, the will is perfectly free, it is the nature of the will to be so free that the will cannot be constrained, our freedom of will is as great as can be conceived. Judgments of this kind naturally provoke skeptical questions, which Albritton articulates as follows:

How could our wills not have their limits, like our digestions? Don't we quite often – or occasionally, at a minimum – have no freedom of will, in some matter or other . . . ? What in the world, that might reasonably be called a freedom, could be so absolute? If the will in the world were some faculty, say, of never mind what, wouldn't it be possible somehow to restrict its exercise? (p. 239)

Of course, Albritton rejects all of these doubts. In his judgment, our wills (unlike our digestions) do not have limits; we never have, in any matter, *no* freedom of will; it is impossible to restrict the will's exercise. Albritton believes, in short, that our wills are unlimited and that their freedom is absolute.

II

What is this all about? What are we to think of these various characterizations, by Descartes and by Albritton, of the will, its limits, and its freedom? For that matter, how are we to go about thinking about what to think of them? The proposal that we try descending deep into ourselves is not really very promising. That approach has not enabled me, at any rate, to see that my will is in its freedom perfect and absolute. The trouble with the approach is that neither the notion of the will nor the notion of its freedom is sufficiently determinate. Consequently, what happens when I go down deep into myself is that I tend to become a bit disoriented. I am too uncertain both about what I am supposed to be looking *at* down there and about what I am supposed to be looking *for*.

Gary Watson says that the doctrine promulgated by Descartes and Albritton is "breathtaking."[2] On the other hand, Albritton himself declares that while the statement that the will is perfectly free may be "prima facie absurd," it is not genuinely extravagant at all. The statement "seems to me not a grandiosity," he explains, "but a simple truth" (p. 243). To be sure, the fact that a truth is simple is quite compatible with its being breathtaking as well. A person's breath might be taken away precisely by the surprising realization that a certain truth is after all quite simple. But that is not the kind of simplicity Albritton has in mind. For the point he makes about the purported truth that the will is perfectly free is that this truth "may be so simple that there's nothing in it, in a sense" (p. 243). The relevant type of simplicity is, in other words, the simplicity of emptiness.

2   "Free Action and Free Will," *Mind* 46 (1987): 163.

What pertinent truth, of which it would be plausible to say that it is in a sense vacuous, can reasonably be gathered from the claims Albritton and Descartes make concerning the will?

III

The assertion that "the will has no limits" might mean that there is no specific limitation, the same for each will, by which every will is necessarily bound. That would leave open the possibility that every will is limited in some particular way of its own. It would entail only that there are no limits binding upon all wills – limits which would presumably be inherent in the nature of the will itself. It is pretty clear, however, that when Descartes states that "God has given us a will with no limits . . . [an] infinite will," he does not intend to leave this possibility open.[3] He does not mean just that there is no single limitation that binds every will. He means that no will can be limited in any way. In asserting that our will has no limits, or that it is infinite, his point is that each of us can will whatever can conceivably be willed by anyone. "The will . . . can in a certain sense be called infinite," Descartes says, "since . . . its scope extends to anything that can possibly be an object of any other will – even the immeasurable will of God."[4] In other words, there is no conceivable willing that we are unable in principle to accomplish.

Albritton is making substantially the same point, I take it, when he insists that there are no limits to our wills except those grounded in considerations that are "'grammatical' or 'conceptual' or 'logical'" (p. 244). On his account, as on Descartes's, we are capable of any willing that can be meaningfully and coherently described – that is, any willing that is conceivable at all. There is nothing that could be willed by anyone that cannot be willed by us.

I wonder whether it is really to an understanding of the will's *freedom* that these assertions about the will are most directly pertinent. Might it not perhaps be more suitable to understand what Descartes and Albritton say as pertaining more to the *power* of the will than to its freedom? For it seems that their attention is focused most immediately upon what we are *capable* of willing, or upon what our wills *can* do, rather than upon the extent to which our wills are *free from constraint* or the extent to which we are *free to use* them?[5]

---

3 Letter to Mersenne, 25 December 1639; F. Alquié, *Descartes: Oeuvres philosophiques* II, 153.

4 *Principles of Philosophy* I, 35. J. Cottingham, R. Stoothoof, D. Murdoch, *The Philosophical Writings of Descartes* I (Cambridge: Cambridge University Press, 1985), 204. Hereafter, this edition of Descartes's works will be cited as "CSM."

5 The distinction between power and freedom tends generally to be somewhat unstable and elusive. Confusion in this area is compounded by the fact that free will itself is sometimes identified not as a variety of freedom but as itself a sort of power. For instance, Watson explains that free will is "the power of rational beings to will one way rather than another, as alternatives present themselves" (*op. cit.*, p. 163).

Albritton poses, rhetorically, this question: "How could our wills not have their limits, like our digestions?" Let us suppose that our wills *did,* like our digestions, have their limits. How, then, would they be limited? Our digestions are surely not limited with respect to their freedom — what in the world would "freedom of the digestion" be? — but with respect to their capability or power. There are certain conceivable digestive tasks that our digestions cannot effectively perform; there are things we are unable to digest. Albritton believes that our wills are in this respect *not* like our digestions. In his opinion, there is no conceivable volitional task that our wills cannot effectively perform; there is nothing we are unable to will. This sounds to me more like an opinion about the power of the will than about its freedom.

Possessing the power to do something does not entail being free to do it, nor does being free to do something entail possessing the corresponding power. Hobbes suggests that freedom has to do with the external relationships of a thing while power is an inherent characteristic: "Liberty, or freedom, signifieth, properly, the absence of . . . external impediments of motion. . . . But when the impediment of motion is in the constitution of the thing itself, we use not to say; it wants the liberty; but the power to move; as when a stone lieth still, or a man is fastened to his bed by sickness."[6] Should we presume, then, that when Descartes describes the will as "so free *in its nature* that it cannot be constrained" (emphasis added). Hobbes would have him say instead that the will is "so *powerful* in its nature that it cannot be constrained"? It does seem so. For if the fact that the will cannot be constrained is due to its own inherent characteristics ("the constitution of the thing itself"), as Descartes evidently supposes, then in Hobbes's terms this fact is essentially germane not to the freedom of the will but to its power.

It might nonetheless be germane in a derivative way to the will's freedom too. If something is so powerful that it *cannot* be constrained, then it is impossible to limit its freedom; for no external circumstance can impede its movement. Chains deprive a person of freedom only by virtue of the fact that it is difficult or impossible for the person to break them. They would not in the slightest impair the freedom of a person so strong that he could move through chains as effortlessly as we move through the circlets of air by which our limbs are commonly surrounded. Thus, if the power of the will had no limits, there would be no limits to the freedom of the will either. Unlimited power entails unlimited freedom.

But is it reasonable for us to think that what makes our wills entirely and absolutely free is the fact that they are more powerful than anything that might constrain or impede them? Is it at all plausible that the perfection of our wills should consist fundamentally in the possession of unlimited power? It is not plausible at all. The will surely does not *seem* very powerful. We are not aware, I think, of having in our wills a force or energy or strength so great that it cannot be

6 *Leviathan,* ch. XXI.

defeated or effectively opposed. Many people report, as Descartes does, an immediate consciousness or feeling that their wills are entirely free. No one, so far as I know, claims an immediate awareness or sense that the will has unlimited power. Perhaps we do in some way experience ourselves as utterly free. But we certainly do not, with respect to our wills, feel irresistibly powerful. Whatever the prima facie absurdity of the view that the will is absolutely free, it seems even more preposterous to suggest that there are no limits to its power.

IV

I believe it is unfortunate that the distinction between the freedom of the will and its power is so generally neglected in discussions of free will. However, it does not seem to me to be necessary to consider whether the doctrine maintained by Descartes and Albritton is better understood as having to do primarily with the power of the will or as having to do primarily with its freedom. For the doctrine actually pertains to neither. The assertion that the will is unlimited is most appropriately understood, it seems to me, as not bearing upon these parameters of the will at all.

Descartes insists that the freedom of his will is as extensive as it could possibly be. He cannot "conceive of anything," he declares, "which surpasses him in freedom of the will." Thus it is clearly his view that *no will could be more free than his*. It is important to notice, however, that Descartes also commits himself to *another* view concerning the extent to which his will is free – namely, the view that *no will could be less free than his!*

This is apparent in the *Fourth Meditation,* where he elaborates his contention that the will is "so perfect and so great that the possibility of a further increase in its perfection or greatness is beyond my understanding."[7] He glosses this contention as being tantamount to a claim that not even God's will is greater than his, at least when the divine will is "considered as will in the essential and strict sense." And he explains that the wills of God and man are in this sense equal "because the will simply consists in the ability to do or not to do something (that is, to affirm or deny, to pursue or avoid)."[8] Descartes clarifies this explanation in the course of discussing why God cannot be blamed for having made humans liable to error. The reason we are liable to error, he asserts, is that our will is more extensive than our intellect. But God could not have given us a less extensive will: "for since the will consists simply of one thing which is, as it were, indivisible, it seems that its nature rules out the possibility of anything being taken away from it."[9]

Thus Descartes cannot conceive of any will that is surpassed in freedom by ours. Since nothing can be taken away from the will, no will can be less than any other.

7 AT VII, p. 57; CSM II, p. 39.
8 AT VII, p. 57; CSM II, p. 40.
9 AT VII, p. 60; CSM II, p. 42.

In other words, the extent or magnitude of our will is, with respect to its freedom, as small as it could possibly be. This does not contradict the claim that the freedom of our will is so great that it could not be increased. It merely makes the additional and compatible claim that the freedom of our will is so small that it could not be diminished. Descartes's overall position on the subject is simply that no will – whether divine, or human, or belonging to a creature of some other kind – could have either more freedom or less freedom than his own.

According to Descartes, having a will is a matter of possessing a certain ability – namely, "the ability to do or not to do something (that is, to affirm or deny, to pursue or avoid)." It is not wholly clear just what possessing this ability consists in or entails. However, what Descartes says about it makes it apparent that he regards it as an all-or-nothing affair. Either one possesses the ability in question completely or one does not possess it at all. Whenever one possesses it, therefore, what is possessed (at least, "when considered as will in the essential or strict sense") is exactly the same.

This all-or-nothing nature of the will is attributed by Descartes to the fact that the will is simple or indivisible. In his opinion, this "rules out the possibility of anything being taken away from it." The possibility he supposes to be ruled out is that of a will from which some of its ability has been removed, or a will whose scope has been reduced. This is impossible because to diminish a will at all would be to annihilate it altogether. A will ceases to exist entirely if anything is subtracted from it. Thus, according to Descartes's doctrine, neither the will itself nor its possession admits of any variation in degree. All wills are the same. None could possibly be more perfect, or less perfect, than it is.

Although Albritton does not characterize the will as being simple or indivisible, he seems equally committed to maintaining that the freedom of the will is not only as great, but also as small, as can be conceived. On his account, the fact that the will is perfectly free is not a mere contingency but a matter of necessary truth: the idea of "unfreedom of will" is, he suggests, "incomprehensible, a picture without application" (p. 250). This implies that there can be no difference in the amounts of freedom enjoyed by different wills. The will's freedom is a matter of necessity. Therefore, every will must as such have precisely the freedom that all wills necessarily have. While this means that no will could possibly have greater freedom than ours, it also means that no will could possibly have less.

But it seems to me that freedom is necessarily susceptible to variations in degree, and that the same is true of power. Whenever it makes sense to describe something as enjoying a certain freedom or a certain power, it also makes sense to ask how much of that freedom or power it enjoys; and if something has a characteristic about which the question of its amount or extent cannot reasonably arise, then that characteristic is properly understood neither as a kind of freedom nor as a kind of power. Freedom and power are essentially quantitative and open to comparisons of measure. One may have either more of them or less.

This appears not to be the case with respect to the characteristic of the will that Descartes and Albritton identify as the will's freedom. That characteristic is not quantitative in its nature at all. Whatever it is, the will can have neither more nor less of it. It is not variable in extent or degree, and it therefore makes no sense to consider how much of it a will enjoys. In my opinion, it is misleading to identify it with inherently variable characteristics like freedom or power.

V

I shall recommend shortly what I regard as a more appropriate identification of the characteristic with which I believe the doctrine of Descartes and Albritton is concerned. First, however, I wish to suggest a way of construing and of justifying that doctrine in its own terms. For the moment, in other words, I propose to accept uncritically the presumption that the doctrine does concern freedom and to consider what plausible claim about the will's freedom it might reasonably be understood to make.

Perhaps, then, the simple and more or less vacuous truth to be gathered from Descartes's and Albritton's ascription to the will of perfect freedom is just this proposition: *every willing is free.* The doctrine that the will is perfectly free may be equivalent, in other words, to the claim that there can be no such thing as an unfree willing. Indeed, this is essentially the formulation of his doctrine that Albritton himself provides as he concludes his defense of the will's freedom. "I doubt," he says, "that I am going to see unfreedom of will anywhere in our lives" (p. 250). The primary justification for Albritton's position is perhaps to be found, moreover, in a consideration similar to the all-or-nothing character attributed to the will by Descartes. The most fundamental and compelling basis for asserting that there is no unfreedom of will, or that every willing is free, may lie in the supposition that without freedom there is no will at all.

What would it be to will unfreely? In general, the distinction between what is done freely and what is done unfreely depends upon whether the doing is by the doer's own choice. A person remains in a room freely when he remains in it because he chooses to do so; and he remains unfreely if it is not by his own choice that he remains in the room. It is on this model that the notions of willing freely and of willing unfreely are to be understood. Thus, a person wills freely when he wills by his own choice, and he wills unfreely if it is not by his own choice that he wills. Willing freely is a matter of willing as one does because one chooses to do so.

In the central cases of unfree doing, a person does something unfreely when it is not merely not by his own choice that he does it but when he does it against his will. The corresponding case of willing unfreely would be that of a person who wills against his will. Accordingly, unfreedom of will is the condition a person is in when it is not by his own will but, rather, against his own will that he wills what he wills.

77

If this is what Albritton means by "unfreedom of will," it is easy to share his doubt that the condition occurs anywhere in our lives. The impossibility of unfreedom of will, or of willing unfreely, seems to follow readily from an elementary aspect of the nature of volitional acts such as choosing and deciding. There can be no discrepancy between choosing to make a certain choice and making that choice, or between deciding to make a certain decision and making that decision.[10] It would not be quite accurate to say that such acts inevitably succeed, for that might suggest misleadingly that implementing them requires the occurrence of some further event in which their successful implementation consists. The point is rather that when a volitional act is in the pertinent respect iterative, the act is tantamount to its own implementation. It is not possible to will in a given mode (e.g., choosing) to perform a volitional act of that mode without thereby actually performing it.

Generally speaking, there is a substantial distinction between choosing to do something and doing it, or between making a decision and carrying it out. However, there is no such distinction when the object of the choice or decision is itself a specific choice or decision. It is certainly possible for a person to decide to make a decision about something and yet not actually make any decision about it, either at that time or later. Similarly, a person can choose to make a choice (instead of, say, choosing to allow someone else to make it) without ever actually getting around to making the choice he has chosen to make. However, choosing not merely *to make some choice or other*, but *to choose this rather than that*, is logically tantamount to *choosing this*; and deciding not merely *to make some decision*, but *to decide to do that rather than to do this*, is logically tantamount to *deciding to do that*. When the object or content of one volitional act is not merely to perform some volitional act or other, but to perform a volitional act whose identity is specified, the occurrence of the one act entails the occurrence of the other.

The conclusion that it is impossible to will unfreely can be derived from this. Suppose that a person chooses to do X. Under what conditions would he in that case be choosing unfreely, or choosing against his will? He would be choosing unfreely to do X only if it were also true of him that he chooses to make a choice contrary to his choice to do X — only if, in other words, he chooses to choose not to do X.[11] But this could not be true of him. For choosing to choose not to do X entails choosing not to do X, which is incompatible with choosing to do X.[12] If

---

10 The same is true of trying. Anyone who tries to make a certain attempt thereby makes that attempt.

11 I shall omit consideration of the possibility that what is against his will is not choosing in particular to do X, but just *choosing* as such – i.e., the possibility that it is against his will to make any choice at all.

12 This may not be obvious. But suppose a person who has been trying to make up his mind how to vote in a certain matter declares that he has concluded his deliberations by making two choices – to vote affirmatively and not to vote affirmatively. It seems to me that unless there is some trick in

someone actually wills to do X, then, it cannot also be the case that he wills not to will to do X. Thus, his willing to do X – his choice or decision to do it – cannot be unfree, or against his will.

If Albritton's doctrine that the will is perfectly free depends in this way just upon the fact that volitional acts are iteratively self-implementing, then it does not seem unreasonable to describe the doctrine as being, in his terms, "so simple that there's nothing in it, in a sense." But it seems to me inappropriate to construe this more or less vacuous doctrine as concerned with the will's *freedom*. It is better, I think, to construe it as concerned with the distinction between activity and passivity. Reformulating it in terms of this distinction makes its truth more perspicuous. It also conveys a more authentic identification and understanding of the characteristic of the will that is at issue.

The doctrine as reformulated is just this proposition: *the will is absolutely and perfectly active.* In other words, there can be no such thing as a passive willing. All of the movements of my will – for instance, my choices and decisions – are *movements that I make.* None is a mere impersonal occurrence, in which my will *moves without my moving it.* None of my choices or decisions merely happens. Its occurrence *is* my activity, and I can no more be a passive bystander with respect to my own choices and decisions than I can be passive with respect to any of my own actions. It is possible for me to be passive when my arm rises, but I cannot be passive when I raise it. Now every willing is necessarily an action; unlike the movements of an arm, it is only as actions that volitions can occur. Thus, activity is of the essence of the will. Volition precludes passivity by its very nature.

VI

Finally, what of the notion that the will is unlimited? There is indeed a sense, which should already be clear, in which the will is unlimited. It is impossible for our volitional capacity to be limited at all by the character of any object that can conceivably be willed. Our physical and intellectual faculties are limited, in that there are physical and intellectual tasks that might conceivably be performed but that are beyond us. But since the possession of the will is an all-or-nothing affair, a person who can perform one conceivable act of will can perform any. It may not be easy for someone to reach the point at which he performs a given volitional act. He may have been reluctant to make any decision or choice, or he may have been powerfully drawn to make a different one. But the act of choosing or of deciding, taken strictly in itself and apart from whatever leads up to it or stands in its way, is the same no matter what its circumstances or its object. It is no more difficult to perform one act of will than it is to perform another. Everyone can make, under

what he says, he has not made any choice at all. He *says* he has chosen, and perhaps he *believes* he has chosen, but no choice has really been made.

suitable conditions, any choice whatever. There are no volitional objects with which any person's will is inherently unable to cope.

On the other hand, there is an important sense in which the activity, and the freedom, of our wills are subject to significant limitations. From the fact that there is something we cannot do passively or unfreely, it does not follow that it is an action we are always able or free to perform. There is no choice I cannot make if I choose to make it; it can never happen that I choose to choose X but fail to choose it. It does not follow from this, however, that I can make any choice whatever. Plainly, there may be certain choices that I cannot choose to make.

Albritton says that "what we propose to do is up to us, if our wills are free" (p. 241). What does it mean to assert that what we propose to do is up to us? I suppose it means (more or less) this: we will propose whatever we want to propose. Now this does not entail that we can propose absolutely anything. After all, there may be certain things that we cannot propose because it is impossible for us to want to propose them. Undoubtedly, we would propose them if we wanted to do so. But we may be incapable of having that desire.

It does appear to be true, of some people at least, that there are volitional acts which they simply cannot bring themselves to perform. Luther said, "Here I stand; I can do no other." Albritton evidently supposes Luther to have meant that his reasons for taking that stand were so incontrovertible that he had no reasonable alternative. In that case, Albritton correctly suggests, Luther still had the alternative of refusing to allow those reasons to count for so much with him. "Luther's reasons," he observes, "were only *reasons*" (p. 247). But I suppose that when Luther insisted that he could do no other he was very likely not, as Albritton supposes, merely talking about his reasons. What he meant to convey was not that those reasons left him with no reasonable alternative to the stand he had decided to take. Rather, he was trying to convey something about himself. I understand him to have meant to say about himself something like this: that he could not help being driven by the considerations supporting his stand; that even when he attempted to give countervailing weight to considerations tending to lead to a different stand, he found it impossible to do so; that whatever the objective logical or moral value of the considerations that moved him, he experienced them as irresistible.

Regardless of what Luther meant, there are surely cases in which people do find it impossible to bring themselves to perform certain volitional acts. For some people, there are propositions to which they cannot bring themselves to assent no matter how weighty they consider the grounds for assenting; or there are choices or decisions which they cannot bring themselves to make no matter how fully they recognize the obligation or the desirability of making them. It is against their nature, as we sometimes say, to perform those particular volitional acts. The fact that they cannot bring themselves to perform those acts means that their wills are limited. They are subject to a kind of volitional necessity, in virtue of which there are conceivable acts of willing that they are unable to perform. This necessity limits the will. But, since the necessity is grounded in the person's own nature, the freedom of the person's will is not impaired.[13]

13 I have elaborated and tried to clarify the notion of volitional necessity in two essays, "The Importance of What We Care About" and "Rationality and the Unthinkable," both of which may be found in Harry Frankfurt, *The Importance of What We Care About* (Cambridge: Cambridge University Press, 1988).

7

On the Usefulness of Final Ends

1. Of the various conceptual formats that are designed to help us organize our thoughts concerning what we do, the distinction between means and ends is among the most widely employed. This is only to be expected. After all, the distinction is a very elementary one, and easy to grasp. Moreover, a schematism grounded in any plausible version of the distinction is bound to be exceptionally well-suited to its task. For the notion of an arrangement of ends and means comprehends both the purposefulness and the rationality that are essential features of our active nature; and it also facilitates considering the relationship by which they are connected. That is, it focuses quite naturally on the ways in which our goals are linked to the processes of reasoning by which we attempt to determine how to achieve them.

A familiar approach to the differentiation of means and ends, and to conceptualizing the relationship between them, invokes two sharply distinct types of consideration. Considerations of the first type have to do with the usefulness of the proposed object. They pertain to the *instrumental* value that it derives from being a means to some desirable end external to itself. This external end may be desirable, of course, only as a means to some still further end. In that case, it is not a final end; it is intermediate or subordinate, and its value too is wholly instrumental. Considerations of the second type pertain to the desirability of the proposed object of choice apart from its usefulness as a means to other things. That is, they pertain to its *terminal* value – the value of an object considered as a final end or end in itself.

Correspondingly, there are two sorts of justification that a person may have for trying to bring about a certain activity or state of affairs: its usefulness as a means, and its terminal value. Sometimes, both sorts of justification are available. In such cases, an object might be pursued partly on account of its instrumental value and partly on account of its desirability as a final end.

This is a somewhat cursory sketch of the notions of means and ends, and of their respective kinds of value; but, as far as it goes, it seems quite plausible. Indeed, it is very close to the inclinations and presumptions of reflective common sense. It is also rather close to Aristotle's account of means and ends, which provides, in the *Nicomachean Ethics,* the general structural framework for his investigation into the nature and conditions of the good life.

In my opinion, however, the framework is too narrow and too rigid. It cannot accommodate a realistic appreciation of the issues we confront when we try to decide upon a good way of living. Our conception of the relationship between means and final ends has to be more spacious and more supple. Otherwise, it will impede our efforts to develop a comprehensive and authentic representation of what actually concerns us when we concern ourselves about how we should live.

2. The Aristotelian approach is rooted in a fundamental asymmetry. A means derives its instrumental value from the relationship in which it stands to its end, but an end derives no value from the relationship between itself and the means to it. Means are valued for the sake of their ends; ends are not valued for the sake of the means that are instrumental in attaining them. The trajectory of the derivation of value is an irreversible vector. This unidirectionality is a primitive and indispensable feature of any Aristotelian account. Without it, an account of that type could not coherently define the distinction between means and ends upon which it rests.

Another central tenet of Aristotelian accounts may seem even more obvious. A means acquires no terminal value from being useful. The relationship in which it stands to its end can endow a means only with instrumental value. Of course, what has instrumental value may have terminal value as well. But it cannot have the latter by virtue of the fact that it has the former. Otherwise, something might be a final end just because it is a means; and that would radically undermine the distinction between means and ends. The fact that something is desirable *for its own sake* cannot possibly be explained, on an Aristotelian account, by its desirability *as a means* to something other than itself.

That these two features are integral to the Aristotelian way of construing the relationship between means and ends is due to the fact that the Aristotelian approach is in a certain respect impersonal. Consider the opening sentence of the *Nicomachean Ethics*: "Every art and every inquiry, and similarly every action and pursuit, is thought to aim at some good; and for this reason the good has rightly been declared to be that at which all things aim" (1094a1–3). Now it is not really actions and pursuits that have ends or aims. It is *agents*. It is only in a manner of speaking that the ends of agents can be assigned to their activities. Speaking strictly, whatever aims are attributable to inquiries and arts are just the aims of those who engage in them.

Because of its impersonality – because it diverts attention from the fact that every end is the end of an agent – the Aristotelian approach tends to separate the task of developing a theory of final ends from an appreciation of the complex role that final ends play in the lives of people. This masks some important aspects of the relationship between means and ends. It obstructs a clear understanding of how final ends function. As a consequence, it obscures the bases upon which any reasonable attempt to evaluate such ends must be made.

3. How, then, do final ends function? To understand this, we must begin by considering a somewhat different question: What is the point of having final ends? Why are we better off with aims, for the sake of which we act, than we would be if

no such things figured in our lives? The issue is not the importance of recognizing what our goals are. It goes without saying that to someone who has goals, a perspicuous appreciation of them will be helpful. After all, he is more likely to hit his target if he can see it clearly. But why aim at anything at all?

We are creatures who cannot avoid being active. Therefore, we will still be active even if we have no aims; but we will be active without purpose. Now being without purpose does not entail having no preferences concerning the possible outcomes of behavior, nor does it entail being invulnerable to harm. Someone who has no goals may be fully susceptible to suffering and to benefitting from his conduct. He may also be quite capable of recognizing the value of its effects upon him. This means that regardless of how empty we are of intent, what we do may nonetheless be important to us. It may serve our interests, or defeat them, even though our interests do not guide it.

This provides the most obvious reason for having goals; namely, the fact that it is important to us that certain possible states of affairs come about and that others be avoided. Given that some outcomes are of greater value to us than others, it is undesirable to behave at random. Rather, it is important for us to guide our activity in accordance with the requirements of what we care about. At least part of the point of having goals, accordingly, is to enhance the likelihood that the result of what we do will be something that we want. Aiming is important because it makes a difference to us what we hit. From this point of view, the problem of choosing goals is fundamentally a matter of deciding what ends it would be most desirable to reach.[1]

What having an end actually accomplishes, however, is more than simply to enhance the likelihood that a state of affairs corresponding to that end will come about. Indeed, Aristotle himself suggests as much: "Desire would be empty and vain," he says, "[unless] there is some end of the things we do which we desire for its own sake" (1094a18–21). This attributes to final ends a function other than that of affecting outcomes. Having a final end, Aristotle indicates, may also affect the character of desire; it may keep desire from being empty and vain. But Aristotle's point here is too weak. If we had no final ends, it is more than desire that would be empty and vain. It is life itself. For living without goals or purposes is living with nothing to do.

Without ends, there are no means. And if no activity serves as a means, then no activity is useful. Thus, having a final end is a condition of engaging in useful activity. Now the fact that an activity is useful endows it with meaning.[2] Suppose that we never acted in order to attain or to accomplish something which we

---

1 It is also essential to calculate both the cost of trying to reach those ends and the likelihood that the effort to reach them will succeed. The most central issue in the selection of some state of affairs as a final end is, however, the value of having that state of affairs prevail.
2 Where the activity is valued for its own sake, it may be considered not only as an end but also as a means to itself.

regarded as desirable. Suppose, in other words, that we never did anything that we believed to be useful. In that case, our activity would appear to us to serve no purpose. We would find it empty and vain, for it would seem to have no point. It would be, to our minds, altogether meaningless. A life constituted entirely by activity of that sort would be, in an important sense, a meaningless life. Life cannot be meaningful in this sense, then, without final ends.

4. What makes a life meaningful in the sense that is pertinent here? It is not that the life, considered as an object, has a specific meaning that can be understood and described. The emptiest and most vapid of lives might have that sort of meaning, as exemplifying or illuminating some principle or as an indicator of something other than itself. Indeed, the very emptiness of the life might be significant in some such way. So the fact that a person's life is meaningless because it is devoid of purpose does not entail that it is also meaningless either in the sense that it is unintelligible or in the sense that there is nothing of interest to be learned from it.

Similarly, a life that is without meaning for the one who lives it might nonetheless be very important. The importance of a life is essentially a matter of its impact. If a microbe initiates a devastating epidemic, which critically alters the course of human history, then the life of that microbe is of considerable importance. But this clearly does not entail that the microbe lives a meaningful life. On the other hand, a human life may be full of meaning for the person who lives it, even though it has no significant impact upon history or upon the world and is therefore in that sense quite unimportant.

Living a life that has meaning for oneself also does not require that the life be happy, or even that it be a good life. It is generally thought that living a meaningful life is, taken by itself, a good thing. But it is surely not the only good thing; and it might not be good enough. A life might be full of meaning, then, and yet so gravely deficient in other ways that no reasonable person would choose to live it.

It cannot even be assumed that a meaningful life must always be preferable to one that lacks meaning. What fills a certain life with meaning may be some intricate and demanding conflict, or a terribly frustrating but compelling struggle, which involves a great deal of anxiety or pain and which is extremely destructive. Thus the very circumstances that make the life meaningful may be deeply objectionable. It might be better to live an empty life than to generate or to endure so much suffering and disorder.

Living a meaningful life does not entail, then, that the life has a meaning, that it is an important life, or that it is good. What it does entail is that whoever lives the life engages during its course, to some considerable extent, in activity that is important to him. But when *is* activity important to a person? It is important to him only when it is devoted to something that he cares about.[3] Thus, a person's life

---

3 Someone may be mistaken, of course, concerning what is important to him. This will happen when he fails to appreciate what he himself really cares about.

is meaningful only if he spends it, to some considerable extent, in activity that is devoted to things that he cares about. It is not essential that the activity he devotes to the things he cares about be successful. The extent to which a life is meaningful depends less upon how much it accomplishes than upon how it is lived. What counts primarily is the extent to which the person cares about the final ends at which he aims.

5. Final ends are possible states of affairs, which someone values for their own sakes. It must not be supposed, however, that the measure of how a life is lived is given by the *value* of his final ends. Rather, how a life is lived is a function of what it is like for the person to *pursue* them. The problem of selecting final ends is not the same, then, as the problem of measuring the inherent or terminal value of possible states of affairs.

According to G. E. Moore, the most fundamental question of ethics is "the question: 'What things are goods or ends in themselves?' "[4] There are at least two difficulties with this. One is that it ignores considerations of degree. That something is good in itself means that its value is not exclusively instrumental. This pertains to the *kind* of value it possesses; but it has nothing to do with the *quantity* of its value. To say of something that it is good in itself is not to say anything at all concerning how much goodness in itself the thing has. And in fact, it is quite possible for what is good in itself to be not really very good at all. Its value may be terminal, but the quantity of that value may be trivial.

However, it is another difficulty with Moore's question that is more immediately germane here. Moore speaks in one breath of "goods or ends in themselves," as though the notion of something being good in itself were freely interchangeable with the notion of its being an end in itself. It seems to me that this aspect of his formulation is out of focus. Whether or not something is good in itself depends exclusively upon its inherent characteristics. On the other hand, whether it is an end in itself depends upon whether someone adopts it or pursues it.

Moreover, considering whether to adopt a certain final end is quite a different matter from estimating its intrinsic goodness. From the supposition that a certain state of affairs would be superior to all others that might be brought about, it does not follow that pursuing as a final end some other state of affairs instead would be a mistake. The goals that it would be most desirable to achieve are not necessarily those that it would be best to seek.

This is not only because there are differences in the probabilities and in the costs of attaining various goals. It is also because there are differences in the kinds of activities, and in the patterns of activity, by which various final ends may be pursued. Adopting one final end may lead a person to become engaged in a network of feeling, emotion, thought, and action that differs very considerably

4 *Principia Ethica* (Cambridge University Press, 1903), p. 184.

from the network in which he would be engaged if he were to adopt another. The life he will have if he pursues the one may therefore be much richer in meaningful activity, and in overall desirability, than the life he will have if he pursues the other.

There is no reason to assume that the relative values of these two sets of activities will be commensurate with the relative values of the final ends to which they are respectively devoted. The activity that is required in order to attain a certain final end of great value may be, after all, extremely meager; and insofar as a person devotes his life to pursuing that final end, his life would be nearly empty. On the other hand, a certain final end of much less inherent value might require invigoratingly complicated and wholehearted attention; adopting that end, then, would fill the person's life with purposefulness, and in this respect his life would be more meaningful.[5] So a person might have good reason for adopting final ends whose terminal value is relatively inferior. Pursuing ends of lesser terminal value might make for a more meaningful life than activity devoted to bringing about states of affairs whose inherent value is greater.

6. What determines whether or not something is important to a person? At first glance, it might appear that the person's beliefs and attitudes are decisive in some cases but not decisive in others. Certain things are important to a person whether or not he recognizes their importance to him – regardless, indeed, of whether he cares about them at all. They are important to him because of how they are capable of affecting him, even if he is unaware that they have that capacity. For example, vitamins are important to people who know nothing about such things. On the other hand, certain things are important to a person only because in fact he does care about them. Consider, for example, a person's friends. If he did not know those people, or if he were altogether indifferent to them, he might very well not be susceptible either to being hurt or to being pleased by them. It may be entirely on account of his own attitudes toward them, in other words, that they have the capacity to affect him and that they are, accordingly, important to him.

In cases of the first kind, the person is passive with respect to the fact that the object is important to him. Its importance to him is wholly independent of whether he has any active intentions concerning it or whether he even thinks about it. In cases of the second kind, the object's importance to the person depends essentially upon his activity. To care about something is not merely to be attracted by it, or to experience certain feelings. No one can properly be said to care about something unless, at least to some degree, he guides his conduct in accordance with the implications of his interest in it. This means paying attention to it and to what concerns it; it means making decisions; it means taking steps. Thus, with

---

5 For instance, it might be possible for someone to bring about an enormous benefit to mankind merely by pressing a button. A life devoted to bringing about that benefit, in which the only meaningful activity was pressing the button, would be less meaningful than one devoted to a final end that was of smaller value but that could be pursued only by complex and varied activity.

respect to those things whose importance to him derives from the fact that he cares about them, the person is necessarily active.[6]

Even in cases of the first kind, however, an object cannot be important to someone who does not care about *anything*. Suppose a person is unaware that a certain object exists, and hence does not care about it. It might nonetheless be important to him by virtue of having a capacity to affect him. But suppose he does not care about any of the effects upon himself that it might produce; suppose he is entirely indifferent to whether he is affected in those ways or not. In that case, the object would be of no importance to him whatever.

In all cases, then, it is what people care about that determines what is important to them. If they cared about nothing, then nothing would be important to them. But would that itself have any importance? Is there any reason why it should be important to a person whether anything is important to him? After all, if there were someone to whom absolutely nothing was important, then, as Thomas Nagel observes, *that* would not be important to him either.[7]

Something that is important to a person is capable of affecting him in ways that he cares about. Since he cares about those effects, he is motivated to take steps in order to enjoy them or to avoid them. But suppose nothing were important to him. Then he would have no motive for taking any such steps. So far as deliberate purposeful activity is concerned, he would languish. Being interested in nothing, he would neither seek anything nor seek to avoid anything. The results would be a fragmentation of life, passivity, and boredom. It is true that even a person who cared about nothing might still make voluntary movements. But he would not make them because he considered it important to make them. He would make them without being personally involved in what he was doing – that is, without caring whether he did it or not.[8]

7. A life in which it were actually the case that nothing was important would be, by hypothesis, a life without important final ends. It follows that it would be a life without meaningful activity. Anyone who lived that life would be indifferent and unengaged with respect to whatever it might be that he did. Furthermore, he

---

6 I have attempted to provide a fuller explanation of what is entailed by caring about something in the final essays of this collection.

7 "If *sub specie aeternitatis* there is no reason to believe that anything matters, then that does not matter either, and we can approach our absurd lives with irony instead of heroism and despair" (Thomas Nagel, *Mortal Questions* [Cambridge University Press, 1979], p. 23).

8 Is it self-evident that caring about nothing means having a bad life? Certain Eastern systems of thought actually appear to recommend it. Their adherents are encouraged to strive toward a condition in which the will is annihilated – in which one no longer exists as a volitional agent. They acknowledge, however, that annihilating the will requires a sustained program of rigorously disciplined effort. The task of extinguishing the self is complicated, protracted, and difficult; endeavors to accomplish it are inevitably strenuous, and they often fail. Thus, even for those to whom the most important thing is that nothing should be important to them, caring about *that* involves extensive volition and action.

would be bored. I believe that the avoidance of boredom is a very fundamental human urge. It is not a matter merely of distaste for a rather unpleasant state of consciousness. Being bored entails a reduction of attention; our responsiveness to conscious stimuli flattens out and shrinks; distinctions are not noticed and not made, so that the conscious field becomes increasingly homogeneous. The general functioning of the mind diminishes. It is of the essence of boredom that it involves an attenuation of psychic liveliness. Its tendency is to approach a complete cessation of significant differentiation within consciousness; and this homogenization is, at the limit, tantamount to the cessation of conscious experience altogether.

A substantial increase in the extent to which we are bored undermines the very continuation of psychic activity. In other words, it threatens the extinction of the active self. What is manifested by our interest in avoiding boredom is therefore not simply a resistance to discomfort but a quite elemental urge for psychic survival. It is natural to construe this as a modification of the more familiar instinct for self-preservation. It is connected to "self-preservation," however, only in an unfamiliarly literal sense − in the sense of sustaining not the *life* of the organism but the *persistence of the self.*

8. What is important to someone depends upon what he cares about. This might well seem to imply that there can be nothing whose importance to anyone is inherent in it. The fact that something is important to a person is invariably a function of that person's feelings, attitudes, and intentions. Considered just in itself, entirely apart from any consideration of what the person in question cares about, nothing can be said either to be or not to be important to him. For the extent to which something is important to him depends essentially upon considerations other than its own inherent characteristics alone.

However, there is an exception to this principle that the importance of anything depends upon considerations outside itself. People are capable of making themselves important. If a person is important to himself, then this importance is manifestly self-endowed; for he is important to himself simply by virtue of the fact that he cares about himself. In this one case, the source of importance lies in the characteristics of the object. The importance of a person to himself is unique in that it is in no way extrinsic. From this it follows, of course, that someone who enjoys this importance cannot be deprived of it by anything other than himself. Only if a person does not care about himself can he fail to be important to himself.

Now whether a person is or is not important to himself may appear to be a straightforwardly contingent matter. It depends just upon whether he cares about himself; and surely, it seems, he might either do so or not. The importance of a person to himself is clearly intrinsic, in that it depends exclusively upon his own characteristics. If the characteristics upon which it depends are indeed contingent, however, then it is also conditional. But is it actually possible for there to be a person who does not care about himself? Perhaps caring about oneself is essential to being a person. Can something to whom its own condition and activities do not matter in the slightest properly be regarded as a person at all? Perhaps nothing that is entirely indifferent to itself is really a person, regardless of how intelligent or emotional or in other respects similar to persons it may be.

Suppose that the sort of reflexivity in question here were, indeed, a conceptually essential characteristic of persons. Then there could not possibly be a person of no importance to himself. To be sure, the importance of a person to himself would still be conditional. But no person could fail to meet the required condition.

9. Let us return to the point concerning means and ends that Aristotelian treatments of the relationship between them fail to take sufficiently into account. It is that, since living a meaningful life is important to us for its own sake, useful activity possesses for us not merely instrumental value but terminal value as well. Being engaged in the pursuit of a desirable state of affairs is not desirable exclusively because it is desirable that the state of affairs should obtain. The pursuit is also desirable as an end in itself. This is because working to reach desirable ends is essential to a meaningful life; a person's life is meaningful, indeed, only to the extent that it is devoted to pursuing goals that are important to him. That we have instrumentally valuable work to do is thus of considerable importance to us for its own sake.

Since there can be no useful work for a person unless he has final ends, the relationship between instrumental and terminal values is not straightforwardly unidirectional. Rather than being unequivocally asymmetric, the relationship is reciprocal. For our final ends derive a certain instrumental value from the very fact that they are terminally valuable. One reason for pursuing them is, of course, that they are (by hypothesis) valuable in themselves. However, pursuing them is also justified in part because pursuit of an intrinsically valuable state of affairs is itself intrinsically valuable. By virtue of the fact that this intrinsically valuable activity is impossible without a final end, its final end possesses instrumental value.

The point here is not that an activity may possess inherent terminal value. Aristotle himself observes that activities may be desired as final ends and not merely as means to ends other than themselves. But in allowing that activities may be undertaken just for their own sakes, Aristotle does not recognize that they may possess terminal value precisely because they are instrumentally valuable. His notion is just that an activity may be desirable on account of its inherent character, quite apart from whatever value it may derive from being a means to something else.

An invigorating workout, with its zestful glow of unimpeded vitality, is good in itself regardless of whether it is good for anything else. The same holds for intellectual activity of various kinds, and for listening to music. On the other hand, consider the work of making bridles for horses. Aristotle regards this activity as desirable exclusively on account of the military ends to which it is a means.[9] He evidently takes it for granted that making a bridle is not inherently enjoyable or fascinating; it is not, he supposes, an activity in which anyone would engage for its own sake, as an end in itself. He regards its value as being exclusively instrumental. The making of bridles provides an instance, then, of Aristotle's conviction that "the activity of the craftsman derives its value only from the value of what it produces."[10]

Let us concede that making bridles is an activity without inherent value, which would be entirely pointless if bridles were not worth having. Still, we cannot presume that the importance to a person of making bridles is wholly coincident with the importance to him of having bridles. It may be, as Aristotle asserts, that arts and inquiries aim just at their products or, if they are worth pursuing for their own sakes, at themselves. But *people* aim also at having useful work. Moreover, they do not desire useful work only because they desire its products. In fact, useful work is among their final ends. They desire it for its own sake, since without it life is empty and vain.

Any rational decision concerning the adoption of final ends must be made partly on the basis of an evaluation of the kinds of activities by which the various prospective ends would be pursued. It requires a consideration not only of the value that is inherent in these activities taken by themselves, but also of the terminal value they possess as contributors of meaning to life. Pursuing one final end rather than another may lead a person to engage in activities that are in themselves more enjoyable. It may also lead him to live a life that is more meaningful. It will do this if it entails a richer and more fully grounded purposefulness – if, that is, the network of activity to which it gives rise has greater complexity and if it radiates more extensively within the person's life.

In evaluating a prospective final end, accordingly, it is essential to consider how much terminal value that end would convey to the means by which it would have to be pursued. In this sense, final ends must be judged on the basis of their usefulness. From one point of view, the activities in which we pursue our terminally valuable final ends have only the instrumental value that is characteristic of means. From another point of view, however, these activities are themselves terminally valuable, and they imbue with instrumental value the final ends for the sake of which they are undertaken.

10. When someone undertakes to choose his final ends, he is proposing to identify the goals and the values that will most basically guide and constrain his conduct. In other words, he is seeking to resolve the question of how he should live. Now

9   *Nicomachean Ethics* 1094a10–15.
10   H. H. Joachim, *The Nicomachean Ethics, A Commentary* (Oxford: Clarendon, 1951), p. 20.

this question suffers from being what may be described as "systematically incho-ate." The problem with it is that the meaning of the question cannot confidently be construed until after the question has been answered. How the question is to be understood depends, that is, upon how it is to be resolved. Thus, it seems that we must attempt to settle the question before knowing exactly what question it is.

A decision concerning how to live must take into account considerations of a variety of types. Some of these are ethical: they have to do with what kinds of life are morally permissible, or morally desirable, or obligatory. Others pertain to the feelings and attitudes of the person whose life is in question: what gives him satisfaction, for instance, or what he really wants. Enumerating and elucidating these considerations involve substantial problems. However, there is a more gen-eral difficulty that is more fundamental than these.

In any reasonable deliberation about how he is to live, a person must assess and compare the values of those things that he regards as important to him. He must define the respective roles that are to be played in his life by feelings, by desires, by morality, by various personal commitments and ideals, and by whatever else he cares about. The most critical issue he has to face, in deciding upon his final ends, is to determine the relative importance that he will accord to each of these. Answering the question of how to live is tantamount, indeed, to making that determination.

But this means that there is no substantial difference between answering the question and specifying the basis upon which it is to be answered. Assigning weights to the various considerations that are pertinent to a decision concerning how to live is the same as deciding how to live. It is on this account that the question may be characterized as systematically inchoate. Until it has been an-swered, it is impossible to understand fully what it asks.

What moves us to ask how we should live? We are moved to ask this question because we want to identify the principles and the purposes to which we should be devoted and by which we should be limited. Our motivation is, in other words, an interest in articulating what we are to care about. We are anxious to get clear concerning what is to be important to us. Now it is precisely on this account that the question is so irredeemably elusive. For the notion of importance is similarly inchoate. Also, it is not susceptible to orderly and analytically definitive elucidation.

Nothing is important unless it makes a difference. For suppose something makes no difference at all: everything else will be exactly the same whether it exists or not. Then, surely, it has utterly no importance. Making a difference is a neces-sary condition, then, for being important. But this condition is not sufficient; the mere fact that something makes a difference is not enough to endow it with importance. After all, everything does make some difference; nonetheless, certain things are entirely without importance. They are unimportant, even though they make a difference, because the only difference they make is trivial.

Something that makes a difference is important, then, only if the difference that it makes is not trivial. It must make an important difference. It follows that we cannot determine whether something is important unless we are already able to distinguish between differences that are trivial and those that are important. Any attempt to formulate a defining criterion for the concept of importance is therefore bound to be circular.

11. Suppose there is someone to whom nothing is important. Such a person has no basis upon which to decide that something is important to him. If it is really true that he cares about nothing, then it is not possible for him to make any reasoned decision to care about anything. To care about anything, or to regard it as important to oneself, means being motivated by a concern for it. The concern may be positive or negative: hatred or love, a desire to possess or a desire to avoid, an interest in sustaining the object or in destroying it. When a person cares about something, his will is necessarily in some such way determinate or fixed. That is, he is not thoroughly indifferent to everything. Now it is only if his volitional nature is in certain respects already fixed that a person can effectively consider what his final ends should be — what is to be important to him, or what to care about. He will not be in a position to inquire into the question of how he should live unless it is already the case that there are some things about which he cares.

This means that someone who is interested in making a reasonable decision concerning how to live cannot propose to start out by refusing to take any determination of the will for granted. If he insists upon being entirely impartial, and upon evaluating the available options unguided by any volitional predisposition, his inquiry is hopeless. The pan-rationalist demand for selfless objectivity is in this context not a reasonable one. It makes no sense to attempt an impersonal approach, from no particular evaluative point of view, to the problem of how one should live.

The fact that the will must be antecedently fixed does not mean that it must be fixed unalterably. What is important to a person depends, just as his other characteristics do, upon a variety of causally influential factors. These will differ at different times. We may therefore come to care about certain things to which we were previously indifferent, and we may cease to care about others. Volitional changes of this sort do not in themselves impair our capacity for judging what is important. In order to have a basis for judging what is important to him, a person must already care about something. But it need not be what he cared about at some earlier time, or what he will care about later.

While what is antecedently important to the person may be alterable, it must not be subject to his own immediate voluntary control. If it is to provide him with a genuine basis for evaluations of importance, the fact that he cares about it cannot be dependent simply upon his own decision or choice. For suppose he were actually in a position to change the fact in that way — i.e., by the exercise of a mere act of will. Suppose it were simply up to him whether or not to continue caring about it.

How could he decide? On what reasonable basis, without arbitrariness, could he make the necessary choice?

He would have to ask himself the following question: "Is it more important to me to keep my will fixed as it is, or is it more important to me to alter it?" But he clearly would be in no position to answer this question. For by the very act of raising the question, and asking what his will should be, he suspends the authority of any antecedent volitional state that could have provided the basis for answering it. Here again, the possibility of being rational requires renouncing the self-denial that is mandated by the pan-rationalistic ideal.

In order for a person to have an appropriate basis for deciding upon his final ends, then, there must not only be something that is antecedently important to him; in addition, its importance to him must be outside his immediate voluntary control. In other words, there must be something about which he *cannot help* caring. This does not entail either that his caring about it must be impervious to all possibility of change or that he cannot change it himself. Rather, it means that his caring about it is not up to him as a matter of free choice: whether he cares about it does not depend upon his simply making up his mind one way or the other. The fact that it is important to him must be due to a feature of his will which he can neither sustain nor alter by just deciding to do so.

In discussing matters pertaining to moral theory, a number of philosophers customarily rely to one extent or another upon reports of "moral intuitions": i.e., what people are inclined to say about issues of how to behave. While this can be helpful, something different is required when investigating how one should live. What we then particularly need to know is not what we are *inclined* to care about or what we are *inclined* to regard as important. We need to know what there is, if anything, that we *cannot help* considering important or about which we *cannot help* caring.

Moreover, this is not merely helpful; it is indispensable. A person who is not antecedently in the grip of some such necessity fails to satisfy a necessary condition for making a rational choice of final ends. If his volitional character is unfixed, or if it is under the direct control of his own will, he cannot proceed in any reasoned way to determine how he should live.

8

The Faintest Passion

1. My title is taken from an observation by A. E. Housman. "The faintest of all human passions," he wrote, "is the love of truth."[1] There are two senses in which a passion may be faint: it may be weak, or it may only be difficult to discern. Housman certainly intended the former. But be that as it may, there is a passion that, in both senses, is even fainter than our love of truth. Surely the very faintest human passion – both the least salient and the least robust – is our love of the truth about ourselves.

The ability both to believe something and at the same time to conceal this from oneself is a bit paradoxical. Philosophers have found it difficult to explain how we do this. There is no problem, however, in understanding *why*. The facts about ourselves are often hard to take. When they move us to self-deception, it is because we find them irreconcilable with what we want to believe. We hide from the truth, it seems clear, because it conflicts with our self-love. My theme here, however, is not self-deception. I am aiming at another enemy of the truth about ourselves – one whose relation to self-love is rather more complex and uncertain. My approach will be somewhat oblique. I begin with a question about lying.

2. When we object to being the victim of a lie, just what is it that we find so objectionable? I am not asking why lying is wrong. My question has to do not with the morality of lying, but with our experience of it. What offends us when we are offended that someone has told us a lie? What accounts for how the lying affects us?

Much is often made of the notion that lying undermines the cohesion of human society. Kant says that "without truth social intercourse and conversation become valueless."[2] And he argues that because it threatens society in this way, "a lie always harms another; if not some particular man, still it harms mankind gener-ally. . . ."[3] Montaigne makes a similar claim: "our intercourse being carried on solely by means of the word, he who falsifies that is a traitor to society."[4] "Lying is

---

I dedicate this address to my first teachers in philosophy, George Boas and Albert Hammond, of blessed memory.

1   A. E. Housman, M. *Manilii, Astronomicon I* (London, 1903), p. xliii.
2   *Lectures on Ethics*, p. 224.
3   "On a Supposed Right to Lie from Altruistic Motives."
4   "Of Giving the Lie."

an accursed vice," Montaigne declares; and then he adds, warming rather frenetically to his subject, that "if we did but recognize the horror and gravity of it, we should punish it with flames more justly than other crimes."[5]

Montaigne and Kant certainly have a point, but they exaggerate. Profitable social intercourse does not really depend, as they maintain, upon people telling each other the truth; nor does conversation lose its value when people lie. The actual quantity of lying is enormous, after all, and yet social life goes on. That people often lie hardly renders it impossible to benefit from living with them. It only means that we have to be careful. We can quite successfully negotiate our way through an environment full of lies, as long as we can reasonably trust our own ability to discriminate more or less effectively between instances in which people are lying and those in which they are telling the truth. General confidence in the honesty of others is not essential as long as we are justified in having confidence in ourselves.

In any case, however, it is not because we think that lies threaten or encumber the order of society that we are upset by them in the first place. Our concern when someone lies to us is not the concern of a citizen. What is most immediately aroused in our reaction to the liar is not public spirit. The reaction is personal. As a rule, we are dismayed far less by the harm the liar may have done to others than by his conduct toward ourselves. What stirs us against him, whether or not he has somehow managed to betray all of mankind, is that he has certainly injured us.

Lying is a rather complicated act. Someone who tells a lie invariably attempts to deceive his victim about matters of two distinct kinds: first, about the state of affairs to which he explictly refers and of which he is purporting to give a correct account; second, about his own beliefs and what is going on in his mind. In addition to misrepresenting a fact about the world, then, the liar also misrepresents various facts about himself. Each of these aspects of what he does is significant in its own way.

First of all, the liar aims at inducing his victims to regard as real a world that he himself has designed. To the extent that he is successful in this, he is the originator of what they take to be reality. How the facts appear to them is determined by what he says. Thus he arrogates to himself something like the divine prerogative of creative speech, simulating the omnipotent will by which God (according to Genesis) brought a world into being merely by stipulating that it should be so. This arrogance offends our pride. We are angered by the liar's insulting effort to usurp control over the conditions in which we understand ourselves to live.

Second, by imposing a false world on his victims, the liar excludes them from his world. Insofar as he places them within an understanding of reality that differs from his own, he separates them radically from himself. This is what leads Adrienne Rich to observe, with poetic exactitude, that "the liar leads an existence

5   "Of Liars."

of unutterable loneliness."[6] The loneliness is precisely *unutterable* because the liar cannot even reveal that he *is* lonely without disclosing that he has lied. By hiding his own thoughts, he makes it impossible for others to be in touch with him – to understand him or to respond to him as he really is, or even to be aware that they are not doing so. This forecloses a mode of human intimacy that is both elementary and normal, and for this reason it too is insulting. Like his presuming to exercise the creative prerogative of a god, the liar's refusal to permit himself to be known is an injury to his victim's pride.

3. In certain cases, lies cause a deeper damage. Adrienne Rich says that "to discover that one has been lied to in a personal relationship leads one to feel a little crazy."[7] Here again, her observation is perspicuous and exact. When we are dealing in an important matter with someone whom we hardly know, we can be confident that what he says coincides with what he believes only on the basis of a more or less deliberate evaluation of his reliability; and, ordinarily, this evaluation only covers specific communications. With our close friends, as a rule, both of these conditions are relaxed. We suppose that our friends are generally truthful with us; and we take this pretty much for granted. We tend to trust whatever they say; and we do so, mainly, not on the basis of a particular calculation that they are telling the truth, but because we feel comfortable with them. As we familiarly put it, "we just know they wouldn't lie to us."

With friends, the presumption of intimacy has become natural. It derives most immediately from our feelings – that is, from our sense of our own state, rather than from an evaluation of pertinent evidence about them. It would be too much to say that a person's inclination to trust his friends belongs to his essential nature. But it could properly enough be said that trusting them has come to be second nature to him.

This is why finding that we have been lied to by a friend engenders a feeling of being crazy. The discovery exposes something about ourselves more disturbing than that we have merely miscalculated or made an error of judgment. It reveals that our own nature (i.e., our second nature) is unreliable, leading us to count on people who cannot be trusted. Needless to say, the deception of a friend implies a fault in the one who tells the lie. But it also shows that the victim is defective too. The liar betrays him, but he is betrayed by his own feelings as well.

Self-betrayal pertains to craziness because it is a hallmark of the irrational. The essence of rationality is to be consistent; and being consistent, in action or in thought, means proceeding so as not to defeat oneself. Aristotle explains that an agent acts rationally insofar as he conforms his actions to the mean. Suppose that, for the sake of good health, a person follows a diet either so meager or so indulgent that it actually leads him away from his goal of well-being. It is in this self-betrayal

---

6 "Women and Honor: Some Notes on Lying," in *On Lies, Secrets and Silence* (New York, 1979), p. 191.
7 Ibid., p. 186.

that the irrationality of his divergence from the mean consists. Intellectual activity is similarly undermined by logical incoherence. When a line of thought generates a contradiction, its further progressive elaboration is blocked. In whatever direction the mind turns, it is driven back: it must affirm what it has already rejected, or deny what it has already affirmed. Like behavior that frustrates its own ambition, contradictory thinking is irrational because it betrays itself.

When a person discovers that someone he had found it natural to count on has lied to him, this shows him that he cannot rely upon his own settled feelings of trust. He sees that his sense of whom he can have confidence in has betrayed him. It has led him to miss the truth rather than to attain it. His assumption that he could guide himself by it has turned out to be self-defeating, and hence irrational. He may well feel, accordingly, a little crazy.

4. According to Aristotle, philosophy in the ancient world began in wonder.[8] In the modern world, of course, it began in doubt. These are both attitudes of uncertainty. We are moved to wonder when the phenomena are unclear. On the other hand, the uneasiness that lying may arouse in us, concerning our own cognitive capacities, is more like the mode of uncertainty that beset Descartes. What disturbed him was not how to think about the phenomena, but what to make of himself. The doubt in which his epistemological and metaphysical enterprise began was self-doubt.

The ancient philosophers, Aristotle explains, "philosophised in order to escape from ignorance."[9] Descartes was moved to philosophize less by ignorance than by anxiety, less by a lack of knowledge than by a lack of self-confidence. What worried him was that he might be by nature so profoundly defective that his intellectual ambitions would be betrayed by the very cognitive capacities upon which he needed to rely in pursuing them. "How do we know," he asked, "that we have not been made in such a way that we constantly deceive ourselves?" In other words, how do we know that rationality is possible at all? Descartes's particular fear was that we might perceive, with equally irresistible clarity and distinctness, both that certain propositions are true and that they are not true. That would show reason to be hopelessly divided. It would mean that anyone who attempted persistently to be rational would end up not knowing what to think.

Spinoza defines a condition of our affective nature that is analogous to this division within reason. The "constitution of the mind which arises from two contrary affects," he says, "is called vacillation of mind, which is therefore related to the affects as doubt is to the imagination."[10] Now I want to consider a somewhat different, but still analogous, type of psychic instability or conflict. I shall call it "ambivalence." Here what is divided is neither a person's reason nor his

8 *Metaphysics* I, 2: 982b12.
9 Ibid., 982b20.
10 *Ethics*, 3P17S.

affects, but his will. Insofar as someone is ambivalent, he is moved by incompatible preferences or attitudes regarding his affects or his desires or regarding other elements of his psychic life. This volitional division keeps him from settling upon or from tolerating any coherent affective or motivational identity. It means that he does not know what he really wants.[11]

Ambivalence is constituted by conflicting volitional movements or tendencies, either conscious or unconscious, that meet two conditions. First, they are inherently and hence unavoidably opposed; that is, they do not just happen to conflict on account of contingent circumstances. Second, they are both wholly internal to a person's will rather than alien to him; that is, he is not passive with respect to them. An example of ambivalence might be provided by someone who is moved to commit himself to a certain career, or to a certain person, and also moved to refrain from doing so.

Conflicts involving first-order psychic elements alone – for instance, between an attraction and an aversion to the same object or action – do not pertain to the will at all. They are not volitional, but merely impulsive or sentimental. Conflicts that pertain to the will arise out of a person's higher-order, reflective attitudes. But even conflicts that do implicate a person's will are nonetheless distinct from ambivalence if some of the psychic forces they involve are exogenous – that is, if the person is not identified with them and they are, in that sense, external to his will.

An addict who struggles sincerely against his addiction is contending with a force by which he does not want to be moved and which is therefore alien to him. Since the conflict is not wholly within his will, he is not volitionally divided or ambivalent. The unwilling addict is wholeheartedly on one side of the conflict from which he suffers, and not at all on the other. The addiction may defeat his will, but does not as such disrupt its unity.

A person is ambivalent, then, only if he is indecisive concerning whether to be for or against a certain psychic position. Now this kind of indecisiveness is as irrational, in its way, as holding contradictory beliefs. The disunity of an ambivalent person's will prevents him from effectively pursuing and satisfactorily attaining his goals. Like conflict within reason, volitional conflict leads to self-betrayal and self-defeat. The trouble is in each case the same: a sort of incoherent greed – trying to have things both ways – which naturally makes it impossible to get anywhere. The flow of volitional or of intellectual activity is interrupted and reversed; movement in any direction is truncated and turned back. However a person starts out to decide or to think, he finds that he is getting in his own way.

The extent and the severity of ambivalence nowadays are probably due in some part to conditions especially characteristic of our time. But volitional disunity itself is, of course, nothing special and nothing new. Saint Augustine observed that

---

11 There are degrees of the sort of conflict I am considering. In discussing ambivalence, I am concerned with conflict sufficiently severe that a person: (a) cannot act decisively; or (b) finds that fulfilling either of his conflicting desires is substantially unsatisfying.

"it is . . . no strange phenomenon partly to will to do something and partly to will not to do it." Division of the will, he believed, is "a disease of the mind" from which we suffer in punishment for Original Sin.[12] At least in his view, then, ambivalence in one degree or another is inherent in the destiny of man.

5. If ambivalence is a disease of the will, the health of the will is to be unified and in this sense wholehearted. A person is volitionally robust when he is wholehearted in his higher-order attitudes and inclinations, in his preferences and decisions, and in other movements of his will. This unity entails no particular level of excitement or warmth. Wholeheartedness is not a measure of the firmness of a person's volitional state, or of his enthusiasm. What is at issue is the organization of the will, not its temperature.

As in the case of the unwilling addict, the unity of a healthy will is quite compatible with certain kinds of virulent psychic conflict. Wholeheartedness does not require that a person be altogether untroubled by inner opposition to his will. It just requires that, with respect to any such conflict, he himself be fully resolved. This means that he must be resolutely on the side of one of the forces struggling within him and not on the side of any other. Concerning the opposition of these forces, he has to know where he himself stands. In other words, he must know what he wants.

To the extent that a person is ambivalent, he does not really know what he wants. This ignorance or uncertainty differs from straightforwardly cognitive deficiency. There may be no information concerning his will that the ambivalent person lacks. The problem is rather that, since his mind is not made up, his will is in fact unformed. He is volitionally inchoate and indeterminate.

This is why ambivalence, like self-deception, is an enemy of truth. The ambivalent person does not hide from some truth or conceal it from himself; he does not prevent the truth from being known. Instead, his ambivalence stands in the way of there being a certain truth about him at all. He is inclined in one direction, and he is inclined in a contrary direction as well; and his attitude toward these inclinations is unsettled. Thus, it is true of him neither that he prefers one of his alternatives, nor that he prefers the other, nor that he likes them equally.

Since ambivalence is not a cognitive deficiency, it cannot be overcome merely by acquiring additional information. It also cannot be overcome voluntaristically. A person cannot make himself volitionally determinate and thereby create a truth where there was none before, merely by an "act of will." In other words, he cannot make himself wholehearted just by a psychic movement that is fully under his immediate voluntary control.

The concept of reality is fundamentally the concept of something which is independent of our wishes and by which we are therefore constrained. Thus, reality

12 *Confessions* VIII, 9.

cannot be under our absolute and unmediated volitional control. The existence and the character of what is real are necessarily indifferent to mere acts of our will.

Now this must hold as well for the reality of the will itself. A person's will is real only if its character is not absolutely up to him. It must be unresponsive to his sheer fiat. It cannot be unconditionally within his power to determine what his will is to be, as it is within the unconstrained power of an author of fiction to render determinate – in whatever way he likes – the volitional characteristics of the people in his stories.

Indeterminacy in the life of a real person cannot be overcome by preemptive decree. To be sure, a person may attempt to resolve his ambivalence by deciding to adhere unequivocally to one of his alternatives rather than to the other; and he may believe that in thus making up his mind he has eliminated the division in his will and become wholehearted. Whether such changes have actually occurred, however, is another matter. When the chips are down he may discover that he is not, after all, decisively moved by the preference or motive he supposed he had adopted. Remember Hotspur's reply when Owen Glendower boasted, "I can call spirits from the vasty deep." He said: "Why, so can I, or so can any man; but will they come when you do call for them?"[13] The same goes for us. We do not control, by our voluntary command, the spirits within our own vasty deeps. We cannot have, simply for the asking, whatever will we want.

We are not fictitious characters, who have sovereign authors; nor are we gods, who can be authors of more than fiction. Therefore, we cannot be authors of ourselves. Reducing our own volitional indeterminacy, and becoming truly whole-hearted, is not a matter of telling stories about our lives. Nor, unless we wish to be as foolish as Owen Glendower, can we propose to shape our wills by stipulating peremptorily at some moment that now we are no longer divided but have become solidly resolute. We can be only what nature and life make us, and that is not so readily up to us.

This may appear to conflict with the notion that our wills are ultimately free. But what is the freedom of the will? A natural and useful way of understanding it is that a person's will is free to the extent that he has whatever will he wants. Now if this means that his will is free only if it is under his entirely unmediated voluntaristic control, then a free will can have no genuine reality; for reality entails resistance to such control. Must we, then, regard our wills either as unfree or as unreal?

The dilemma can be avoided if we construe the freedom of someone's will as requiring, not that he originate or control what he wills, but that he be whole-hearted in it. If there is no division within a person's will, it follows that the will he has is the will he wants. His wholeheartedness means exactly that there is in him no endogenous desire to be volitionally different than he is. Although he may be

13 *Henry IV, Part 1.*

unable to create in himself a will other than the one he has, his will is free at least in the sense that he himself does not oppose or impede it.

6. Being wholehearted is not always warranted. There are circumstances in which it is only reasonable, no matter how uncomfortable it may be, for a person to be drawn in several directions at once. But while accepting ambivalence may sometimes be helpful or wise, it is never desirable as such or for its own sake. And to remain persistently ambivalent concerning issues of substantial importance in the conduct of life is a significant disability. Moral and political theorists often emphasize how valuable it is for people to have extensive repertoires of worthwhile options from which they are free to choose. The actual value to people of possessing these options depends to a large extent, however, upon their capacities for wholeheartedness.

After all, what good is it for someone to be free to make significant choices if he does not know what he wants and if he is unable to overcome his ambivalence? What is the point of offering a beguiling variety of alternatives to people who can respond to them only with irresolute vacillation? For someone who is unlikely to have any stable preferences or goals, the benefits of freedom are, at the very least, severely diminished. The opportunity to act in accordance with his own inclinations is a doubtful asset for an individual whose will is so divided that he is moved both to decide for a certain alternative and to decide against it. Neither of the alternatives can satisfy him, since each entails frustration of the other. The fact that he is free to choose between them is likely only to make his anguish more poignant and more intense.

Unless a person is capable of a considerable degree of volitional unity, he cannot make coherent use of freedom. Those who care about freedom must therefore be concerned about more than the availability of attractive opportunities among which people can choose as they please. They must also concern themselves with whether people can come to know what they want to do with the freedom they enjoy. It may be, as Saint Augustine supposed, that a thoroughly unified will comes only as a gift of God. Still, the extent to which people suffer from volitional indeterminacy is not entirely independent of the social, political, and cultural conditions in which they live. Those conditions may either facilitate or impede the development of unambivalent attitudes, preferences, and goals.

7. So far I have provided for wholeheartedness only a brief conceptual sketch, elaborated primarily in relation to an equally sketchy account of the notion of ambivalence. Now I will try to develop a more fully articulated understanding of what it is to be wholehearted, by construing it as tantamount to the enjoyment of a kind of self-satisfaction. In speaking of self-satisfaction, I do not mean to refer pejoratively to a state of narcissistic complacency or smugness. The state I have in mind – a state of satisfaction with the condition of the self – is utterly inoffensive

and benign. Clarifying its structure will actually help not only to illuminate what is involved in being wholehearted. It will also help in coping with an alleged difficulty in hierarchical analyses of the self. And I believe that, in addition, it will enhance our understanding of a rather troublesome notion — the notion of identification — that is fundamental to any philosophy of mind and of action.

Consider a person who believes something wholeheartedly, who is wholehearted in some feeling or attitude, or who intends wholeheartedly to perform a certain action. In what does his wholeheartedness with respect to these psychic elements consist? It consists in his being fully satisfied that they, rather than others that inherently (i.e., non-contingently) conflict with them, should be among the causes and considerations that determine his cognitive, affective, attitudinal, and behavioral processes.

This is compatible with his also being wholehearted with respect to other psychic elements, which contingently (i.e., due to particular circumstances) conflict with these and which are more important to him. The fact that a person is satisfied with an intention, a feeling, or a belief does not entail that he is committed to acting on it. Being wholehearted with respect to one element is consistent with assigning a higher priority to another. Someone may be satisfied to have both elements play active roles in his psychic economy, though not roles that are equally urgent or compelling. The element that is less important to him is not necessarily alien, threatening him from outside the structure of his self. It may be as much a part of him as those other elements that are more important parts of him.[14]

Now what does it mean to say of a person that he is satisfied with his psychic condition, or with some element or aspect of it? It does not mean that he considers it the best condition available to him. Some people may be so demanding that they are never willing to settle for anything less than that. But as a rule, satisfaction is not conditioned by an uncompromising ambition to maximize. People often settle gladly for less than what they think it would be possible for them to get. From the fact that someone is satisfied with his condition, then, it does not follow that no alteration of it would be acceptable to him. It goes almost without saying, of course, that he would be satisfied with an improved condition. However, he might also be satisfied even with a condition inferior to the one he is in.

What satisfaction does entail is an absence of restlessness or resistance. A satisfied person might willingly accept a change in his condition, but he has no active interest in bringing about a change. Even if he recognizes that he could be better off, the possibility does not engage his concern: being better off is simply

14 It is only to persons that wholeheartedness and ambivalence are attributable. For this reason, wholeheartedness is not exactly equivalent to the absence of ambivalence: the fact that there is no inherent conflict among the various elements of someone's psychic state does not quite entail that he is wholehearted with respect to them. To be a person, as distinct from simply a human organism, requires a complex volitional structure involving reflective self-evaluation. Human beings that lack this structure may be free of inherent volitional conflict, but they are not persons. Therefore, they are neither ambivalent nor wholehearted.

not interesting or important to him. This is not because he believes that becoming better off would be too costly, or because it is too uncertain. It is just that, as a sheer matter of fact, he has no ambition for improvement; he accepts the state of things as it is, without reservation and without any practical interest in how it compares with other possibilities. Perhaps his condition could be improved at no net cost, and perhaps he is aware of this, but he simply does not care.[15]

To be satisfied with something does not require that a person have any particular belief about it, nor any particular feeling or attitude or intention. It does not require, for instance, that he regard it as satisfactory, or that he accede to it with approval, or that he intend to leave it as it stands. There is nothing that he needs to think, or to adopt, or to accept; it is not necessary for him to do anything at all. This is important, because it explains why there is no danger here of a problematic regress.

Suppose that being satisfied did require a person to have, as an essential constitutive condition of his satisfaction, some deliberate psychic element — some deliberate attitude or belief or feeling or intention. This element could not be one with which the person is at all dissatisfied. How could someone be wholehearted with respect to one psychic element by virtue of being halfhearted with respect to another? So if being satisfied required some element as a constituent, satisfaction with respect to one matter would depend upon satisfaction with respect to another; satisfaction with respect to the second would depend upon satisfaction with respect to still a third; and so on, endlessly. Satisfaction with one's self requires, then, no adoption of any cognitive, attitudinal, affective, or intentional stance. It does not require the performance of a particular act; and it also does not require any deliberate abstention. Satisfaction is a state of the entire psychic system — a state constituted just by the absence of any tendency or inclination to alter its condition.

Of course, a person may make the judgment that he is well enough off; and on that basis he may decide to refrain from doing anything to improve his situation. Making this judgment or this decision does not, however, either make him satisfied or entail that he is satisfied. His decision to refrain from trying to change things is, in effect, a decision on his part to act *as though* he is satisfied. Refraining from trying to change things *simulates* the equilibrium in which satisfaction consists. But to simulate satisfaction is not the same as being satisfied. A person is actually satisfied only when the equilibrium is not contrived or imposed but is integral to his psychic condition — that is, when that condition is settled and unreserved apart from any effort by him to make it so.

Being genuinely satisfied is not a matter, then, of choosing to leave things as they are or of making some judgment or decision concerning the desirability of

---

15 A satisfied person may become dissatisfied upon realizing that things might be better. The realization may cause his expectations to rise. This does not mean, of course, that he was dissatisfied before they rose.

change. It is a matter of simply *having no interest* in making changes. What it requires is that psychic elements of certain kinds *do not occur*. But while the absence of such elements does not require either deliberate action or deliberate restraint, their absence must nonetheless be reflective. In other words, the fact that the person is not moved to change things must derive from his understanding and evaluation of how things are with him. Thus, the essential non-occurrence is neither deliberately contrived nor wantonly unselfconscious. It develops and prevails as an unmanaged consequence of the person's appreciation of his psychic condition.[16]

8. Let me try briefly to sketch how this bears on the hierarchical approach to analysis of the self and on the notion of identification. On hierarchical accounts, a person identifies with one rather than with another of his own desires by virtue of wanting to be moved to action by the first desire rather than by the second. For example, someone who is trying to quit smoking is identified with his first-order desire not to smoke, rather than with his concurrent first-order desire for another cigarette, if he wants the desire not to smoke to be the one that effectively guides his conduct. But what determines whether he identifies with this second-order preference?

Considered in itself, after all, his desire to defeat the desire to smoke is just another desire. How can it claim to be constitutive of what he really wants? The mere fact that it is a second-order desire surely gives it no particular authority. And it will not help to look for a third-order desire that serves to identify the person with this second-order preference. Obviously, the same question would arise concerning the authority of that desire; so we would have to find an even higher-order desire; and so on endlessly. The whole approach appears to be doomed.

Hierarchical accounts of the identity of the self do not presume, however, that a person's identification with some desire consists simply in the fact that he *has* a higher-order desire by which the first desire is endorsed. The endorsing higher-order desire must be, in addition, a desire with which the person is *satisfied*. And since (as I tried to explain earlier) satisfaction with one psychic element does not require satisfaction with any other, being satisfied with a certain desire does not entail an endless proliferation of higher orders and desires. Identification is constituted neatly by an endorsing higher-order desire with which the person is satisfied. It is possible, of course, for someone to be satisfied with his first-order desires without in any way considering whether to endorse them. In that case, he is identified with those first-order desires. But insofar as his desires are utterly

16 Being or becoming satisfied is like being or becoming relaxed. Suppose that someone sees his troubles recede and consequently relaxes. No doubt it is by various feelings, beliefs, and attitudes that he is led to relax. But the occurrence of these psychic elements does not constitute being relaxed, nor are they necessary for relaxation. What is essential is only that the person stop worrying and feeling tense.

unreflective, he is to that extent not genuinely a person at all. He is merely a wanton.

9. Is it possible to be satisfied with ambivalence? A person may certainly come to accept the fact that he is ambivalent as unalterable. It seems to me, however, that it is not a fact with which he can possibly be satisfied. No one can be wholeheartedly ambivalent, any more than someone can desire unequivocally to betray himself or to be irrational. That someone accepts his ambivalence can mean only that he is resigned to it; it could not mean that it satisfies him. Perhaps conditions are imaginable in which a person might reasonably regard ambivalence as worthwhile in order to avoid some even more unsatisfactory alternative. But no one can desire to be ambivalent for its own sake.

It is a necessary truth about us, then, that we wholeheartedly desire to be wholehearted. This suggests a criterion for use in the design of ideals and programs of life, and generally in determining what to regard as important and to care about. What we care about should be, to the greatest extent possible, something we are able to care about wholeheartedly. We do not wish to work against ourselves, or to have to hold ourselves back. There are many things to which we find ourselves attracted. In trying to decide which of them is to be important to us, we must anticipate the extent to which each can be coherently elaborated in our lives.

This may be quite different than the extent to which, considered in itself, it is worthy of being cared about. The fact that something is important to us does not primarily consist in our estimate of its own value. The question of what we are to care about is not settled by arriving at judgments as to the inherent or comparative merits of various possible objects of devotion. The fact that a person cares about or is devoted to something – an ideal, or another person, or a project – means that, whatever he may *think* about it, to one degree or another he *loves* it. The problem has to do most fundamentally, then, with what we are capable of loving.

What about self-love? That a person is fully satisfied with himself means that he is wholehearted in his feelings, his intentions, and his thoughts. And insofar as being wholehearted is tantamount to loving, wholeheartedness with regard to such things is the same as self-love. Now someone who is engaged in self-deception in a matter concerning what he is or what he is doing is conceding thereby that he is not satisfied with himself. Like everyone else, of course, he would like to be wholehearted; as all of us do, he wants to love himself. Indeed, this is his motive for self-deception. It is his desire to love himself that leads him to replace an unsatisfying truth about himself, which he cannot wholeheartedly accept, with a belief that he can accept without ambivalence.

Of course, the effort is misguided. Psychic unity obviously cannot be achieved by dividing oneself. However, the self-deceiver is in fact attempting to escape from being ambivalent. He is trying to overcome the indeterminacy of his cognitive state. What he desires, in other words, is that there be an unequivocal truth

106

concerning what he thinks. We might even say, if we are fond of paradox, that what moves him to deceive himself is the love of truth.

10. Unfortunately it is rare, as we know, for our desire to love ourselves to be fulfilled. We are not often satisfied with our conduct or with what we are. Our lives are marred, to one degree or another, by ambivalence. Saint Augustine thought that a transition to psychic unity from a state of volitional division requires a miracle. So he prayed for conversion. That is not actually such a bad approach to the problem. In any case, it seems to have worked out well for him.

I have another suggestion, however, which he appears not to have considered. I will offer it by relating a conversation I had a few years ago with a woman who worked in an office near mine. She and I did not know each other very well, but one day our talk somehow became a bit more personal than usual. At a certain point in the conversation she told me that, in her opinion, in a serious relationship only two things are really important: honesty and a sense of humor. Then she thought for a moment and said: "You know, I'm really not all that sure about honesty; after all, even if they tell you the truth, they change their minds so fast, you can't count on them anyhow."

Sometimes a person is so ambivalent, or vacillates so fluidly, that there is no stable fact concerning what he thinks or feels. In cases like that, when the only truth is too limited to be helpful, meticulous honesty may not be such an important virtue. No doubt the best thing would be for the person to settle down: give up trying to have things both ways and find some coherent order in which he can be more or less wholehearted. But suppose you are simply unable to make up your mind. No matter how you twist or turn, you cannot find a way of being satisfied with yourself. My advice is that, if your will is utterly divided, and volitional unity is really out of the question, be sure at least to hang on to your sense of humor.

9

On the Necessity of Ideals

FREEDOM, INDIVIDUALITY, AND NECESSITY

Our culture places a very high value on a certain ideal of freedom according to which a person is to have varied alternatives available in the design and conduct of his life. For a long time we have been fundamentally committed to encouraging a steady expansion of the range of options from which people can select. This commitment has been rather lavishly provided with technological, institutional, and ideological support. Moreover, it has become morally entrenched: we admire individuals and societies that promote freedom, and we deplore practices or circumstances that impair it. The more a society leaves it up to its members to determine individually the direction of their energies and the specification of their goals, and the more reasonable possibilities it offers them, the more enlightened and humane we consider it.

Our conception of ideal freedom is limited, to be sure, by considerations of legitimacy. Even those most enthusiastically devoted to freedom acknowledge that some courses of action are morally or in other ways unacceptable. As time has gone on, however, these constraints have been progressively relaxed. Corresponding to the proliferation of possibilities engendered by increasing technological and managerial sophistication, there has been a steady and notable weakening of the ethical and social constraints on legitimate choices and courses of action. Thus the expansion of freedom has affected not only what can be done but what is permissible as well. This combination of endlessly more masterful technical control and increasingly uncritical permissiveness has generated a tendency whose limit would be a culture in which everything is possible and anything goes.

Another ideal also enjoys considerable vitality, though devotion to it is perhaps not quite so pervasive or so orthodox as the commitment to freedom. This is the ideal of individuality, construed in terms of the development of a distinctive and robust sense of personal identity. To the extent that people find this ideal compelling, they endeavor to cultivate their own personal characters and styles and to decide autonomously how to live and what to do. Insofar as men and women have attained genuine individuality, they know their own minds. Furthermore, they have formed their minds not by merely imitating others but through a more personalized and creative process in which each has discovered and determined independently what he himself is.

108

Enlarging the range of available and permitted alternatives entails, of course, diminishing the scope of necessity in human life. It narrows the extent to which people find that circumstances allow them no choice but to follow a particular course of action. But as the ideal of freedom is more closely approached, the progressive reduction of necessity tends to undermine that ideal; and it also tends to undermine the ideal of individuality. For it is true both of freedom and of individuality that they *require* necessity.

FREEDOM AND AUTONOMY IN CONFLICT

We very commonly assume that whenever our freedom is expanded, our lives are thereby enriched. But this is true only up to a point. Reducing the grip of necessity may not in fact enhance our enjoyment of freedom. For if the restrictions on the choices that a person is in a position to make are relaxed too far, he may become, to a greater or lesser degree, disoriented with respect to where his interests and preferences lie. Instead of finding that the scope and vigor of his autonomy are augmented as the range of choices open to him broadens, he may become volitionally debilitated by an increasing uncertainty both concerning how to make decisions and concerning what to choose.

That is, extensive growth in the variety of a person's options may weaken his sense of his identity. The task of evaluating and ranking a considerably enlarged number of alternatives may be too much for him; it may overload his capacity to make decisions firmly grounded in a steady appreciation of what he really values and desires. Though he may have been able to find his way easily among a relatively small number of options, when he confronts a substantially wider array of possibilities, his understanding of his own interests and priorities will likely become less decisive. He may well discover, then, that his confidence in his preferences and predilections – a confidence established when the alternatives he needed to consider were fewer and more familiar – is drastically undermined. He may experience an unsettling diminution in the clarity with which he comprehends who he is. His grasp of his own identity may thus be radically disturbed.

Now suppose that someone is in a position to select from a field of alternatives that has not merely been extended but has no boundaries at all. Suppose, in other words, that every conceivable course of action is both available and eligible for choice. If the limits of choice have genuinely been wiped out, some possible courses of action will affect the person's desires and preferences themselves and hence bring about profound changes in his volitional character. It will be possible, then, for him to change those aspects of his nature that determine what choices he makes. He will be in a position to redesign his own will.

In that case, however, he will have to face his alternatives without a definitive set of goals, preferences, or other principles of choice. If his will becomes whatever he chooses to make it, no will can be unequivocally his until he has decided what will to choose. Any volitional characteristics that he may have prior to making that choice will be merely adventitious and provisional, for he has not committed himself to them and can alter them as he wants. Accordingly, no choice to which these characteristics lead will be fully or wholeheartedly his own. He is not volitionally equipped to make truly autonomous choices until he chooses how his choices are to be made.

But how is it possible for him to make that choice? What is to guide him in choosing, when the volitional characteristics by which his choices are to be guided are among the very things that he must choose? Under these conditions there is in him no fixed point from which a self-directed volitional process can begin. Erasing the boundaries within which his freedom was confined leaves him with too little volitional substance. No choice that he makes can be regarded as having originated in what we could meaningfully identify as his own will.

Unless a person makes choices within restrictions from which he cannot escape by merely choosing to do so, the notion of self-direction, of autonomy, cannot find a grip. Someone free of all such restrictions is so vacant of identifiable and stable volitional tendencies and constraints that he cannot deliberate or make decisions in any conscientious way. If he nonetheless does remain in some way capable of choice, the decisions and choices he makes will be altogether arbitrary. They cannot possess authentically personal significance or authority, for his will has no determinate character.

There is, then, a reciprocal conflict or strain between freedom and individuality. The latter requires limits that the former tends to erase. With total freedom, there can be no individual identity. This is because an excess of choice impairs the will. Without individuality, on the other hand, freedom loses much of its point. The availability of alternatives counts, after all, only for someone who has a will of his own. It should come as no surprise that when there is a steady inclination *both* to urge a general expansion of freedom *and* to encourage the development of autonomy, things begin to go wrong.

LIMITS OF THE WILL

What limits does an autonomous will require? What are the volitional necessities whose elimination or attenuation threatens individuality and freedom? The most fundamental, I believe, pertain to what a person cares about, what he considers important to him. This is not primarily either a cognitive or an affective matter. Cognitive and affective considerations are its sources and grounds. But though it is based on what a person believes and feels, caring is not the same as believing or feeling. Caring is essentially volitional; that is, it concerns one's will. The fact that a person cares about something or considers it important to himself does not consist in his holding certain opinions about it; nor does it consist in his having certain feelings or desires. His caring about it consists, rather, in the fact that he *guides* himself by reference to it. This entails that he purposefully direct his attention, attitudes, and behavior in response to circumstances germane to the fortunes of the object about which he cares. A person who cares about something is, as it were, invested in it. By caring about it, he makes himself susceptible to benefits and vulnerable to losses depending upon whether what he cares about flourishes or is diminished. We may say that in this sense he *identifies* himself with what he cares about.

About certain things that are important to him, a person may care so much, or in such a way, that he is subject to a kind of necessity. Because of this necessity, various courses of action that he would otherwise be able to pursue are effectively unavailable to him. It is impossible for him to pursue them. He may well possess the knowledge and skill required for performing the actions in question; nonetheless, he is unable to perform them. The reason is that he cannot bring himself to do so. It is not that he cannot muster the necessary *power.* What he cannot muster is the *will.* He is held in the grip of a volitional necessity that renders certain actions impossible for him — not by depriving him of the capacity to perform them but by making it impossible for him to use that capacity.

Consider a mother who reaches the conclusion, after conscientious deliberation, that it would be best for her to give up her child for adoption, and suppose that she decides to do so. When the moment arrives for actually giving up the child, however, she may find that she cannot go through with it — not because she has reconsidered the matter and changed her mind but because she simply cannot bring herself to give her child away. Similarly, there are reports that military officers refused to carry out orders to begin launching nuclear weapons when they believed that the orders were not part of a test but were intended actually to bring about a nuclear strike. Since these officers had volunteered for their assignments, they were presumably unaware of the limits within which their wills were bound. When the chips were down, however, they discovered that in fact they could not bring themselves to do what they had believed they would be willing to do.

When a person is subject to this sort of volitional necessity, it renders certain actions *unthinkable* for him. These actions are not genuinely among his options. He cannot perform any of them, because he is prevented by a volitional constraint; that is, he cannot *will* to perform them. Even though he may think it would be best for him to perform one of the actions, he *cannot bring himself* to perform it. He cannot volitionally organize himself in the necessary way. If he attempts to do so, he runs up against the *limits of his will.* This is shown by the fact that he is unable to perform the action even when all the nonvolitional conditions for his performing it (e.g., opportunity, knowledge, and power) are satisfied.

A person who cannot bring himself to perform a certain action has a powerful aversion, which effectively limits his conduct. But finding it unthinkable to perform an action is not the same as being irresistibly averse to performing it. In cases of volitional necessity, the aversion is not only irresistible; it is also in some way endorsed by the person. Furthermore, endorsing the aversion is something that he cares about. Indeed, his conduct is constrained so effectively precisely because of the fact that, whether consciously or not, he endorses the aversion and cares about maintaining it. Thus, he resists making any efforts to do what he remains deeply averse to doing.

This distinguishes situations in which one finds an action *unthinkable* from those in which one's inability to choose effectively is due to addiction, terror, or some other variety of overwhelming compulsion or inhibition. In situations of the former kind, but not in those of the latter, the effectiveness of the person's incapacity derives from the fact that the person considers that incapacity to be important to him. This also accounts for the rather notable peculiarity that when a person discovers that it is unthinkable for him to perform a certain action, or to refrain from performing it, he does not ordinarily experience the constraint as moving or obstructing him against his will. Although he may not know it, the fact is that the constraint is itself imposed by his will. For this reason he experiences his submission to it less as a defeat than as a liberation.

The necessities of the will are, of course, subject to change. What is unthinkable for a person at one time may not be unthinkable for him at another, as a consequence of alterations in the contingent circumstances from which volitional necessities derive. A person may even find it possible deliberately to alter the necessities that bind his will. Needless to say, however, he cannot alter them by a sheer act of will. A person cannot redesign his own volitional nature simply by making up his mind that what has been unthinkable for him is no longer so. Ordinary inhibitions and aversions may sometimes be overcome by strenuous efforts of will. But a genuine necessity of the will could hardly be susceptible to alteration in that way.

A person for whom an action is unthinkable may be in a position to alter his will by means less immediate and direct than the exercise of willpower alone. However, undertaking to make the unthinkable thinkable might itself be something that the person cannot bring himself to do. Then it is not only unthinkable for him to perform the action in question; it is also unthinkable for him to form an effective intention to become willing to perform it. His will is constrained by an aversion to the very idea of making that change in himself. He cannot bring himself to endorse that idea. To be sure, changes in circumstances might bring about a change in his will. But he cannot change his will by any deliberate effort of his own. He is subject to a necessity that, in this sense, defines an absolute limit. And this necessity is unequivocally constitutive of his nature or essence as a volitional being.

VOLITIONAL NECESSITY AND IDENTITY

In every triangle, the sum of the interior angles is equal to 180 degrees. The triangle may be scalene, isosceles, or equilateral, but in no triangle does the sum of the interior angles equal either more or less than 180 degrees. This is a necessary condition for being a triangle; it constitutes part of the essence of triangularity. Triangles have, as it were, no choice. They cannot help satisfying the condition in question; doing so defines the generic identity of a triangle as the type of thing it is. The idea that the identity of a thing is to be understood in terms of conditions essential for its existence is one of the oldest and most compelling of the philosophical principles that guide our efforts to clarify our thought. To grasp what a thing is, we must grasp its essence, namely, those characteristics without which it cannot be what it is. Thus the notions of necessity and identity are intimately related.

Of course, the necessity that binds a triangle to its essential nature is only a conceptual or logical necessity. This type of necessity has to do with the organization of our ideas and our language. It governs how things are described and classified. But it does not govern, nor is it even pertinent to, the careers of the things themselves. It is not a real force, and it has no effect on what actually happens in the world. The fact that a figure cannot be a triangle unless it possesses the characteristics essential to triangularity has no influence on whether or not a certain triangular figure retains these characteristics or is altered in such a way as to lose them.

It seems to me that when we talk about the essential nature of a person, the issue is analogous. It is likewise a matter of the person's necessary characteristics. In this case, however, the necessity is not merely conceptual. Here the necessity does not pertain only to how the person is to be classified or described. The constraints imposed by volitional necessity are not constraints merely upon thought and language. Volitional necessity constrains the person himself, by limiting the choices he can make.

The essential nature of a person is constituted by his necessary *personal* characteristics. These characteristics have to do particularly with his nature as a person, rather than with his nature as a human being or as a biological organism of a certain type. They are especially characteristics of his will. In speaking of the personal characteristics of someone's will, I do not mean to refer simply to the desires or impulses that move him. We attribute impulses, desires, and motives even to infants and animals, creatures that cannot properly be said either to be persons or to possess wills. The personal characteristics of someone's will are reflexive, or higher-order, volitional features. They pertain to a person's efforts to negotiate his own way among the various impulses and desires by which he is moved, as he undertakes to identify himself more intimately with some of his own psychic characteristics and to distance himself from others.

To be a *person* entails evaluative attitudes (not necessarily based on moral considerations) toward oneself. A person is a creature prepared to endorse or repudiate the motives from which he acts and to organize the preferences and priorities by which his choices are ordered. He is disposed to consider whether what attracts him is actually important to him. Instead of responding unreflectively to whatever he happens to feel most strongly, he undertakes to guide his conduct in accordance with what he really cares about.

To the extent that a person is constrained by volitional necessities, there are certain things that he cannot help willing or that he cannot bring himself to do. These necessities substantially affect the actual course and character of his life. But they affect not only what he does: they limit the possibilities that are open to his will, that is, they determine what he cannot will and what he cannot help willing. Now the character of a person's will constitutes what he most centrally is. Accordingly, the volitional necessities that bind a person identify what he cannot help being. They are in this respect analogues of the logical or conceptual necessities that define the essential nature of a triangle. Just as the essence of a triangle consists in what it must be, so the essential nature of a person consists in what he must will. The boundaries of his will define his shape as a person.

IDEALS

Without attempting to analyze the nature or basis of volitional necessity, I suggest that its force is in certain respects similar to the force of love. This force is somewhat paradoxical. Love *captivates* us, but even while we are its captive we find that it is in some way liberating. Love is *selfless*, but it also enables us in some way to feel most truly ourselves. Moreover, it seems that love would not be so liberating or so enhancing if its grip on us were not so overpowering and so far outside our immediate voluntary control.

Only by virtue of the necessity that it imposes upon us does love intensify our sense of identity and of freedom. We cannot help loving what we love, nor can we make ourselves love by a mere act of will. The value of loving for us derives precisely, at least in part, from the very fact that whether we love is not up to us. The importance of loving to us would be lost if we could love something or cease to love it merely by deciding to do so. The self-fulfillment and freedom that love provides depend upon the very necessity that love entails.

If someone loves nothing, it follows that he has no ideals. Now an ideal is a limit. A person's ideals are concerns that he cannot bring himself to betray. They entail constraints that, for him, it is unthinkable to violate. Suppose that someone has no ideals at all. In that case, nothing is unthinkable for him; there are no limits to what he might be willing to do. He can make whatever decisions he likes and shape his will just as he pleases. This does not mean that his will is free. It means only that his will is anarchic, moved by mere impulse and inclination. For a person without ideals, there are no volitional laws that he has bound himself to respect and to which he unconditionally submits. He has no inviolable boundaries. Thus he is amorphous, with no fixed identity or shape.

If someone has no ideals, there is nothing that he cannot bring himself to do.

Moreover, since nothing is necessary to him, there is nothing that he can be said essentially to be. To be sure, he may have a number of persistent psychological dispositions or traits; he may exhibit various consistent patterns of inclination and choice. But any stable volitional characteristics he may have are products of impersonal causal influences. They are not consequences of his wanting to be a person of a certain sort or to devote himself to a certain kind of life; they are not fixed by his will itself but by contingencies external to it. In other words, his will is governed entirely by circumstances rather than by any essential nature of its own. None of his volitional characteristics is necessary to him, since none derives from his own nature.

This means that he lacks a personal essence, which would comprise the necessary conditions of his identity. For this reason, there is no such thing for him as genuine integrity. After all, he has no personal boundaries whose inviolability he might set himself to protect. There is nothing that he is essentially. What he is at any given time is no more than what he happens then to be, which is merely accidental.

The ideals that define the essential nature of a person need not be moral ideals, in the sense in which morality is especially a matter of how a person relates himself to the interests of others. The most decisive boundaries of a person's life may derive from imperatives of tradition, of style, of intellect, or of some other mode of ambition. This leaves open what characteristics an ideal must possess to serve its function of limiting a person and specifying his identity. To a surprising extent, philosophers have neglected this important question, and I will not pursue it here. Another important question, which has also been neglected and which I shall also not undertake to discuss, concerns the basis on which a person can reasonably make a choice from among various worthy ideals.

It may seem inappropriate to suggest that problems of choice and justification can arise with respect to what I have characterized as necessities. What cannot be helped, it would appear, does not depend upon being chosen, nor, accordingly, does it require justification. But while it is true that a person can no more choose or decide on the limits of his will than he can simply choose or decide on what he will love, we must not conclude from this that he has nothing whatever to say about the matter. From the fact that what binds us to our ideals is love, it does not follow that our relationship to them is wholly noncognitive. There is considerable room for reason and argument in the clarification of ideals and in the evaluation of their worthiness. Even in romantic love, after all, there is generally more to the story than being swept blindly off one's feet.

REASON AND LOVE

It is widely supposed that the two most precious capacities of our species, which make human life distinctively valuable and interesting, are that we can reason and that we can love. Each of these capacities is fully realized only when a person finds himself constrained by a kind of necessity. In the former case, it is the cognitive necessity of logic; in the latter, it is the volitional necessity of love. Reason is universal, in the sense that its dictates are equally binding on everyone. On the other hand, love is particular: the fact that I am devoted to certain ideals, or the fact that I love someone, does not lead me to think that anyone who does not do the same is making a mistake. The question of whom one is to love cannot be settled by developing a rigorous proof, nor can one rigorously demonstrate which ideals are properly to define the boundaries of one's will. This should not be taken to entail, however, that our volitional necessities must merely be acknowledged as givens – that is, accepted passively as brute facts with respect to which deliberation and rational critique have no place. The relationship between love and reason is an ancient philosophical theme, which it would be well for us to explore anew.

10

On God's Creation

Leazar said in Bar Sira's name: About what is too great for thee inquire not; what is too hard for thee investigate not; about what is too wonderful for thee know not; of what is hidden from thee ask not; study what was permitted thee; thou hast no business with hidden things.

— *Midrash Rabbah*

1. I propose to ignore these instructions.[1] I shall consider certain hidden things. In just what way did God create the world? What was the state of affairs before He created it? What was the nature of the creative process? What, exactly, did He do? And how may we understand, in the light of what He did, His relationship to the world and to mankind?

Of course these questions are too great, too hard, and too wonderful. It is true that we have no business with them. Still, there are other things in life besides business.

2. No one has yet produced, so far as I am aware, an adequate biography of God. We have no systematic developmental account of the character and activities of the deity whose career is related in the Old Testament. It is plain, however, that He is responsive to human behavior, and that He often reacts to it with great intensity. Moreover, it often seems that He regards Himself as being in some way dependent on the conduct of mankind. The things people do appear at times to affect Him in ways that even suggest a certain vulnerability on His part.[2]

A rather striking manifestation of this dependency is God's recurrent interest in executing covenants with human beings. Insofar as a covenant is a contract, it is an agreement entered into for mutual advantage. If it is to rest neither on ignorance nor coercion, it must offer benefits of comparable magnitude to everyone who is to be bound by it. Now it is not difficult to understand how humans might profit by entering into contractual arrangements with a being of enormous power and energy who is in an incomparably effective position to promote and protect their interests. But what is in it for God? In what way might He expect to benefit from

---

1 The epigraph is from *Midrash Rabbah*, ed. H. Freedman and M. Simon (London: Soncino Press, 1939), vol. 1 (Gen. 1), p. 56.
2 Thus God responds to the sin of Adam and Eve not simply with anger and curses but also with fear (cf. Genesis 3:22).

any human performance? How could it be in His interest to obligate Himself to man? What difference can it make to Him how people act? Why does He care about it at all?

One line of response to these problems is grounded in the familiar image of God as an absolute and imperious ruler, an exigent and all-powerful issuer of commands and decrees. On this account, the reason people are obliged to obey and to worship God is not that doing so is inherently desirable or that it is beneficial to anyone. They are required to submit to God's will only because He demands their submission; and He demands this just because, whether out of pride or out of jealousy or out of sheer willfulness, He wants it. Thus the considerations that define the relationship between man and God are, from a moral point of view, quite arbitrary: human beings must do what God commands, and He commands it simply because it is what He wants. The ultimate relevant fact is that it pleases Him to be worshipped and obeyed. There is nothing more to be said about the matter than that.

Another line of response invokes a far different, though equally familiar, image of God as a loving parent. On this account, God is not motivated in His relationship with mankind by any willful desire for glorification. He does not regard people primarily as His subjects, but as His children. It is because He wishes them well, rather than because He is concerned with Himself, that He is preoccupied with their behavior. What He fears is that they may act in ways that will be detrimental to their best interests. For this reason, He devotes Himself paternalistically to instructing them and to guiding their conduct. When He berates them or provides them with inducements to do this or that, He does so entirely for their benefit. Since people are not always capable of understanding what is good for them, they cannot be left to themselves. For their own sakes, accordingly, God requires them to accept His authority.

Neither of these two lines of response goes deep enough. In both cases, the problem of understanding the relationship between man and the divine remains wholly isolated from the problem of understanding creation. But there must be a profound connection between these problems. It could hardly fail to be the case that God's view of human beings is in some way determined or conditioned by how their relationship began. Thus, there is every reason to think that a clarification of God's creation would illuminate the curious symbiosis between Him and his most notable creature. After all, before God was Lord or Father of mankind, He was the Creator of the world.

3. What was the state of affairs when the process of creation began? Here is what we are told:

When God began to create heaven and earth, the earth was unformed and void, and darkness was over the surface of the deep; and the spirit of God hovered over the water. And God said, "Let there be light." And there was light. (Gen. 1:1–3)[3]

This is manifestly not an account of a creation ex nihilo. Whatever basis there may be for supposing that the world was created out of nothing, these opening lines of Genesis appear to be flatly inconsistent with that supposition. They seem to make it quite explicitly clear that before God performed His first creative act – that is, prior to His creation of light – there was already something. Indeed, quite a bit. The text mentions three things: the earth, the deep, and the spirit of God.

It may appear to be somewhat uncertain whether we are to understand that the earth was actually in existence at the beginning of the creative process. The assertion that the earth was "unformed and void" might naturally be construed as describing the condition of the earth at a certain time in its history; and in that case it would imply that the earth, although it did not yet have a specifiable form or character, did then exist. But the assertion could also plausibly be taken to imply instead that, at the time in question, the earth did not yet exist. Everything depends on what is meant by saying of the earth that it was "unformed and void."

Suppose that we accept Rashi's suggestion concerning how to understand this key phrase.[4] Then we will probably have to conclude that the earth did already exist when God's creative activity began. The Hebrew words translated as "unformed" and "void" are, respectively, *tohu* and *bohu*. Rashi says that "the word *bohu* has the meaning of emptiness and void." As for the other element of the phrase, he explains that "the word *tohu* has the meaning of astonishment and amazement . . . ; for a person would be astonished and amazed at the void in the world."

Now, if we take this seriously, it is difficult to construe the assertion that the earth was *tohu* and *bohu* as consistent with the supposition that the earth did not exist. After all, what would be so surprising about the non-existence of the earth before creation began? No one examining the state of affairs prior to the creation of light would be astonished or amazed to discover an empty space at the location destined in due course to be occupied by the earth. That would surely not be surprising at all. On the contrary: before creation gets under way, one would naturally *expect* to find emptinesses and voids.

Perhaps, then, "the void in the world" does not refer to a simple vacancy or to an absence of matter. Perhaps it refers to a deficiency of another sort, which permits the supposition that the earth did in some way already exist. Rashi says that the

---

3   The translation is based on the New JPS Translation, in *Tanakh: The Holy Scriptures* (Philadelphia: Jewish Publication Society, 1988).

4   Abraham ben Isaiah and Benjamin Sharfman, *The Pentateuch and Rashi's Commentary (Genesis): A Linear Translation into English* (Brooklyn, N.Y.: S. S. & R. Publishing Company, 1949), p. 3.

void in the world is astonishing and amazing. Now what is it to be astonished or amazed? It is a matter of being more or less *dumbfounded;* and this means being to some degree *speechless.* A person who is struck with astonishment, or with amazement, is not immediately capable of giving an orderly and informative account of what has struck him that way.

The experience disorganizes him, and therefore he cannot readily describe it. This may happen when the experience is so unexpected that the person is thrown off balance. Then, because he is startled, the person is for the moment unprepared to grasp the nature of the experience confidently even though it is not something that is inherently difficult to comprehend. However, this is not to the point here. For, as has already been suggested, the terms employed to characterize the earth at the beginning of creation do not mean that the condition of the earth at that time was unexpected.

What the terms *tohu* and *bohu* convey is that prior to creation the condition of the earth was *indeterminate.* Genuine indeterminacy would certainly be dumbfounding. It would inevitably leave one speechless, because indeterminacy is precisely a matter of being insusceptible to coherent description. So the reason a person could not grasp the pre-creation condition of the earth discursively is not that the earth does not then exist; nor is it that the nature of the earth before creation would be so surprising that anyone observing it would be irresistibly taken aback. Rather, the person would be dumbfounded by the fact that the earth does not possess a definite nature at all: it exists, but it lacks distinct and fully articulated properties. This is the sense in which the earth is said to be "unformed." It is in a similar sense that the earth is said to be "void." It is void in the sense of being blank, with no identifiable character.

Prior to creation the earth was inchoate and hence not describable in the categories of intelligible speech. That is why anyone encountering it at that time would have been, as Rashi intimates, amazed, astonished, and (necessarily) speechless. Now this way of understanding what the passage says about the earth is confirmed by what it goes on to say about the deep. Here the text is quite unequivocal: the deep does already exist. Moreover, we may legitimately suppose that the deep was as inchoate as the earth, even though the text does not explicitly assert that it was unformed and void. For water is naturally and paradigmatically fluid, and this fluidity evokes by itself the notion of something that lacks a stable and determinate character. It is essentially characteristic of water to have no fixed place and no inherent form. Water flows and spreads freely, without inner constraint; and it accepts as its own whatever shape surrounds it. By its very nature, then, the deep is "unformed and void."

4. Although it was unformed when creation began, the deep did have a surface. We are told that there are two things over this surface: darkness, and the spirit of God

(*ruach elohim*). Now why does the text refer here to the *spirit* of God? What is the significance of the fact that it does not refer simply to God Himself? The *spirit of God* and *God* are surely not the same. There is a difference between the spirit of a thing and the thing itself. Roughly speaking, the former provides the latter with its distinctive mode of animation. Of course, not everything has a spirit. Something has a spirit only insofar as (again, roughly) it is integral to its nature to be energetically purposeful. Then its spirit is the general tendency or style that informs its various purposes. It is what sustains and guides the direction of its energy.[5]

Suppose the energy of an active being is sharply focused, its purposefulness wholly determinate. In that case, its spirit is fully defined. But it may be that a purposeful being does not have an altogether certain or determinate purpose. Although it is capable of purposefulness and is tending toward purposeful activity, it may not yet have settled into guiding itself steadily by any specific purpose. In that case, its purpose is not entirely actualized or clearly defined. Its spirit is, to one degree or another, still unformed. And its own nature is correspondingly indistinct.

The difference between the spirit of God and God is the difference between a relatively unactualized and a more completely actualized mode of divine existence. This corresponds to the difference between the formless state of the world before creation and the fully determinate state of the world subsequent to the creative process. At the beginning of creation, God was as unformed as the world. The divine was present and active only as an indistinct spirit; its reality was not yet that of God Himself. The nature of this divine spirit was indefinite, and its activity was vague. In the still indeterminate condition of things that prevailed prior to creation, neither the world nor God was wholly developed. The specific character of the deity – i.e., the exact direction of its purposefulness and power – had not yet been articulated or realized. Like the unshaped and fluid world itself, the divine presence was inchoate.

Consider how the text represents the divine before the sequence of creative acts and compare this with how it refers to the divine when that sequence of acts begins. With respect to the time prior to creation, we have: "*the spirit of God* hovered over the water." With respect to the initial performance in the creative sequence, however, we have: "And *God* said: 'Let there be light.'" The spirit of God is present in the world before the initial creative act. When it comes to the performance of that act, however, it is not by the spirit of God that the act is performed. The act is performed by God Himself. Each subsequent act in the process of creation is also reported as having been performed by God rather than by the divine spirit.

A fundamental difference between the spirit of God and God is that the former,

5   Thus, "the spirit of '76." The same notion is involved when we say such things as "His spirit will live on in the institution to which he devoted so much of himself," and "Although I cannot be present, I am with you in spirit."

since it has no definite nature, cannot be genuinely active. Thus there is nothing in the text to suggest that it ever accomplishes anything or even that it ever attempts anything. One activity (and only one) is attributed to it: "the spirit of God *hovered* over the water." Now, hovering is a peculiarly vague and unproductive sort of activity. While it requires energy and may involve some movement, it closely resembles being completely at rest. Indeed, hovering is specifically designed to avoid any passage from one location to another. Its purposefulness is in this respect indecisive and without ambition. The distinctive goal of hovering is precisely to have no direction and to bring about no significant change of place. It is devoted essentially to going nowhere. Its whole purpose is to simulate and to approach total inactivity.

As long as it is devoted to nothing more than an indecisive hovering over the shapeless waters of the deep, the energy of the divine agency is basically inactive. Divine agency is then nothing more than the potentiality of an incipient but as yet unrealized God. The text explicitly marks the transition from this state of affairs to one in which the divine is more fully actualized and determinate. It does so by abandoning the term "the spirit of God" and by shifting to the term "God."

5. This transition is simultaneous with the start of the creative activity that transforms an inchoate world into an ordered cosmos. But there is more to be said. The process by which the divine becomes actualized and determinate not only *begins at the same time* as the series of acts by which divine agency fashions the cosmos. The two sequences *coincide*. Thus, each *begins with the same event* – viz., the creation of light. This first creative act both transforms a dark world into a lighted one and transforms the spirit of God into God.

What is the nature of the act? It is, of course, an act of speech: "God said, 'Let there be light.'" Moreover, this act of speech is evidently effective *without any intermediation:* "God said, 'Let there be light'; and there was light." Between the utterance and its outcome, nothing intervenes. The act is not like the utterances of magic; creation is not accomplished by the work of some arcane power, subordinate to God, which is summoned and deployed by the casting of a verbal spell. Accordingly, the creative act of speech is not a command. Nor is the act effective by causing a response in something other than itself. The effectiveness of the act is provided entirely by its own creative power. It does not require or depend on anything else. Some words are spoken and, in the very speaking of these words, both the world and the divine are thereby altered. The world is lighted, and the divine spirit becomes God.

How are we to understand the relationship between these initial alterations of the world and of the divine? Consider the fact that the Hebrew word translated as "spirit," in the phrase "the spirit of God," is *ruach*. In certain other translations of the passage at hand, this word is translated as "wind"; and, in still others, it is translated as "breath."[6] Now each of these three words refers to something elusive

6 Rashi says, in commenting on Genesis 1:2: "The throne of glory stands [suspended] in the air and

and indeterminate. Spirits, winds, and breaths are difficult to pin down. For one thing, they lack recognizable shapes or boundaries; for another, it requires considerable scientific sophistication to identify the material of which each is composed. With respect to each, then, neither its form nor its matter is easy to grasp.

Before God began creating, the divine nature was indefinite. It was present in the world only as a breath, or a wind, or a spirit. This changed when the divine began to speak. Uttering words involves shaping the breath. Similarly, the formation of a thought entails ordering the mind or spirit. Both speaking and thinking are matters of articulation, which create form by imposing distinctions upon what is previously undifferentiated. Whether it is considered an act of speech or an act of thought, then, "Let there be light" is an ordering or an articulation by which something with a distinct identity is formed. As its identity becomes definite, the spirit of God – previously formless and indeterminate – becomes God.

We must ask why the creation of the world began with the creation of light. The primary relevant difference between darkness and light is that in the light it is possible to make clear distinctions. In the darkness, no (visual) distinctions can be made. Under ordinary circumstances, of course, turning on a light reveals distinctions that already existed but that were concealed by the darkness. But the creation of light effects a more radical change. It makes possible, for the first time, the introduction of stable distinctions into a world that was previously fluid and unshaped. That is to say, it provides for the possibility of making a cosmos – an ordered and determinate system of being – out of what had hitherto existed only inchoately.

Before He began to articulate the utterances by which He created the world, God's will was formless and undefined. He had no determinate intentions or desires; and he did nothing but hover indecisively. It was only in formulating the clear-cut volitions expressed in His successive creative acts of speech that His active nature became focused and specific. These acts of speech were not addressed to anyone or to anything. They were resolutions, or determinations of intention, by which the spirit of God was transformed into a purposeful and active being. Thus *God was created by creating.* He was defined by His creation, just as the nature of the world that He created was defined by Him.

This sounds a bit like Spinoza's doctrines that God and the world are somehow one and that the order of the world is identical with the mind of God. Of course, Spinoza regards the divine order as necessary and thus as self-explanatory, while the view I am here attributing to Genesis is that a world without order is possible and

---

hovers over the face of the waters by the breath of the mouth of the Holy One. Blessed be He, and at His command, like a dove – which hovers over the nest" (ben Isaiah and Scharfman, *The Pentateuch and Rashi's Commentary*, pp. 3–4). Similarly, Freedman and Simon, eds., *Midrash Rabbah*, p. 20: "R. Berekiah commenced in the name of R. Judah b. R. Simon: By the word of the Lord were the heavens made, and all the host of them by the breath of His mouth (Ps. 39:6): not by labor or toil but only by a word; thus, And God said: Let there be light."

123

in fact preceded creation. The Genesis account, as I construe it, is not rationalistic. It does not even attempt to explain *why* the inchoate became ordered; it offers no understanding of what made the spirit of God transform itself into God. Perhaps the spirit of God possesses an inherent tendency toward order; or perhaps it *is* this tendency. Perhaps the assumption that there exists a divine spirit in the world means, in other words, precisely this: that the universe tends to acquire and sustain determinate characteristics and a stable order.

6. The final creative act is, of course, the creation of man. Now what God does in creating a man differs quite markedly and suggestively from what He does in His earlier creative activities. At each of the eight steps in the sequence of creation, God declares that something is to happen or to be done. The first seven declarations are uniform in pattern: (i) "Let there be light," (ii) "Let there be an expanse in the midst of the water," (iii) "Let the water below the sky be gathered into one area," (iv) "Let the earth sprout vegetation," (v) "Let there be lights in the expanse of the sky," (vi) "Let the waters bring forth swarms of living creatures, and birds," and (vii) "Let the earth bring forth every kind of living creature." The eighth declaration diverges strikingly from this pattern. God's final utterance is: (viii) "Let *us make* man." When He comes to the creation of man, God's resolution is for the first time not that something should happen or should be done, but that *He should do it Himself.*

Man is unique, then, in not having been created by an act of speech. The statement "Let us make man" enunciates the intention to create man, but it does not itself accomplish the creation. The actual creation of man is reported separately, as follows: "And God created man in His image, in the image of God He created them, male and female He created them." That the creation of human beings was not accomplished by speech is confirmed by the second account of creation. At Genesis 2:7, there is no reference to any utterance. The text there refers instead to another sort of activity altogether. "The Lord God formed man from the dust of the earth, He blew into his nostrils the breath of life, and man became a living being." In forming man out of dust, God created him, so to speak, *by hand.*[7]

In the earlier stages of the creative process, the "Let . . . " utterances are creative by themselves. They require no further or separate activity of implementation. Thus, in the account of every earlier stage except one, the report of the utterance is followed immediately, and with no indication of any intervening events, by a report ("And it was so") that the relevant creation has been accomplished.[8] There is

---

7 Rashi says: "For everything was created by [divine] decree but he was created by the hands [of God]. For it is said (Ps. 139:5), 'And thou hast laid thy hand upon me.'" Ben Isaiah and Scharfman, *The Pentateuch and Rashi's Commentary*, p. 14.

8 The one exception is the sixth utterance ("Let the waters bring forth swarms of living creatures, and birds that fly above the earth across the expanse of the sky"), which is not followed by "And it was

no suggestion of mediation between the act of speech and the realization of the intention it expresses. In order for the first seven features of the world to be created, it suffices that the divine spirit or will be resolved. God creates them simply through the formation of His own nature.

When it comes to creating man, however, that is not how God does it. He begins by making up His mind, or by becoming resolved, to create man. But this resolution of His will does not suffice. It is only preliminary to the activity by which the creation of man is actually accomplished. Unlike every other step in the sequence of creation, God's final creative act is manifestly not an act of self-definition. He does not create man by forming Himself but by shaping some dust – that is, by *doing something to something else.* The creation of man does not come about by a simple articulation of God's volition or thought or breath. It is a mediated process, in which forming the intention is one thing and implementing it effectively is another. God does not create man by a purely reflexive act, which is creative just by advancing the development of His own nature. The creation of man requires work.

This has a large and resonant import. It means that man, unlike all other creatures of God, is genuinely an artifact. Human existence and human nature are not created sheerly through the self-definition of the divine; God's formation of humans is not tantamount to His formation of Himself. Their coming into being is distinct from any modification of the divine will. The creation of man is unique in being emphatically not identical with the articulation of an intention. And since human existence was not begun by a determination of God's volitional nature, human history is therefore not unequivocally subject to the determinations of God's will.

This implies that, with respect to man, God's omnipotence is limited. Just as the creation of human beings required that God do some real work – it being evidently insufficient for Him merely to resolve that humans should exist – so God

---

so." Instead, it is followed immediately by this: "God created the great sea monsters, and all the living creatures of every kind that creep, which the waters brought forth in swarms, and all the winged birds of every kind." In this respect, the account of the sixth step may seem to resemble that of the eighth; for both appear to report that God does something in addition to speaking. But I think that the significance of this resemblance must be discounted. First of all, it makes no theological sense. Second, there is a more reasonable way to explain the resemblance than by assimilating the creation of sea creatures to the creation of human beings. The statement that God created the sea monsters and the rest may be understood as merely an elaborated report of what His sixth utterance accomplished rather than as the report of additional activity undertaken to implement the sixth utterance. That utterance is creative by itself, and the report that "God created the great sea monsters" does not mean that He performed a further implementing act. It simply reports what the sixth utterance created. This way of construing the sixth step clearly cannot be employed with respect to the eighth. For the eighth utterance ("Let us make . . .") is unmistakably *prospective.* It cannot be understood except as proposing to perform a further act of creation.

cannot exercise direct power over mankind by mere acts of the divine will.[9] In creating human beings, God created something separate — something whose being is distinct and radically other than His own. In other words, mankind does not exist just as an articulation of God's will. Therefore, human beings are not wholly dependent on divine volition or immediately subject to it.

Man is a product of God's handiwork. In producing people, God produced creatures whose nature is independent of the direct or unmediated control of His will. This explains, for example, why God, when He expels Adam and Eve from Eden, posts guards at the gates. He cannot achieve His intention that Adam and Eve stay out of Eden simply by forming a volition that they do so. Insofar as the world is formed by the formation of His own will, God can shape it by shaping Himself — i.e., by articulating His own thoughts and volitions. But in dealing with man, whose being is distinct and separate from Himself, God can exercise control only through intermediaries.

But why did God create something distinct from Himself? By introducing into the world a being other than His own, whose behavior is determined by its own nature rather than by His will, He appears to abandon unequivocal control over His creation. Thus he seems deliberately to undermine His own omnipotence. Why would He do this? Perhaps He did it because in a world in which everything is determined simply by His will, there would really be nothing other than Himself; and His omnipotence would therefore be meaningless. God's control of the world would in that case be nothing more than self-control. It would be power over nothing but Himself!

There is a kind of paradox in the notion of omnipotence. A being enjoys absolute omnipotence only if its effective exercise of unlimited power requires nothing more than a determination of its will. If its intentions themselves do not suffice but must be implemented by further exertions, its power is to that extent qualified. The insufficiency of its volition implies some external resistance, which cannot be overcome without work. It follows that a being possesses unlimited omnipotence only if there is nothing other than itself over which to exercise its power. For (a) unequivocal omnipotence entails unmediated control, while (b) the being of anything that is subject to unmediated control belongs to whatever exercises that control.

Thus, a wholly omnipotent being would necessarily be alone. There would be nothing other than itself over which to exercise power. It could do nothing but form intentions and thereby alter its own nature. In a sense, then, it would be quite powerless. God needs a being other than Himself, then, in order to exercise His

9 Of course God can exercise *indirect* power over human beings by volition alone, since the rest of nature does respond without mediation to His will. So God can endeavor to control man indirectly by directly affecting conditions (i.e., just by making up His mind) which are important to human interests.

power at all meaningfully. But this means that for the meaningful exercise of His power, He needs a being over which His power is not absolute.

7. The fact that God and man are separate is the source of an ineradicable tension in the careers of each. The story of man's yearning to diminish the distance between himself and the divine has often been explored. Less familiar is the story of God's struggle to accommodate the reality of a being other than His own.

The texts make it clear that God has found this struggle frustrating and even demoralizing. Indeed, at the time of Noah it actually led Him to believe for a while that His creation of man had been a mistake:

And the Lord regretted that He had made man on earth, and His heart was saddened. The Lord said, "I will blot out from the earth the men whom I created – men together with beasts, creeping things, and birds of the sky; for I regret that I made them." (Gen. 6:6–7)

Only by the heartening example of Noah was God persuaded to change His mind about this:

Noah was a righteous man; he was blameless in his age; Noah walked with God. (Gen. 6:9)

Despite his distinctness as an independent being, and his capacity therefore to diverge from God's will, Noah was not distant from God. On the contrary, he "walked with God." It was in this cohesion with God that his righteousness and his blamelessness consisted. The example of Noah convinced God that, even though men are beyond the control of His unmediated will, it is not inevitable that there be a distance between His will and the will of man.

God yearns, just as man does, to overcome the distance between them. Since man is separate and can therefore act only by his own will, this cannot be accomplished unless man accedes voluntarily to the divine order. Accordingly, it is necessary for God to threaten, to persuade, and to bargain. This accounts for the importance of covenant.

But why does God care whether men act in harmony with His will? Why does He so badly want man to walk with Him? The answer is that He requires man to accept a divine order so as to complete His creation both of the world and of Himself. It is through the articulation of order that God's being is realized and defined. And it is only to the extent that the inchoate is transformed into a cosmos that He exists with a determinate and actualized nature. As long as there is anything outside that cosmos, neither the world nor God Himself is complete. They remain to some extent formless and unactualized.

If man's will is disharmonious with the will of God, there is a boundary beyond which divine order does not prevail. In that case, God is not omnipresent. Being is ultimately fragmented. As there is a limit to the extent of divine order, so the cosmos is incomplete and the actualization of the divine is unfinished. It is for this reason that the distance of man is a threat to God.

127

It is understandable why Genesis does not report that, after creating man, "God saw that this was good." Nor is it any wonder that God may sometimes be inclined to think that He made a mistake in creating man. But God has resolved not to destroy mankind. Instead He negotiates, He cajoles, He tries to make a deal. Endlessly, he seeks to induce man to accept at least some kind of coherence with the divine. This would not erase the separateness of God and man; human volition would be as independent as before. But it would at least entail that human life is ordered as God wishes it to be ordered. Hence it would entail that His order prevails universally, albeit not exclusively, by His unmediated volitional control. God has no better hope for completion. God and humans can never be one and the same as God is one and the same with the rest of His creation. He needs man to walk with Him. He depends on mankind's cooperation. Without it, divine order cannot be sustained throughout the world.

According to one Talmudic view, God reckons the creation of the world as having been finished only when the Tabernacle was erected. That is, there was a complete and fully ordered cosmos only when His law was decisively established as determining the affairs of Israel.[10] The point is not merely that the created world is *unsatisfactory* until human beings accept the divine law, but that it is not *complete* until then.[11] Until there is a coherent harmony between man and God, there is no universal order; that is, the cosmos is unfinished. God cannot complete the process of His creation alone.[12]

---

10 "At the erection of the Tabernacle, as it says, And he that presented his offering *the* first day (Num. 7:12) meaning, the first of the world's creation, for God said, 'It is as though on that day I created My world'" (*Midrash Rabbah*, p. 25).

11 As the editors of the Midrashic text point out: "The world is not really created until man does God's will, here symbolized by the erection of the Temple, and thereby His original design to be at one with man is fulfilled" (ibid., n. 4).

12 The ideas I have tried to develop in this essay derive from conversations with R. Sidney Morgenbesser.

Autonomy, Necessity, and Love

I. There are several kinds of actions that, in one sense or another, we *must* perform. These actions are not coerced; nor are the movements we make when we perform them spasmodic, or in any other manner beyond our physical control. What we do is neither compulsive nor compelled. The actions are wholly voluntary. Nonetheless, we have no real alternatives to performing them.

One category of such actions is made up of the various things that we have to do because they are indispensable to the attainment of our settled goals. These are the *necessities of ambition and prudence.* In a second category, there are the more peremptory imperatives of moral obligation. They are the *necessities of duty.* These two categories do not exhaust the significantly distinct kinds of actions concerning which we recognize that we have no choice. Besides what is conditionally indispensable to us on account of our prudential interests and our ambitions, and besides the demands that are made upon us categorically in the name of duty, there are in addition the *necessities of love.*

I shall not attempt to provide a comprehensive analysis of the concept of love. As I shall deploy the concept, it has a very wide scope: love is a species of caring about things, and its possible objects include whatever we may care about in certain ways. Thus loving something — at least, as I propose to construe the matter — is not merely a matter of liking it a great deal or of finding it deeply satisfying, as in "loving" chocolate ice cream or the piano music of Chopin. To love differs from having feelings of a certain type, such as those of powerful attraction or of intense desire or of compelling delight. It is also not equivalent to or entailed by any judgment or appreciation of the inherent value of its object. To love something is quite different from considering it to be especially appealing or precious. The fact that a person recognizes that an object is valuable or that it is good does not imply that he cares about it or, indeed, that he has any particular interest in it at all.

Of course, love does ordinarily involve various strong feelings and beliefs that express, reveal, and support it. The heart of love, however, is neither affective nor cognitive. It is volitional. That a person cares about or that he loves something has less to do with how things make him feel, or with his opinions about them, than with the more or less stable motivational structures that shape his preferences and that guide and limit his conduct. What a person loves helps to determine the choices that he makes and the actions that he is eager or unwilling to perform.

Since people are often mistaken about what is moving them in their choices and in their actions, they may also be mistaken concerning what they love.

The object of love is very commonly a specific concrete individual: for instance, another person, or a country, or an institution. The beloved may also be an object of a more abstract sort: for instance, a moral or a non-moral ideal. Greater emotional color and urgency may often be manifest when the object of love is an individual than when it is something like social justice, or scientific truth, or a family tradition. This is not invariably the case, however, and in any event it is not a defining feature of love that it must be hot rather than cool.

The requirements of prudence and of ambition are not only conditional. They are also contingent. The intentions and needs from which they derive are not logically necessary; hence they are neither a priori nor universal, but can only be determined empirically on the basis of personal considerations. The essential characteristics of the requirements of duty are rather more controversial. Let us suppose, however, that Kant and others are correct in maintaining that these requirements are entirely impersonal and that they are neither contingent nor conditional. As for the requirements of love, they are certainly not logically necessary. Nonetheless, despite their manifest contingency, they may be quite categorical. They differ, accordingly, both from the conditional requirements of ambition and prudence and from the impersonally a priori requirements of duty.

Love is irredeemably a matter of personal circumstance. There are no necessary truths or a priori principles by which it can be established what we are to love; nor do the constraints that bind the lover to his beloved also impartially and indifferently bind everyone else to it as well. On the other hand, devoted love and its commands are often strictly unconditional. Like the impersonal mandates of duty, the imperatives of love too may be starkly uncompromising, providing no loopholes and offering no recourse. The claims that are made upon us by our love of our children, or of our countries, or of our ideals may be just as unequivocally categorical as those that are made upon us by the moral law. In cases of both kinds, there is no room for negotiation: we simply *must not* violate our moral obligations, and we simply *must not* betray what we love.

Needless to say, the claims of love and those of duty may conflict. My purpose in this essay, however, is not to assess the relative weight of the authority that is properly to be accorded to each. Nor shall I consider the possibility that, even when they are incompatible, the authority of each may be absolute. I am not here interested either in morality or in reason, but in autonomy.

II. According to Kant, autonomy can be achieved only through obedience to the rational dictates of the moral law. Indeed, he insists that a person "proves his freedom in the highest degree by being *unable* to resist the call of duty."[1] I agree

---

1 *The Metaphysics of Morals*, pp. 381–2 fn. (emphasis added), translated by Mary Gregor (Cambridge University Press, 1991).

that a person may be free without having alternatives from which he can choose as he pleases. Moreover, I believe that the most genuine freedom is not only compatible with being necessitated; as Kant suggests, it actually requires necessity. I do not share Kant's view, however, that autonomy consists essentially and exclusively in submission to the requirements of duty. In my opinion, actions may be autonomous, whether or not they are in accordance with duty, when they are performed out of love.[2]

The idea of autonomy is the idea of self-government. An autonomous political entity is one that is independent of external control; it manages its own affairs. Similarly, individuals are autonomous to the extent that they govern themselves. In examining what this entails, it is important to avoid being misled by etymology. The term "autonomy" derives from two Greek words: one meaning "self," and the other meaning "reason" or "principle" or "law." This fact is sometimes regarded as supporting the Kantian notion that "autonomy of the will is the property the will has of being a *law* to itself."[3] The relation between autonomy and law cannot be established, however, by consulting a dictionary. Whether being self-governed necessarily involves following general principles or rules of action is a philosophical question, not an etymological one.

No doubt it is sensible to fear that government without law may be tyrannical, chaotic, and inhumane. Nevertheless, a government that is arbitrary or inconsistent or vicious is hardly the same as no government at all. Perhaps it is also true of individuals that they cannot govern themselves very satisfactorily, and cannot lead desirable or even decent lives, unless they govern themselves by principles or laws. Nevertheless, they are in fact governing themselves to the extent that the commands that they obey, whether based upon rules or not, are their own commands. It cannot simply be taken for granted that any commands by which people govern themselves must be commands that are derived by the rational application of general principles. The capacity to rule does not belong uniquely to reason. There are ruling passions as well.

III. Kant argues that someone whose conduct is motivated merely by his own personal interests is inevitably heteronomous. What interests a person is a contingent matter, of course, which is determined by circumstances that are outside his control. Kant understands this to entail that personal interests are not integral to the essential nature of a person's will. In his view, they are volitionally adven-

---

2   On Kant's account, our capacity for recognizing and accepting our moral obligations is what raises us above the non-rational animals. But we are distinguished from these animals also by virtue of the fact that they are incapable of love. If "reason" is to refer to whatever makes us distinctively human, then we should not understand it to be exclusively a faculty for grasping reasons or applying rules. It must also include our capacity to form attitudes toward our own wills. This volitional self-reflection, rather than any discursive or inferential activity, is at the heart of our capacity to love.

3   *Groundwork of the Metaphysics of Morals*, p. 440 (emphasis added), translated by James W. Ellington (Indianapolis: Hackett Publishing Company, 1981).

titious: they do not depend wholly upon the person's inherent volitional character, but at least partly upon causes that are logically external to it. Since the person's interests do not derive strictly and entirely from himself, autonomy cannot be grounded in interests. To the extent that a person's conduct is guided by his interests, he is being governed by circumstances that do not essentially belong to himself. Therefore, he is necessarily heteronomous.

The autonomous will can only be one that incorporates what Kant calls a "pure" will. It must conform, in other words, to the requirements of a will that is indifferent to all personal interests – that is entirely devoid of all empirical motives, preferences, and desires. Now this *pure will* is a very peculiar and unlikely place in which to locate an indispensable condition of individual autonomy. After all, its purity consists precisely in the fact that it is wholly untouched by any of the contingent personal features that make people distinctive and that characterize their specific identities. What it wills can be determined entirely a priori, as a matter of universally valid necessary truth. The pure will has no individuality whatsoever. It is identical in everyone, and its volitions are everywhere exactly the same. In other words, the pure will is thoroughly *impersonal.* The commands that it issues are issued by no one in particular.

An autonomous agent is, by definition, governed by himself alone. He acts entirely under his own control. It seems natural and reasonable to presume that when a person is acting under his own control, he will guide his conduct with an eye to those things that he considers to be of the greatest importance to him. If he is in charge of his own life, we cannot plausibly expect that he will systematically neglect what he most cares about for the sake of considerations in which he has less interest or no interest at all. Now it is not very likely, in my opinion, that what each of us considers most important to himself is exactly the same. It seems to me even less likely that the one thing about which each of us cares most is the moral law.

A person acts autonomously only when his volitions derive from the essential character of his will. According to Kant, a person's volitions are related to his will in this way only insofar as he is following the austerely impersonal dictates of the moral law. In fact, however, the same relation between volition and will holds when a person is acting out of love. Love is, of course, paradigmatically personal. Nevertheless, the unconditional commands of love are not, as Kant suggests, adventitious elements of a person's will. They are essentially integral to it, for what a person loves is a defining element of his volitional nature. When he acts out of love, accordingly, his volitions do derive from the essential character of his will. Thus, the personal grip of love satisfies the conditions for autonomy that Kant believes can be satisfied only by the impersonal constraints of the moral law.

IV. Someone is heteronomous when what he wills is not determined exclusively by the inherent nature of his will but at least partly by considerations that are conceptually inessential to it. These conceptually inessential considerations are separable from his will, and in that respect they are logically external to it. Now insofar as a person's will is affected by considerations that are external to it, the person is being acted upon. To that extent, he is passive. The person is active, on the other hand, insofar as his will determines itself. The distinction between heteronomy and autonomy coincides, then, with the distinction between being passive and being active. If it is indeed possible to be autonomous by virtue of submitting to the ruling passion of love, it must be possible to be ruled by love without thereby being passive.

In many of its instances, love is fundamentally passive. It is passive when the lover is motivated by an expectation that obtaining or continuing to possess the object of his love will be beneficial to him. The expectation may not be self-consciously explicit; it certainly need not be the result of any deliberate calculation or assessment. In one way or another, however, the object strikes the lover as being capable of providing him with gratification or with joy or with some other desirable state. This is the essential basis upon which his loving the object depends: his love is conditional upon his attribution to his beloved of a capacity to improve the condition of his life. What mainly binds him to the object of his love, whether he is prepared to acknowledge this or not, is a preoccupation with his own good.

To be sure, he may devote himself with enormous intensity, and at extravagant cost, to protecting and advancing the interests and ends of his beloved. Insofar as he does so, however, it is either because he supposes that it may increase the likelihood that his desire for his beloved will be fulfilled or because he understands that his beloved must flourish if it is to be optimally capable of providing him with the benefits that he hopes to obtain from it. Despite any appearances or affirmations to the contrary, his devotion to the object of his love is motivated by self-interest.

But love need not be based upon self-interest. It may be fundamentally active, differing from passive love in the nature of the lover's motivation and in his concern for whatever it is that he loves. Loving of any variety implies conduct that is designed to be beneficial to the beloved object. In active love, the lover values this activity for its own sake instead of for the sake of advantages that he himself may ultimately derive from it. His primary goal is not to receive benefits but to provide them. He is motivated by an interest in serving the interests and ends of his beloved rather than by an interest in serving his own.

The loving activity of the passive lover is motivated essentially by a self-regarding interest in sustaining or enhancing the likelihood that the object of his love will be useful to him. In active love, the lover is not motivated by any interest of this sort in the utility to him of his beloved. Rather, he is motivated by an interest in the loving itself. This must not be understood to mean that what motivates him is the inherent appeal of the activities in which loving leads him to engage, considered entirely apart from their effects on his beloved. To be sure, it may well be that he is attracted by those activities when he considers them strictly as such and for their own sakes; he may find them to be, by virtue of their intrinsic characteristics alone, compellingly gratifying or enjoyable. In that case, however, his love is just as self-interested, just as conditional, and just as passive as if he valued the loving activity in which he engages solely for its utility in bringing him the benefits that he hopes to receive from his beloved.

Caring for a child may involve activities and experiences whose desirability to the parent is as inherent in them as the desirability of an invigorating workout or of listening to good music. The parent may value them for their own sakes, quite independently of how they affect the child. But suppose that the parent also loves the child, and that this love for the child is wholly active and unconditional. Suppose, in other words, that it depends neither upon an anticipation of benefits of any sort from the child nor upon an interest for their own sakes in the activities and experiences that loving involves. No doubt it might be said that, even though the love is genuinely unconditional, the parent is nonetheless motivated by a self-regarding personal interest. What motivates him, after all, is his interest in the welfare of the child. It is essential to appreciate, however, that his interest in the child is entirely *disinterested*. It can be satisfied completely and only by the satisfaction of interests that are altogether distinct from and independent of his own. The interest that moves the devoted parent is unquestionably *personal,* but it is also utterly *selfless*.

Although active love as such is valuable to the lover only for the sake of the benefits that it provides to his beloved, it is also true that it is valuable to him for its own sake. The loving is valuable to him for its own sake, however, *precisely* and *only* because of its utility. Serving the ends and interests of his beloved is something that he values as an end in itself. If he did not consider his loving devotion to be instrumentally valuable in providing benefits to his beloved, it would not be intrinsically valuable to him.[4]

V. Kant imagines that except when we are acting in submission to the moral law, "we everywhere come upon the dear self."[5] He believes that the renunciation of interest is impossible except when the will accedes to the austerely impersonal constraints of duty. But to leave the dear self behind it is not necessary, as he supposes, to renounce all interests. We need not render ourselves volitionally pure.

4 The active lover values the ends and interests of his beloved for their own sakes. Their intrinsic value to him makes them in a certain way instrumentally valuable to him, since the fact that they are intrinsically valuable to him is a condition of the intrinsic value to him of his devotion to them. Thus his devotion is intrinsically valuable to him because of its utility, and the ends and interests of the beloved are instrumentally valuable to him because of their intrinsic value. I have explored these somewhat unfamiliar and paradoxical aspects of the relationship between ends and means in my essay "On the Usefulness of Final Ends" (see Chapter 7).
5 *Groundwork*, p. 407.

We can keep our interests, as long as they are disinterested. What is essential for leaving the dear self behind is not that the will be pure or impersonal, but only that it be selfless.

To the extent that its interests are personal rather than purely a priori, even the most selfless will is of course determined by contingencies. Kant insists that the pursuit of *any* contingent interest is unavoidably heteronomous. This view depends upon his assumption that insofar as a will is determined by contingencies, what it wills is adventitious rather than entailed by its own inherent nature. From this assumption, it follows that a will motivated by personal interests is moved by circumstances external to itself and is therefore passive and heteronomous.

In my opinion, Kant's assumption is mistaken. Even though a person's interests are contingent, they can belong to the essential nature of his will. Thus, despite the fact that unconditional love is a personal matter, what a person loves may be among his essential volitional characteristics. What autonomy requires is not that the essential nature of the will be a priori, but that the imperatives deriving from it carry genuine *authority*. Kant insists that the requisite authority can be provided only by the necessities of reason. I believe that it can also be provided by those of active love.

In active love, the lover cares selflessly about his beloved. It is important to him for its own sake that the object of his love flourish; he is disinterestedly devoted to its interests and ends. Now this is not the only essential constitutive feature of active love. Another of its defining characteristics is that the unconditional importance to the lover of what he loves is not a voluntary matter. The lover cannot help being selflessly devoted to his beloved. In this respect, he is not free. On the contrary, he is in the very nature of the case *captivated* by his beloved and by his love. The will of the lover is rigorously constrained. Love is not a matter of choice.

Kant says of the hypothetical imperatives of prudence and ambition that, since the needs and inclinations in which they are grounded are merely contingent, we can escape the force of these imperatives whenever we have a will to do so. Only in the precepts of the moral law, he claims, do we find imperatives from whose authority we cannot freely choose to turn away:

What is necessary merely in order to attain some arbitrary purpose can be regarded as in itself contingent, and the precept can always be ignored once the purpose is abandoned. Contrariwise, an unconditioned command does not leave the will free to choose the opposite at its own liking. Consequently, only such a command carries with it that necessity which is demanded from a law.[6]

On this account, the rational imperatives of the moral law are uniquely categorical. Hence they alone enjoy the necessity, or the inherent authority, that laws must have. All other commands are merely hypothetical, and they lose all their force when the contingent conditions upon which they rely no longer prevail.

6   Ibid., p. 420.

But the commands of selfless love are also categorical. The claims that are made upon us by our ideals or by our children, or by whatever we may love disinterestedly and without conditions, are as unconditional and as unyielding as those of morality and reason. It goes without saying that love is a contingent matter; unlike the dictates of the pure will, those of love are not supported by rational necessity. The fact that love and its commands are logically arbitrary does not mean, however, that they can be abandoned or invalidated at will. We are certainly not free to decide "at our own liking" what to love or what love requires of us.

It is true, of course, that over the course of time the objects of a person's love may vary. Love may appear or disappear; one beloved object may be replaced or joined by another. Changes of these kinds alter the configuration of the will. But the fact that they are changes in the will does not mean that they are up to us. In fact, they are not under our deliberate volitional control. It may sometimes be possible for a person to manipulate conditions in his environment or in himself so as to bring it about that he begins or that he ceases to love a certain object; but this does not imply that for him love is a matter of free choice. So far as what he loves is concerned, he cannot directly affect his will by a mere act of will. It is not up to him whether he is intimately susceptible to the object that he loves. The captivity of love cannot be entered or escaped just by choosing to do so.

VI. It may seem that in this respect love does not differ significantly from a variety of other familiar conditions. There are numerous emotions and impulses by which people are at times gripped so forcefully and moved so powerfully that they are unable to subdue or to resist them. We are vulnerable not only to being captivated by love, but also to being enslaved by jealousy or by a compulsion to take drugs. These passions too may be beyond our voluntary control, and it may be impossible for us to elude their rule.

When conditions like jealousy and addiction enslave us, they do so by virtue of their sheer overwhelming intensity or strength. They are then so powerful that we are simply unable to keep ourselves from acting as they require. The force with which they move us is literally irresistible. It may well be that we would truly prefer not to accede to it, but we cannot help giving in. In cases like these, the effective impetus of the emotion or compulsion is more or less independent of our own deliberate intentions and desires. It is capable of determining what we do regardless of how we might prefer to act.

In many circumstances we regard forces of these kinds as alien to ourselves. This is not because they are irresistible. It is because we do not identify ourselves with them and do not want them to move us. Thus, we may wish that we could be free of the driving influence of jealousy or of addiction. We may prefer to conduct ourselves in accordance with other motives; and we may endeavor strenuously, whether successfully or not, to do so. But irresistible forces do not invariably oppose or conflict with desires or intentions by which we would prefer to be moved. They may move us irresistibly precisely in ways that we are wholeheartedly pleased to endorse. There may be no discrepancy between what we must do and how we would in any event wish to behave. In that case, the irresistible force is not alien to us at all.

The volitional attitudes that a person maintains toward his own elementary motivational tendencies are entirely up to him. Passions such as jealousy and craving merely provide him with psychic raw material, as it were, out of which he must design and fashion the character and the structure of his will. They themselves do not essentially include any affirmative or negative volitional attitudes toward the motivational tendencies in which they consist. Whether a person identifies himself with these passions, or whether they occur as alien forces that remain outside the boundaries of his volitional identity, depends upon what he himself wants his will to be.

However imposing or intense the motivational *power* that the passions mobilize may be, the passions have no inherent motivational *authority*. In fact, the passions do not really make any *claims* upon us at all. Considered strictly in themselves, apart from whatever additional impetus or facilitation we ourselves may provide by acceding to them, their effectiveness in moving us is entirely a matter of *sheer brute force*. There is nothing in them other than the magnitude of this force that requires us, or that even encourages us, to act as they command.

Love is different. The fact that a person loves something does not merely present him with primary volitional raw material. Love is not an elementary psychic datum, which in itself implies no particular evaluative or practical attitude on the part of the lover toward its motivational tendency. To be sure, a person may regret loving what he loves. He may have attempted to avoid loving it; and he may try to extinguish his love. No doubt there are many possible varieties of volitional complexity and ambivalence. But since love is itself a configuration of the will, it cannot be true of a person who does genuinely love something that his love is entirely involuntary.[7]

This does not mean, of course, that a person necessarily assigns the very highest priority to serving the interests of whatever he loves. After all, there may be more than one thing that he loves; and they cannot all come first. The fact that a person loves something does imply, however, that he cannot help caring about its interests and that their importance to him is among the considerations by which he cannot help wanting his choices and his conduct to be guided. His readiness to serve the interests of his beloved is not just a primitive feeling or an impulse toward which his attitude may be as yet totally indeterminate. It is an element of his established volitional nature, and hence of his identity as a person.

People are sometimes ambivalent. That is, they are sometimes in part opposed

---

7 This accounts for the fundamental difference, both in tone and in substance, between being "captivated" by love and being "enslaved" by passion.

to a motivational tendency with which they are also in part identified. Accordingly, there are circumstances in which it might reasonably be asserted that a person is "overwhelmed" by love. Such an assertion could not properly be taken to imply, however, that in being overwhelmed by love the person has been made to succumb in a struggle with an alien force. An ambivalent person is simultaneously on both sides of the struggle within himself. His will itself is divided; therefore, it cannot be thoroughly or decisively defeated by either of the opposing forces. To be overwhelmed by love is necessarily tantamount, then, to being overwhelmed not by an external or alien power but by part of oneself.

VII. I believe that this sheds some light on why it is that the claims of love, unlike the mere pressures of emotion and desire, possess not simply power but authority. The authority for the lover of the claims that are made upon him by his love is the authority of his own essential nature as a person. It is, in other words, the authority over him of the essential nature of his own individual will.

What is meant here by the "essential nature" of a person? The essential nature of triangles, or of triangularity, includes the characteristics that any figure correctly identified as triangular must necessarily possess. The essential characteristics of triangles are those that no genuine triangle can help having. The essential nature of a person is to be understood similarly, as including the characteristics that define his essential identity. The essential identity of an individual differs, however, from that of a type of thing. The essence of triangularity is an a priori matter of *definitional* or *conceptual* necessity. The essence of a person, on the other hand, is a matter of the contingent volitional necessities by which the will of the person is as a matter of fact constrained.

These constraints cannot be determined by conceptual or logical analysis. They are substantive rather than merely formal. They pertain to the purposes, the preferences, and the other personal characteristics that the individual cannot help having and that effectively determine the activities of his will. In other words, they are specified for any given person by what he loves. Our essential natures as individuals are constituted, accordingly, by what we cannot help caring about. The necessities of love, and their relative order or intensity, define our volitional boundaries. They mark our volitional limits, and thus they delineate our shapes as persons.

This means that love is in a certain way reflexive. Insofar as a person loves something, the fact that he cares about it as he does requires that he must care similarly about how he acts in matters that concern it. Because love entails that the lover has certain volitional attitudes toward the object of his love, it also entails that he has corresponding volitional attitudes toward himself. In the very nature of the case, he cannot be indifferent to how what he does affects his beloved. To the extent that he cares about the object of his love, therefore, he necessarily cares about his own conduct as well.

138

Caring about his beloved is tantamount, then, to caring about himself. In being devoted to the well-being of his beloved as an ideal goal, the lover is thereby devoted to an effort to realize a corresponding ideal in himself – namely, the ideal of living a life that is devoted to the interests and ends of his beloved. Someone who loves justice, for instance, necessarily wants to be a person who serves the interests of justice. He necessarily regards serving its interests not only as contributing to the realization of a desirable social condition, but also as integral to the realization of his ideal for himself. His love defines for him, at least in part, the motives and preferences of his ideal self.

A person who fails to act in the ways that caring about his beloved requires necessarily fails to live in accordance with his ideal for himself. In betraying the object of his love, he therefore betrays himself as well. Now the fact that a person betrays himself entails, of course, a rupture in his inner cohesion or unity; it means that there is a division within his will. There is, I believe, a quite primitive human need to establish and to maintain volitional unity. Any threat to this unity – that is, any threat to the cohesion of the self – tends to alarm a person and to mobilize him for an attempt at "self-preservation."

It seems to me that the authority that love has for us is closely related to this compelling and irreducible need to protect the unity of the self. Since the commands of love derive from the essential nature of a person's will, a person who voluntarily disobeys those commands is thereby acting voluntarily against the requirements of his own will. He is opposing ends and interests that are essential to his nature as a person. In other words, he is betraying himself. We are naturally averse to inflicting upon ourselves such drastic psychic injuries.[8]

Insofar as someone violates his own essential nature, he fails to treat himself unequivocally as an end. That is to say, he treats himself without full respect. Self-betrayal is, indeed, plainly and fundamentally inconsistent with self-respect. Since a betrayal of what we love is necessarily a betrayal of oneself, the person who betrays his love manifests a lack of respect for himself. It is our basic need for self-respect, which is very closely related to our need for psychic unity, that grounds the authority for us of the commands of love.[9]

---

8 Situations in which it is impossible for a person to avoid this sort of self-betrayal provide the theme for one variety of human tragedy. Thus, Agamemnon at Aulis is destroyed by an inescapable conflict between two equally defining elements of his own nature: his love for his daughter and his love for the army he commands. His ideals for himself include both being a devoted father and being devoted to the welfare of his men. When he is forced to sacrifice one of these, he is thereby forced to betray himself. Rarely, if ever, do tragedies of this sort have sequels. Since the volitional unity of the tragic hero has been irreparably ruptured, there is a sense in which the person he had been no longer exists. Hence, there can be no continuation of *his* story.

9 Ambivalence as such entails a mode of self-betrayal. It consists in a vacillation or opposition within the self which guarantees that one volitional element will be opposed by another, so that the person cannot avoid acting against himself. Thus, ambivalence is an enemy of self-respect.

VIII. Acting out of love is not a special case of acting out of duty. The authority of love must not be confused with the authority of the moral law. Some thinkers mistakenly identify the commands of love as simply requirements of a certain type of moral obligation. This error is motivated, perhaps, by a reluctance to acknowledge that the importance of moral obligation is rather limited. In any event, misconstruing love in this way facilitates neglect of the fact that there are unconditionally authoritative commands that have nothing particularly to do with the moral law.

Consider this illustration of the view of a leading contemporary moral philosopher: "Because of my special obligation to my own child, for instance, it might be the most important thing in the world *to me* that my child be successful or happy."[10] This suggests that the peculiar importance to parents of their children's welfare has its source or ground somehow in moral principles. Mothers and fathers are supposed to care especially about their children because of their obligations as parents.

But surely the great importance to me of my children's welfare does *not* derive from any alleged "special obligations" that I may have, as their parent, to provide them with care and support. The happiness and success of my children are not important to me because there is some principle to which I adhere and from which I can infer their importance. They are important to me just because I love my children very much. This is quite sufficient to account for my recognition that there are certain things that, precisely because I love my children and not for any principled reason, I must do.

Moral obligation is really not what counts here. Even if parents are somehow morally obligated to love or to care about their children, it is not normally on account of any such obligation that they do love them. Parents are generally not concerned for their children out of duty, but simply out of love; and the love, needless to say, is not a love of duty but a love of the children. To account for the necessities and the authority of parental love, there is no reason to invoke the moral law.

IX. The necessity of Kant's categorical imperative is supposed to derive from the absolute requirements of reason itself. The dictates of the pure will are not only unconditional, but no coherent alternatives to them can even be conceived. This does not mean, however, that no alternative to them will in fact be pursued. Notwithstanding its a priori truth, the moral law may be disobeyed. The fact that its commands are rationally necessary is what gives them their authority. It does not, on Kant's account, directly or inescapably ensure that a person will actually submit to them.

10 The view in question, which pertains to supposed "special obligations," is advanced by Thomas Nagel in *The View from Nowhere*, pp. 164 ff. The illustration of Nagel's view is provided by C. Korsgaard, "The Reasons We Can Share," *Social Philosophy & Policy*, vol. 10, no. 1 (1993), p. 33.

The moral law can influence a person's conduct, Kant believes, only through the mediation of *respect*. It is his respect for the moral law, rather than simply his understanding of it or his perception of its rationality, that leads a rational agent to subordinate his inclinations to the requirements of duty. Whether the agent actually accedes to the demands of obligation is determined, therefore, by whether his respect for the moral law is sufficiently strong to overcome the personal inclinations that compete with it.

The relative strengths of inclination and of respect for the moral law depend upon a variety of contingent empirical circumstances. Hence, the effectiveness of the moral law in determining the actual conduct even of someone who fully understands what that law requires is a contingent matter. Although the moral law is theoretically necessary, this necessity as such does not in practice necessitate. It accounts for the authority of the law, but it does not of itself guarantee that people will obey it.

With regard to love, the situation is quite similar. The necessities of love are not rational, of course, but volitional; love constrains the will rather than the understanding. But just as the moral law cannot be other than it is, so we cannot help loving what we love. Moreover, the dictates of love, like the requirements of the moral law, enjoy an unconditional authority. In radically distinct but nonetheless closely parallel ways, each tells us what we must do.

In both cases, the commands may be disobeyed. We may in matters either of duty or of love negligently or willfully or akratically fail to do what we must do. What supports our obedience in each case is a variety of respect. It is difficult to establish whether it is respect for the moral law or self-respect that is in general the more robust and the more reliable. In any case, it is clear that the categorical requirements both of duty and of love are vulnerable to violation and betrayal. As the theoretical necessity of the one cannot ensure that rational agents will be virtuous, so the volitional necessity of the other cannot ensure that lovers will be true.

12

An Alleged Asymmetry between Actions and Omissions

Do the conditions for moral responsibility differ according to whether what is at issue is an action or an omission? John Fischer and Mark Ravizza claim that they do.[1] In their opinion, someone may be morally responsible for performing an action even though he could not have done otherwise; but a person cannot be morally responsible for omitting to perform or failing to perform an action if he could not have done otherwise – that is, if he could not have performed it. The idea that there is an important asymmetry of this sort between actions and omissions strikes me as rather implausible. There appears to be no fundamental reason why instances of performing actions should be, as such, morally different from instances of not performing them. After all, the distinction between actions and omissions is not a very deep one. Indeed, it is often a rather arbitrary matter whether what a person does is described as performing an action or as omitting to perform one. So it would be surprising if the moral evaluation of actions and of omissions differed in any particularly significant way.

Imagine that a person – call him "Stanley" – deliberately keeps himself very still. He refrains, for some reason, from moving his body at all. Why should our moral evaluation of this situation require attention to considerations – having to do with whether Stanley was free to behave differently – that would have required no attention whatever if we were evaluating a situation in which he deliberately made his body move? What count are his intentions and his carrying them out. Why should it be important whether what he does involves *moving?*

I agree with Fischer and Ravizza concerning how it is that a person may be morally responsible for an action even though he could not have done otherwise. The fact that someone could not have done otherwise may have, in the actual sequence of events, no causal influence on his behavior. It may play no role whatsoever in accounting for his action; he may actually be led to do what he does entirely by other considerations. It is because of this possibility that, as Fischer and Ravizza put it, "moral responsibility for an action does not require the freedom to refrain from performing the action" (p. 262).

Now it seems to me that when we turn from cases of action to cases of omission,

1 John Fischer and Mark Ravizza, "Responsibility and Inevitability," *Ethics* 101 (January 1991): 258–78, cited hereafter by page number in the text. I was the commentator on the Fischer and Ravizza paper when it was presented at the Greensboro Colloquium. The present article conveys the substance of my comments on that occasion.

we find the very same possibility. In the actual sequence of events, the fact that someone could not have performed a certain action – and hence could not have avoided omitting it – may have no causal influence on his behavior. It may play no role whatsoever in accounting for his omitting to perform the action. What actually leads the person to omit the action may be other considerations entirely.

Thus, suppose that there is someone with a powerful interest in having Stanley refrain from making any deliberate movements, who arranges things in such a way that Stanley will be stricken with general paralysis if he shows any inclination to move. Nonetheless, Stanley may keep himself still quite on his own altogether independently of this person's schemes. Why should Stanley not be morally responsible for keeping still, in that case, just as much as if there had been nothing to prevent him from moving had he chosen to do so?

Precisely the same kind of conditional or fail-safe overdetermination, in virtue of which there may be moral responsibility for actions that one cannot avoid, may be present in cases of omissions that one cannot avoid. There should therefore be no morally interesting asymmetry between actions and omissions, unless there is some *other* morally pertinent respect in which these two varieties of behavior differ. Fischer and Ravizza maintain that there is such a difference. They claim that in order to be morally responsible for an action a person must be in "actual causal control" of the bodily movement that performing the action requires. This means that the agent must deliberately produce the movement in question. In order to be morally responsible for an omission, in contrast, a person must be in "regulative control" of the relevant bodily movement. This means that the agent must have the capacity both to produce the movement and to prevent it from occurring. Fischer and Ravizza attempt to derive moral asymmetry by differentiating these two sorts of control.

But what is supposed to account for the difference in the sorts of control that actions and omissions require? Fischer and Ravizza simply provide no reason for believing that cases of the one type require a different sort of control than cases of the other. In my view, there is every reason to prefer an account that is straightforwardly symmetrical. If what moral responsibility requires in a case of action is just "actual causal control" of the relevant *movement,* then what it requires in a case of omission is just the same "actual causal control" of the *omission* of the relevant movement. This implies (as Fischer and Ravizza agree) that a person may be morally responsible for an action if he deliberately produces the relevant movement, regardless of whether he could have prevented that movement. It also implies (contrary to what they assert) that a person may be morally responsible for an omission if he deliberately prevents the relevant movement, even if he could not have produced the movement.

Let us consider some of the examples that Fischer and Ravizza discuss. In "Sloth" (p. 261), John decides against saving a drowning child who (because there are sharks nearby) would have drowned even if John had tried to save him. Fischer

NECESSITY, VOLITION, AND LOVE

and Ravizza suggest that it is discordant to insist that in these circumstances John is morally responsible for not saving the child. They are right about this. But what explains the discordance is not, as they suppose, the fact that it was impossible for John to save the child.

This fact might have been due to circumstances of quite a different sort than those which they describe. Thus, imagine that if John had even started to consider saving the child he would have been overwhelmed by a literally irresistible desire to do something else; and imagine that this would have caused him to discard all thought of saving the child. With this change, the case of John exactly parallels another of Fischer's and Ravizza's examples – that of Matthew ("Hero").[2] They correctly regard Matthew as clearly praiseworthy for his action despite the fact that if he had even started to consider an alternative sequence in which he refrained from acting, he "would have been overwhelmed by literally irresistible guilt feelings," which would have prevented him from refraining. But if Matthew is clearly praiseworthy, then John is as clearly blameworthy for what he does despite the fact that, because of circumstances in the alternative sequence of precisely the same kind, he could not have done otherwise than refrain from acting to save the child.

In Fischer's and Ravizza's version of the example, John bears no moral responsibility for failing to save the child. This is not, however, because he cannot save the child. The real reason is that what he does has no bearing at all upon whether the child is saved. The sharks operate both in the actual and in the alternative sequences, and they see to it that the child drowns no matter what John does. In the revised version of the example, the child is also bound to drown. But the effect of revising the example is that, in the revised actual sequence, the child drowns *only* because John refrains from acting to save him. No factor operating in the revised actual sequence undermines John's sole responsibility for the drowning in that sequence. *That* is why John is morally responsible for failing to save the child even though he cannot prevent him from drowning.[3]

In the light of this, one might perhaps wish to deal more meticulously with the case of Matthew. After all, it was not entirely up to him whether he succeeded in saving the child. It depended upon there being, in the actual sequence, circumstances over which he had no control – for instance, the absence of nearby sharks. One might therefore prefer to say that Matthew is not praiseworthy for actually

2 "Matthew is walking along a beach . . . , he sees a child struggling in the water and he quickly deliberates . . . , jumps into the water, and rescues the child. We can imagine that Matthew does not give any thought to not trying to rescue the child, but that if he had considered not trying to save the child, he would have been overwhelmed by literally irresistible guilt feelings which would have caused him to jump into the water and save the child anyway. . . . Apparently Matthew is morally responsible – indeed praiseworthy – for his action, although he could not have done otherwise" (p. 259).

3 It appears, then, that the original version of the example suffers from the same defect for which Fischer and Ravizza criticize Susan Wolf (p. 260).

saving the child, but that he is praiseworthy only for acting to save him. If this seems reasonable, then one should of course also prefer to say that John is not blameworthy for refraining from saving the child but only for refraining from acting to save him. The two cases are, in any event, entirely symmetrical. If there is any discordance in holding John morally responsible for refraining from saving the child, it is equally discordant to regard Matthew as morally responsible for saving him.

13

Equality and Respect

1. Let me begin with a preliminary caution, and with a statement of intent. I propose to deal here with issues that pertain to the alleged moral value of equality. So far as I am aware, nothing that I shall say concerning these issues implies anything of substance as to the kinds of social or political policies that it may be desirable to pursue or to avoid. My discussion is motivated exclusively by conceptual or analytic concerns. It is not inspired or shaped by any social ideology or political interest.

2. I categorically reject the presumption that egalitarianism, of whatever variety, is an ideal of any intrinsic moral importance. This emphatically does not mean that I am inclined generally to endorse or to be indifferent to prevailing inequalities, or that I oppose efforts to eliminate them. In fact, I support many such efforts. What leads me to support them, however, is not a conviction that equality of some kind is morally desirable for its own sake and that certain egalitarian goals are therefore inherently worthy. Rather, it is a more contingent and pragmatically grounded belief that in many circumstances greater equality of one sort or another would facilitate the pursuit of other socially desirable aims. So far as equality as such is concerned, I am convinced that it has no inherent or underived moral value at all.[1]

3. Some philosophers believe that an equal distribution of certain valuable resources, just by virtue of being egalitarian, is a significant moral good. Others maintain that what actually is of moral importance is not that the resources be distributed equally but that everyone enjoy the same level of welfare. All of these philosophers agree that there is some type of equality that is morally valuable in

---

1 In the introduction to their anthology *Equality: Selected Readings*, Louis Pojman and Robert Westmoreland attribute to me the view that, with regard to economic considerations, "in an affluent society we have a duty to provide for people's minimal needs, but nothing further" (1997, p. 11). That is by no means my view. In an essay entitled "Egalitarianism as a Moral Ideal," which was originally published in *Ethics* in October 1987 and then reprinted in my collection entitled *The Importance of What We Care About*, I argued that what is morally important is not that people have equal incomes or equal wealth but that each person have enough. By "enough" I meant enough for a good life, not – as Pojman and Westmoreland suppose – merely enough to get by.

itself, quite apart from whatever utility it may possess in supporting efforts to achieve other morally desirable goals.

It seems to me that insofar as egalitarian ideals are based upon the supposition that equality of some kind is morally desirable as such, or for its own sake, the moral appeal of egalitarianism is an illusion. In my opinion, equality has no moral value in itself. It is true that, among morally conscientious individuals, appeals in behalf of equality often have very considerable emotional power; moreover, as I have indicated, there are situations in which morally pertinent considerations do indeed dictate that a certain inequality should be avoided or reduced. Nonetheless, I believe that it is always a mistake to regard equality of any kind as desirable inherently. There is no egalitarian ideal the realization of which is valuable simply and strictly in its own right. Whenever it is morally important to strive for equality, it is always because doing so will promote some other value rather than because equality itself is morally desirable.

In addition to equality of resources and equality of welfare, several other modes of equality may be distinguished: equality of opportunity, equal respect, equal rights, equal consideration, equal concern, and so on. My view is that *none* of these modes of equality is intrinsically valuable. Hence, I maintain that none of the egalitarian ideals corresponding to them has any underived moral worth. Once various conceptual misunderstandings and confusions are dispelled, it appears finally that equality as such is of no moral importance.

4. With regard to the inegalitarian conditions that prevail when socioeconomic classes are markedly stratified, Thomas Nagel asks: "How could it not be an evil that some people's life prospects at birth are radically inferior to others?" (1991, p. 28). The question has undeniable rhetorical force. It seems impossible that any decent person, with normal feelings of human warmth, could fail to recognize that radical initial discrepancies in life prospects are morally unacceptable and that a readiness to tolerate them would be blatantly immoral.

And yet, is it really indisputable that such discrepancies must always be so awful? Although the life prospects of those in the lower socioeconomic strata have nearly always been terrible, it is not a necessary truth that this familiar relationship must hold. Having less is compatible, after all, with having quite a bit; doing worse than others does not entail doing badly. It is true that people in the lowest strata of society generally live in horrible conditions, but this association of low social position with dreadful quality of life is entirely contingent. There is no necessary connection between being at the bottom of society and being poor in the sense in which poverty is a serious and morally objectionable barrier to a good life.

Suppose we learn that the prospects of those whose life prospects are "radically inferior" are in fact rather good – not as good as the prospects with which some others begin, but nonetheless good enough to ensure a life that includes many genuinely valuable elements and that people who are both sensitive and reasonable find deeply satisfying. This is likely to alter the quality of our concern. Even if we should continue to insist that no inequality can ever be fully acceptable, discrepancies between life prospects that are very good and life prospects that are still better may not strike us as warranting the hot sense of moral urgency that is evoked by characterizing every discrepancy of this kind as *evil*.

5. The egalitarian condemnation of inequality as inherently bad loses much of its force, I believe, when we recognize that those who are doing considerably worse than others may nonetheless be doing rather well. But the egalitarian position remains misguided even when its moral claims are moderated. Inequality is, after all, a purely *formal* characteristic; and from this formal characteristic of the relationship between two items, nothing whatever follows as to the desirability or the value of either. Surely what is of genuine moral concern is not formal but substantive. It is whether people have good lives, and not how their lives compare with the lives of others.

Suppose it is suggested that a life that is radically inferior to others cannot possibly be a good life. It will presumably be conceded that one good life may be less good than another, and hence that *mere* inferiority does not entail that a life is necessarily bad. It might perhaps be conceded further that this is not entailed even by the fact that the one life is *considerably* inferior to the other. But suppose someone insists that the very notion of being *radically* inferior entails not merely that a life is less good than others, but that the life falls decisively below the threshold that separates lives that are good from lives that are not good.

Let it be accepted as a conceptually necessary truth, then, that radically inferior lives are invariably bad. In that case, it will be entirely reasonable to agree that the radical inferiority of some people's life prospects is indeed – as Nagel says – an evil. But why is it an evil? The evil does not lie in the circumstance that the inferior lives happen to be unequal to other lives. What makes it an evil that some people have bad lives is not that some other people have better lives. The evil lies simply in the unmistakable fact that bad lives are bad.[2]

6. When someone is wondering whether to be satisfied with the resources that are at his disposal, or when he is evaluating the level of his well-being, what is it genuinely important that he take into account? The assessments that we are supposing he wishes to make are personal: they have to do with the specific quality of his own life. What he must do, it seems clear, is to make these assessments on

---

2　The fact that some bad lives are radically inferior to the lives of others may be quite relevant, of course, to social policy. That some have better lives makes it clear, for one thing, that better lives are possible. For another, the radical superiority of the better lives may suggest that the bad lives might be improved by using resources diverted from the better ones. These considerations have nothing to do, however, with whether or not equality itself is inherently valuable.

the basis of a realistic estimate of how closely the course of his life suits his individual capacities, meets his particular needs, fulfills his best potentialities, and provides him with what he himself cares about. With respect to none of these considerations, it seems to me, is it essential for him to measure his circumstances against the circumstances of anyone else. Of course, such comparisons may often be illuminating; they may enable a person to understand his own situation more clearly. Even so, they are at best heuristic rather than criterial.

If a person has enough resources to provide for the satisfaction of his needs and his interests, his resources are entirely adequate; their adequacy does not depend in addition upon the magnitude of the resources that other people possess. Whether the opportunities available to a person include the alternatives from which it would be desirable for him to be able to choose depends upon what opportunities suit his capacities, his interests, and his potentialities. It does not depend upon whether his opportunities coincide with those available to others.

The same goes for rights, for respect, for consideration, and for concern. Enjoying the rights that it is appropriate for a person to enjoy, and being treated with appropriate respect and consideration and concern, have nothing essentially to do with the respect and consideration and concern that other people are shown or with the rights that other people happen to enjoy. Every person should be accorded the rights, the respect, the consideration, and the concern to which he is entitled by virtue of what he is and of what he has done. The extent of his entitlement to them does not depend upon whether or not other people are entitled to them as well.[3]

It may well be that the entitlements of all people to certain things are in fact the same. If this is so, however, it is not because equality is important. It is because all people happen to be the same, or are necessarily the same, with regard to the characteristics from which the entitlements in question derive – for instance, common humanity, a capacity for suffering, citizenship in the kingdom of ends, or whatever. The mere fact that one person has something or is entitled to something – taken simply by itself – is *no reason at all* for another person to want the same thing or to think himself entitled to it. In other words, equality as such has no moral importance.

3 In *Inequality Reexamined,* Amartya Sen claims that "to have any kind of plausibility, ethical reasoning on social matters must involve elementary equal consideration for all at some level that is seen as critical (1992, p. 17). But what does "equal consideration" mean? Surely giving people equal consideration does not mean spending equal time or equal effort in considering their interests or their entitlements. Sen himself suggests that it has to do with avoiding arbitrariness: "the absence of such equality would make a theory arbitrarily discriminating and hard to defend" (ibid.). But avoiding arbitrariness has nothing to do with treating people equally. It is a matter of having a reasonable basis for treating them as one does. It would be arbitrarily discriminating to give greater consideration to one person than to another without having a reasonable basis for discriminating between them; and it would similarly be arbitrary to give both the same consideration when there is a reasonable basis for treating them differently. To avoid arbitrariness, we must treat likes alike and unlikes differently. This is no more an egalitarian principle than it is an inegalitarian one.

II

7. Still, this is not the end of the story. Consider someone who is in no way concerned about equality for its own sake, and who is also quite satisfied that he has as much of everything as he can use, but who happens to have less of certain things than others have. The fact that he has been treated unequally might offend him, even though he does not object to inequality as such. He might consider the inequality between his condition and the condition of others to be objectionable, because it might suggest to him that whoever is responsible for the discrepancy has failed to treat him with a certain kind of respect. It is easy to confuse being treated with the sort of respect in question with being treated equally. However, the two are not the same. I believe that the widespread tendency to exaggerate the moral importance of egalitarianism is due, at least in part, to a misunderstanding of the relationship between treating people equally and treating them with respect.

The most fundamental difference between equality and respect has to do with focus and intent. With regard to any parameter – whether it has to do with resources, welfare, opportunity, respect, rights, consideration, concern, or whatever – equality is merely a matter of each person having the same as others. Respect is more personal. Treating a person with respect means, in the sense that is pertinent here, dealing with him exclusively on the basis of those aspects of his particular character or circumstances that are actually relevant to the issue at hand.[4]

Treating people with respect precludes assigning them special advantages or disadvantages except on the basis of considerations that differentiate relevantly among them. Thus, it entails impartiality and the avoidance of arbitrariness. Those who are concerned with equality aim at outcomes that are in some pertinent way indistinguishable. On the other hand, those who wish to treat people with respect aim at outcomes that are matched specifically to the particularities of the individual. It is clear that the direction in which a desire for equality points may diverge from the direction in which an interest in respect and impartiality lead.

8. Under certain conditions, to be sure, the requirements of equality and of respect will converge. It is important that this convergence not be misconstrued.

---

4 I am uncertain about the relationship between what I am referring to as "respect" and what Avishai Margalit (1996) has in mind when he speaks of respect. In his usage, as I understand it, treating people without respect is closely linked to humiliating them or to giving them reason to feel humiliated. In my usage, this is not obviously the case. For one thing, since the value assigned to respect may be overridden by other values, people often prefer – sometimes for perfectly good and even admirable reasons – to be treated as though they have characteristics that they do not have or as though they lack characteristics that they actually possess. This means that they prefer to be treated without what I am calling "respect," but it is not at all clear that they are inviting humiliation. I recognize that it is rather dissonant to characterize such people, in the way I do here, as trying to avoid being treated respectfully. A disinclination to appear and to be treated as what one is may sometimes suggest a lack of *self*-respect, perhaps, but not always. I have been unable to design a more suitable terminology.

Consider a situation in which no information is available either about any relevant similarities between two people or about any relevant differences between them. In that case, the most natural and the most sensible recourse is to treat both people the same – that is, to treat them equally. Now the fact that an egalitarian policy is the only plausible one under such conditions may give rise to an impression that a preference for equality is – as it were – the default position, which must be implemented in the absence of considerations showing that an alternative is required. Many thinkers do in fact claim that egalitarianism enjoys a presumptive moral advantage over other policies. In their view, it is always desirable for equality to prevail unless the initial moral superiority of an egalitarian policy is overcome by particular features of the situation at hand.

Isaiah Berlin advances this view as follows:

The assumption is that equality needs no reasons, only inequality does so. . . . If I have a cake and there are ten persons among whom I wish to divide it, then if I give exactly one tenth to each, this will not, at any rate automatically, call for justification; whereas if I depart from this principle of equal division I am expected to produce a special reason. (1955–56, p. 132)

This sort of account appeals to many people; indeed, it is widely thought to be confirmed by elementary common sense. In fact, however, the assumption that Berlin enunciates is mistaken. Equality has no inherent moral advantage over inequality. There is no basis for a presumption in favor of egalitarian goals.

If it would indeed be morally correct to distribute Berlin's cake in equal shares, the explanation is not – as he supposes – that equality needs no reasons, or that egalitarian distribution enjoys an initial moral superiority over other alternatives. The critical feature of the situation, as he evidently imagines it, is that he has *neither* a special reason for dividing the cake equally *nor* a special reason for dividing it unequally. In other words, the situation is one in which he does not know *either* that the people among whom the cake is to be shared are alike in ways that warrant giving them equal shares *or* that they differ in ways that justify giving them shares of different sizes. He has no relevant information about these people at all.

This means, of course, that the relevant information available to him about each of the people is exactly the same: namely, *zero*. But if his relevant information about each person is identical with his relevant information about the others, it would be arbitrary and disrespectful to treat the people differently; impartiality requires that he treat everyone the same. So he *does* have a reason that justifies an egalitarian distribution of the cake. It is the moral importance of respect and hence of impartiality, rather than any supposedly prior or preemptive moral importance of equality, that constrains us to treat people the same when we know nothing that provides us with a special reason for treating them differently.

In cases like the one Berlin describes, it is merely a happenstance that the requirements of equality and of respect coincide. There may also be circumstances

151

in which the coincidence of these requirements is not so contingent. Suppose we agree that everyone is entitled to certain things simply in virtue of being human. With regard to these entitlements, individual differences naturally cannot provide any relevant basis for differentiating between one person and another; for the only characteristics of each person that are relevant – to wit, simply those that constitute his humanity – are necessarily shared by every other human being. Therefore, the criteria of impartiality and of equality must inescapably yield, in this case, the same result.

The fact that this sort of case requires equality is not grounded, however, in any moral authority that egalitarianism possesses in its own right. Rather, the claim of egalitarianism is derivative. It is grounded in the more basic requirements of respect and of impartiality. What most fundamentally dictates that all human beings must be accorded the same entitlements is the presumed moral importance of responding impartially to their common humanity, and not the alleged moral importance of equality as an independently compelling goal.

III

9. What is it about impartiality, and about what I have been referring to as "respect," that makes them morally imperative? Why is it important to be guided in dealing with people only by whatever it is about them that is genuinely relevant? There is a sense in which being guided by what is relevant – thus treating relevantly similar cases alike and relevantly unlike cases differently – is an elementary aspect of being rational.[5] Being impartial and respectful is a special case of being rational in this sense. It might be suggested, accordingly, that the moral value of these ways of treating people derives from the importance of avoiding the irrationality that would be entailed by relying upon irrelevancies. But this only raises another question. What is the moral importance of avoiding irrationality?

10. It is desirable that people be rational. On the other hand, this does not mean that irrationality as such is immoral. The fact that adopting a certain belief or pursuing a certain course of behavior contravenes the requirements of rationality does not entail that a moral imperative of some kind has been violated. People who reason badly are surely not, just on that account, morally culpable. So there must be something else about deviations from respect, besides the fact that they are breaches of rationality, that has a more immediate and a more specific moral import.

People who resent disrespectful treatment do so because, by its very nature, it

---

5   What counts as relevant and what counts as irrelevant may often depend heavily, of course, upon moral considerations.

conveys a refusal to acknowledge the truth about them.[6] Failing to respect some-one is a matter of ignoring the relevance of some aspect of his nature or of his situation. The lack of respect consists in the circumstance that some important fact about the person is not properly attended to or is not taken appropriately into account. In other words, the person is dealt with as though he is not what he actually is. The implications of significant features of his life are overlooked or denied. Pertinent aspects of how things are with him are treated as though they had no reality. It is as though, because he is denied suitable respect, his very existence is reduced.

This sort of treatment, at least when it has to do with matters of some conse-quence, may naturally evoke painful feelings of resentment. It may also evoke a more or less inchoate anxiety; for when a person is treated as though significant elements of his life count for nothing, it is natural for him to experience this as in a certain way an assault upon his reality. What is at stake for him, when people act as though he is not what he is, is a kind of self-preservation. It is not his biological survival that is challenged, of course, when his nature is denied. It is the reality of his existence for others, and hence the solidity of his own sense that he is real.

11. Experiences of being ignored – of not being taken seriously, of not counting, of being unable to make one's presence felt or one's voice heard – may be pro-foundly disturbing. They often trigger in people an extraordinarily intense protec-tive response, which may be quite incommensurate in its vehemence with the magnitude of the damage to their objective interests that is actually threatened. The classical articulation of this response is in the limitlessly reckless cry to "let justice be done though the heavens may fall." What leads to such an unmeasured and perhaps even self-destructive demand for redress is plainly not an appraisal of the extent of the injustice that has been done, nor is it an estimate of what it might actually take to undo the injustice. The demand issues in a less calculated manner from the unbearably deep suffering and dread that may be caused when people are treated unjustly – that is, when their personal reality is threatened by a denial of the impartiality that respect requires.

Demands for equality have a very different meaning in our lives than demands for respect. Someone who insists that he be treated equally is calculating his demands on the basis of what other people have rather than on the basis of what will accord with the realities of his own condition and most suitably provide for his own interests and needs. In his desire for equality, there is no affirmation by a person of himself. On the contrary, a concern for being equal to others tends to alienate people from themselves. It leads them to define their goals in terms that are set by considerations other than the specific requirements of their own personal

6 As I suggested in footnote 4, someone who wishes to conceal or to misrepresent the truth about himself may welcome being treated without respect. In what follows, I shall be concerned only with cases in which a person resents disrespectful treatment.

nature and of their own circumstances. It tends to distract them from recognizing that their most authentic ambitions are those which derive from the character of their own lives and not those which are imposed upon them by the conditions in which others happen to live.

Needless to say, the pursuit of egalitarian goals often has very substantial utility in promoting a variety of compelling political and social ideals. But the widespread conviction that equality itself and as such has some basic value as an independently important moral ideal is not only mistaken; it is an impediment to the identification of what truly is of fundamental moral and social worth.

REFERENCES

Berlin, Isaiah. "Equality as an Ideal." *Proceedings of the Aristotelian Society* 56 (1955–56). Reprinted in Frederick Olafson, ed., *Justice and Social Policy* (Englewood Cliffs, N.J.: Prentice Hall, 1961).

Frankfurt, Harry. *The Importance of What We Care About.* New York: Cambridge University Press, 1988.

Margalit, Avishai. *The Decent Society.* Cambridge, Mass.: Harvard University Press, 1996.

Nagel, Thomas. *Equality and Partiality.* New York: Oxford University Press, 1991.

Pojman, Louis, and Westmoreland, Robert. *Equality: Selected Readings.* New York: Oxford University Press, 1997.

Sen, Amartya. *Inequality Reexamined.* Cambridge, Mass.: Harvard University Press, 1992.

14

On Caring

I. CARING AND NECESSITY

1. In their discussions of issues concerning the nature of human action and its essential determinants, and also in their inquiries into the structure of practical reasoning, philosophers typically draw upon a more or less standard and rather limited conceptual repertoire. The most familiar item in that repertoire is the indispensable, ubiquitous, and protean notion of what people *want*, or – synonymously, at least in the somewhat procrustean usage that I shall adopt – the notion of what they *desire*. This notion is deployed routinely, and often rather carelessly, in a variety of different roles. It is important that these roles be carefully differentiated and severally understood. Otherwise, the significance of some fundamental aspects of our lives will tend to be severely blurred. In this connection, I think it may be useful to extend the standard repertoire by articulating certain other notions which, although they too are both familiar and philosophically significant, have been to some extent neglected.

2. What is the point of practical reasoning? One natural and appealingly plausible answer is that people engage in practical reasoning, or deliberate, in order to determine how to attain the goals they desire to reach: a person wants to get certain things, and so he tries to figure out – through the use of practical reason – how best to get them. Now I do not wish to suggest that this account of the matter is incorrect. However, I believe that it masks some significant complexities and variations in the character of our interests and our motivations.

On many occasions, what serves to inspire our thinking and to shape our conduct is not that we merely *want* one thing or another. Often, what moves us is that there is something of which it is both more precise and more pertinent to say that we *care about it* or that we *regard it as important to ourselves*. In certain cases, moreover, it is appropriate to characterize what guides us even more narrowly by referring to a particular mode of caring – namely, *love*. It is especially with these concepts – what we care about, what we consider important to us, and what we love – that I am going to be concerned.

I indicated a moment ago that I propose to treat the verbs "to desire" and "to want" as synonyms. Here is another terminological stipulation. The fact that a person *cares about something* and the fact that he *regards it as important to himself* are to be construed as substantially equivalent. I am not saying that these expressions have the very same meaning; in fact, they do not. My stipulation is only the more limited one that, however the two expressions are rightly to be understood, people necessarily consider whatever they care about to be important to them; and, conversely, they necessarily care about anything that they consider important to them.

3. Philosophically relevant references to desire are by no means limited, of course, to specialized logical and metaphysical analyses of practical reasoning and of the concept of action. They also figure prominently in moral and political discourse. Representations concerning what people want are frequently accorded considerable justificatory authority, and they often also have compelling rhetorical effect, in evaluations of the attitudes, policies, and behavior of individuals and of societies. Any acceptable account of the appropriate prerogatives and responsibilities of government, as well as any convincing account of what morality demands, must provide a measure of the weight that is to be assigned to the claims of desire. It must therefore rely upon some understanding of what the various formations and structures of desire may be.

The philosophy of liberalism is distinctively preoccupied with defining and defending the ideal of a society that maximizes the freedom of its members to do what they want. One argument that may be advanced in behalf of this ideal is that permitting people to do as they please enhances the likelihood that they will get what they want, so that ensuring their freedom facilitates their success in the pursuit of happiness. To be sure, the connection between doing as we please and getting what we want is not very reliable. What is perhaps even more problematic is the connection between getting what we want and actually being happy.

There are people who are evidently quite confident, nonetheless, that the entire character of happiness does really lie in nothing other than the fulfillment of desire. This is the view of Thomas Hobbes, who declares that happiness (his term is "felicity") is simply "continued success in obtaining those things which a man from time to time desireth, that is to say, continual prospering."[1] In other words, happiness entirely and exclusively consists in the complete and regular satisfaction of desire. What makes people happy is just doing and getting whatever they happen to want.

This wholesale reliance upon the sheer fact of desire strikes me as egregiously indiscriminate. Hobbes is apparently not concerned that people may be misguided in what they want; he takes happiness to consist flatly in the satisfaction of whatever desires they actually have. Of course, this does not commit him to maintaining that every satisfaction of desire weighs the same. He can allow that satisfying one desire contributes more to a person's happiness than satisfying

---

1   Thomas Hobbes, *Leviathan*, Part 1, chapter 6.

another when the person wants to satisfy the one more than he wants to satisfy the other — that is, when he *prefers* satisfying the one over satisfying the other. But resorting to the concept of preference does not provide sufficiently for the discriminations that an adequate account of the relation between happiness and desire must be able to support.

For one thing, obviously, a person may be as misguided in his preferences as in his desires. But even apart from this difficulty, there is a decisive flaw of another kind in the doctrine that being happy is unconditionally equivalent to doing or getting what one prefers. Suppose that a person is not misguided and makes no mistakes. The fact that one desire ranks higher than another in the order of his preferences still cannot be presumed to mean that satisfying the former desire will contribute more to his happiness than satisfying the latter. His preference for satisfying the one desire over the other may be entirely sound; it may be quite untainted by any error of fact or failure of judgment. Yet it may nonetheless make no difference to his happiness which of the two desires he fulfills. Indeed, his happiness may be totally unaffected even if he fulfills neither of them.

Whether someone is happy is not determined by what he merely wants, nor even by what he prefers. It is possible that a person's happiness may be neither increased by his success in satisfying his desires nor impaired by his failure to satisfy them. The reason is that some of the things people want, or prefer, are things they do not really care about. The fact that a person wants one thing more than he wants another does not entail that he cares about it more, therefore, because it does not entail that he cares about it at all.[2]

From my desire for some chocolate ice cream, for example, or from my preference for chocolate ice cream over pineapple sherbet, it cannot be inferred that chocolate ice cream is something that I consider to be important to me. It is quite common for people to want various things without actually caring about them, and to prefer satisfying one of their desires rather than another without regarding the object of either desire as being of any importance to them. Surely it cannot reasonably be supposed that their happiness depends at all, much less that it depends essentially, upon the satisfaction of desires or preferences that they themselves do not care about.

4. Getting whatever one wants cannot be tantamount to what we have in mind when we speak of happiness. After all, creatures of numerous subhuman animal species also have desires and preferences. This may make them susceptible both to the pleasures of gratification and to the pains of frustration, but it hardly entails

---

2 A person who does not care about either of two things may nonetheless care about his preference for one of them over the other. That is, he may consider it important to him that his priorities be respected, and thus that desires ranking higher in his order of preference not be frustrated for the sake of desires that rank lower. This point is separate from the one in the text, and I shall not pursue it here.

that they are capable of being happy. They want things, and they want some things more than they want others. But they lack the additional psychic complexity that is required in order to have the capacity to care about anything. The fact that an animal satisfies its desires and preferences is not enough to warrant our regarding it as happy. In my view, at any rate, it makes no sense to attribute either happiness or unhappiness to a creature that does not regard anything as important to itself.

It might perhaps be suggested that although wanting something is admittedly not the same as caring about it, and although many subhuman creatures have desires without having the capacity to care about anything, the situation is different for us. The fact that a *person* wants something, it might be argued, does warrant an inference to the conclusion that he cares about it, at least in cases where he wants it *badly*. For a person who wants something badly will naturally be quite uncomfortable if his desire is frustrated, and we may reasonably presume that whoever is capable of caring about anything will certainly care about avoiding significant discomfort. So however it may be for lesser creatures, it is legitimate to suppose that a *person* who wants something badly does indeed care about it.

But even if it is true that a person who wants something badly does necessarily care about avoiding the frustration of his desire, we cannot assume that he also cares about the *object* of his desire. If satisfying a desire were the *only* way to avoid being frustrated, then whoever cared about avoiding frustration *would* have to care about getting the things he wants. However, people can also avoid frustration without getting the objects of their desires by ceasing to want them. Instead of satisfying their desires, in other words, they may avoid frustration by giving up the desires. Moreover, people do often prefer to avoid the pain of frustration by giving up their desires rather than by satisfying them. In any event, to care about avoiding the frustration of a desire is not the same either as caring about satisfying the desire or as caring about whatever it is by which the desire would be satisfied.

5. To care about something differs not only from wanting it and from preferring it but also from judging it to be valuable. A person who acknowledges that something has considerable intrinsic value does not thereby commit himself to caring about it. Perhaps he commits himself to recognizing that it *qualifies* to be *desired for its own sake* and to be *pursued as a final end*. But this is far from meaning that he does actually desire it or seek it, or that he ought to do either. Despite his recognition of its value, it may just not appeal to him; and even if it does appeal to him, he may have good reason for neither wanting it nor pursuing it. Each of us can surely identify a considerable number of things that we think would be worth doing or worth having for their own sakes, but to which we ourselves are not especially drawn and at which we quite reasonably prefer not to aim.

Suppose, however, that someone does adopt a certain goal, which he values for its own sake and pursues as a final end. It *still* cannot be presumed that he cares about it. We often devote our time and effort and other resources to the pursuit of goals that we desire to attain because we are convinced of their intrinsic value but that we do not really consider to be of any importance to us. For instance, there are numerous more or less inconsequential pleasures that we seek entirely for their own sakes but that we do not truly care about at all. When I want an ice-cream cone simply for the pleasure of eating it, that pleasure is for me a final end. I desire it for its own sake. But this hardly means that it is something I care about. Very likely, the pleasure of eating the ice cream is something that I truly *do not* consider at all important to me. There is no incoherence in appraising something as intrinsically valuable, and pursuing it actively as a final end that is worth having in itself, and yet not caring about it.

In conducting the deliberations through which they undertake to design their lives and to assess their conduct, people have to confront a number of familiar issues – concerning what they want, which things they want more than others, what they consider to be inherently valuable and hence worthy of being pursued for its own sake, and what they propose to adopt for themselves as the final ends that they will actually seek to attain. They also face a further distinct task. They need to decide or discover what it is that they care about, or what they regard as important to them. This is not the same as determining what to want, what to prefer, what to value, or what to pursue for its own sake. The criteria for determining what people care about are not the same as the criteria for identifying their desires and preferences, their attributions of intrinsic value, or their final ends.

6. What does it mean, then, to care about something? Suppose someone is planning to attend a concert that is to be devoted to music he particularly enjoys. There are easily imaginable circumstances in which he might emphatically and sincerely declare that, although he certainly does want to go to the concert, it is not something that he regards as being at all important to him. Consider the following scenario. The prospective concertgoer is asked by a close friend for an important favor. Doing the favor will make it impossible for him to get to the concert. He agrees gladly to do the favor, but incidentally mentions to his friend that doing it will require him to change his plans for the evening. Upon hearing this, his friend becomes confused and apologetic, expresses a reluctance to impose upon his good-natured readiness to forgo the concert, and begins to withdraw the request for the favor. At this point, the music lover interrupts him, saying: "Don't worry about the possibility that you may be taking too much advantage of my friendship for you. The fact is that going to this concert is not at all important to me. I really don't care about missing it."

It is possible here, of course, that the music lover is not being altogether candid. Perhaps he is fully aware that he *does* care about missing the concert but considerately chooses to conceal this in order to protect his friend from embarrassment. I believe that what he says to reassure his friend may be the literal truth: although he would indeed like to attend the concert, missing it may really be of absolutely no importance to him. But suppose that what he says is *not* true? Suppose that his disclaimer misrepresents him, and that he is very well aware that going to the concert actually is of some importance to him. What would that imply?

One thing it would imply, it seems to me, is that forgoing the concert will cost him something: he will be disappointed, and he will suffer an uncomfortable sense of detriment or loss. If he does really care about going to the concert, then missing it will hurt. And if forgoing the concert will hurt, that must be because going to the concert is something that he still wants to do even after he decides to help his friend instead. If he no longer had any desire to attend the concert, there is no reason why he should be bothered by being unable to attend it.

So the supposition that he cares about attending the concert, even after he has agreed to forgo it, entails at least this: he continues to desire to attend the concert — and therefore to be susceptible to pain caused by the frustration of this desire — despite the fact that he now feels that satisfying the desire is less important to him than doing the favor for his friend. Under the circumstances, he is willing to give up going to the concert. But his desire to attend it persists, albeit with a lower priority than before.

This is not, however, the end of the story. In order to establish that a person cares about something, it can hardly be enough to show merely that his desire for it happens to persist after he has set aside his plan for satisfying the desire. In the case of the music lover, the persistence of his desire to go to the concert would have no essential bearing upon whether he cares about the concert if the desire persisted only by virtue of some sort of affective or volitional inertia. If it is to have such a bearing, the desire must endure through an exercise of his own volitional activity rather than by its own inherent momentum.

This volitional activity may not be fully conscious or explicitly deliberate. But his vulnerability to the cost that forgoing the concert will impose on him must be in some way *his own doing*. It cannot be simply a matter of inadvertence or passivity on his part. The reason that missing the concert will cause him to suffer frustration, even after he has decided to forgo the concert for the sake of doing the favor, cannot be that he is too negligent or too indolent or too impotent to revise his inclinations and attitudes appropriately in light of that decision. In other words, the persistence of his desire must be due to the fact that he is unwilling to give it up.

Thus, his caring about going to the concert implies that he is disposed to support and sustain his desire to go to it even after he has decided that he prefers to satisfy another desire instead. Forgoing the concert would frustrate his first-order desire to attend the concert. In itself, on the other hand, it would fail to touch the higher-order desire – which he might or might not have – that this first-order desire not be extinguished or abandoned. His caring about the concert would essentially consist in his having and identifying with a higher-order desire of this kind.

Missing the concert may be costly to him, of course, even if he does not care about it. Needless to say, people are not always able to shape their inclinations as they would like. Thus, his desire to attend the concert may persist despite the fact that he makes no effort to sustain it and would greatly prefer that it disappear. In that case, he has the misfortune of being stuck with a desire he does not want. But his relationship to this desire, and its standing in his psychic economy, are radically affected by his unwillingness for it to persist.

The fact that the music lover does not care about the concert cannot ensure that, when he decides to do the favor for his friend, his desire to attend the concert will conveniently be extinguished. It does imply, however, that in making his decision he dissociates himself from the desire and proposes to cease being moved by its appeal. He does not merely assign it a lower priority than it had before. Rather, he denies it any position at all in his order of preferences. To be sure, he may find that the desire nonetheless remains alive within him. But he has now disenfranchised the desire, so to speak, and has alienated it from himself.

Whether the person cares about the concert is not fundamentally, then, a question either of how enthusiastic he *feels* about going to it or of how beneficial he *believes* or *expects* going to it would be. No doubt beliefs, feelings, and expectations of those kinds *do,* in many situations, more or less reliably indicate whether a person considers something to be important to him. What is at the heart of the matter, however, is not a condition of *feeling* or of *belief* or of *expectation* but of *will.* The question of whether a person cares about something pertains essentially to whether he is *committed* to his desire for it in the way that I have suggested, or whether he is willing and prepared to give the desire up and to have it excluded from the order of his preferences.

Human beings are extremely complicated; they tend to be ambivalent and inconsistent in many respects, and they are resourceful. This makes them elusive. Especially with regard to the most significant aspects of their lives, they are generally hard to pin down, difficult to sort out, and just about impossible to sum up. When it comes to asserting that a person cares about something, it is a good idea to keep in mind that various important qualifications may be in order. So: (a) even though the fact that a person cares about something is constituted by certain of his own desires, it may be that he cannot help caring about what he cares about because he cannot help having those desires; (b) he may care about it, despite seeing clearly that it is foolish or even irrational for him to do so in light of the fact that the desire he is unwilling to abandon is one that he can never satisfy; (c) the person may care about something even though he wishes that he didn't, and despite strenuous efforts to stop; (d) a person may care about things a great deal without realizing that he cares about them at all, and he may not really care at all about things that he believes he considers to be very important to him.

7. Being committed to a desire is not at all equivalent to simply approving of the desire or to merely endorsing it. Commitment goes beyond acceptance of the desire and hence willingness to be moved by it. It entails a further disposition to be active in seeing to it that the desire is not abandoned or neglected. A person who cares about something may not actually pursue it as an end; after all, he may prefer instead to pursue other things that he cares about more. He will necessarily be concerned, however, that his desire for it continue to occupy some meaningful position in the order of his preferences. If the desire should tend to disappear, or be forgotten, he will be disposed to refresh it and to reinforce whatever degree of influence he wishes it to exert upon his decisions and upon his behavior.

Now if this is at least *part* of a correct account of what it means to care about something, then it is of quite fundamental significance to the character of our lives that, as a matter of fact, we do care about various things. Suppose we cared about nothing. In that case, we would be creatures with no active interest in establishing or sustaining any thematic continuity in our volitional lives. We would not be disposed to make any effort to maintain any of the interests, aims, and ambitions by which we are from time to time moved.

Of course, we would still be moved to *satisfy* our desires; that is irreducibly part of the nature of desire. We might also still want to have certain desires, and to be motivated by them in what we do; and we might want not to have certain others and want not to be moved by them to act. In other words, our capacity for higher-order desires and higher-order volitions might remain fully intact. Moreover, some of our higher-order desires and volitions might tend to endure and thus to provide a degree of volitional consistency or stability in our lives. From our point of view as agents, however, whatever coherence or unity might happen to come about in this way would be merely fortuitous and inadvertent. It would not be the result of any deliberate or guiding intent on our part. Desires and volitions of various hierarchical orders would come and go; and sometimes they might last for a while. But in the design and contrivance of their succession we ourselves would be playing no concerned or defining role.

The significance to us of *caring* is thus more basic than the importance to us of *what* we care about. Needless to say, it is better for us to care about what is truly worth caring about than it is to care about things that are inconsequential or otherwise unworthy or that will bring us harm. However, the value to us of the fact that we care about various things does not derive simply from the value or the suitability of the objects about which we care. Caring is important to us for its own sake, insofar as it is the indispensably foundational activity through which we provide continuity and coherence to our volitional lives. Regardless of whether its objects are appropriate, our caring about things possesses for us an inherent value by virtue of its essential role in making us the distinctive kind of creatures that we are.

8. Given that caring about things is a fundamentally constitutive feature of our lives, what more practical function does it serve? What role does it play *in* our lives, apart from the role of making our lives the kind of lives they are? Leaving aside the fact that we consider it desirable for its own sake to be creatures who live lives of this kind, what is the *instrumental* value to us of caring about things? What do we achieve by it?

I believe that it is pertinent to consider, in this connection, the relationship between the notion of importance and the notion of need. As I understand this relationship, things are important to us – whether we recognize their importance to us or not – insofar as we need them; and how important to us they are depends upon how badly we need them. Those things that we do not need at all are of no importance to us; and things are of no importance to us only if they are things for which we have no need. As for what makes something a necessity, I construe the defining characteristic of the things that we need as having to do with what is necessary in order to avoid harm. To assert that a person needs something means just that he will inevitably be harmed in one way or another – he will inevitably suffer some injury or loss – unless he has it. On the other hand, if it is possible for a person to do without a certain thing and yet suffer no harm, then he does not really need that thing.

Harms vary widely, of course, in their severity. Therefore, on this very general way of construing the nature of need – which admittedly tracks ordinary uses of the relevant terms only up to a point – some needs are far more serious than others, and some are not serious at all. If suffering a certain harm would be a relatively inconsequential matter, the need for whatever is an indispensable condition of avoiding that harm will lack urgency and be of very little significance altogether. But it will nonetheless be a genuine need, however uncompelling, by virtue of the fact that satisfying it is the only way to avoid a genuine – albeit minor – harm. No doubt there may be disagreements concerning whether, or to what degree, a certain state of affairs *would* be truly harmful to someone. In that case, the corresponding questions concerning what that person needs, and how badly he needs it, will be similarly controversial.

Given the connection between need and harm, it is plainly in our interest to have what we need. We have an equally clear interest, moreover, in *wanting* what we need. That is to say, it is naturally in our interest to want those things that are in fact important to us. If we do really need them, and if therefore they are indeed important to us, then it is to our advantage that we desire to get them. After all, our getting them might be quite a bit less likely if we did not want them. Things are likely to go worse for us if there are things that we need but do not desire, and that we are therefore not inclined either to go after or to accept. Insofar, then, as a person considers something important to him and hence something that he needs, he will normally also consider it important to him to desire it. Furthermore, he will be similarly motivated to prevent himself from losing his desire for it. It is good for us that we be motivated to satisfy our needs. So it is a good idea for us to sustain that motivation and to support it whenever it might otherwise tend to fade.

9. Now there are many good things that we consider genuinely valuable, that we want, and that we pursue, but that we do not need. We do not need them because, however attractive or valuable they may be, they are not indispensable to us. Failure to obtain them need not cause us harm, because wholly adequate substitutes for them are available to us at no greater cost. Whatever satisfactions they provide can be replaced without any additional expense by other satisfactions that are attainable in other ways. Thus, we can get along just as well without them.

On the other hand, of course, things that we do not need may nonetheless satisfy our needs. Many of our needs are in fact disjunctive. That is, they can be satisfied by any one of a number of different means, each of which is capable of satisfying the need by virtue of some feature that all of the disjuncts share. What actually serves in the end to satisfy a disjunctive need may not itself be anything that is really needed, as the needy person may be in a position to satisfy his need equally well in other ways.

This does not mean that we want the things that satisfy our disjunctive needs only because they are valuable instrumentally rather than because of value that is intrinsic to them. In fact, we may desire them strictly for their own sakes – that is, for their intrinsic value alone. After all, what a person needs on a certain occasion may be simply to possess or to do *something or other* that is intrinsically valuable. His need then is disjunctive, and there may be a variety of things that would satisfy it at more or less the same cost. But his need can be satisfied by these various things only because each of them is indeed intrinsically valuable. If the disjunct that the person chooses meets his need, it does so precisely because it is valuable for its own sake. When he chooses it, accordingly, he chooses it as a final end and not as a means to enjoying the value of something other than itself.

Suppose it is literally true that the person in my example, who had initially planned to go to the concert, does not really care about going to it. That is to say, suppose he does not regard going to the concert as being of any importance to him. Then he does not believe that he needs to go to it; in other words, he does not expect that missing the concert will unavoidably bring him any incremental cost. We may imagine that he is interested in spending his evening in some manner that is intrinsically worthwhile, but that this interest of his is disjunctive (or perhaps one might say "generic"). He wants to avoid squandering the evening, but he understands that going to the concert is not the only way for him to accomplish this. He appreciates that listening to the music at the concert would have the intrinsic value he seeks. But the alternative proposed by his friend offers him an opportunity to do something that he considers to be no less intrinsically valuable; and, for one reason or another, he prefers it. Thus, a person who desires something exclusively for its intrinsic value (e.g., listening to music) may be happy to accept instead something else (e.g., helping a friend) that also possesses intrinsic value but possesses it by virtue of characteristics of a quite different sort.

10. These considerations have a bearing upon certain aspects of the peculiar structure, and of the significance in our lives, of *love*. Loving is a mode of caring. Among the things that we care about there are some that we cannot help caring about; and among the things that we cannot help caring about are those that we love. I am not going to attempt to develop a rigorous and comprehensive articulation of the nature of love. It may well be that the notion, as it is commonly and carelessly invoked, is too inchoate ever to be perspicuously and conclusively grasped and charted. I must certainly do something, though, at least to point in the general direction of the class of phenomena that I have in mind.

Roughly speaking, then, when I refer here to love I am referring to a concern for the well-being or flourishing of a beloved object – a concern that is more or less volitionally *constrained*, so that it is not a matter of entirely free choice or under full voluntary control, and that is also more or less *disinterested*. Like other modes of caring, this concern is neither equivalent to nor entailed by any type of feeling or cognition. Loving something is not the same as – or even implicit in – liking it very much, or wanting it very badly, or deriving or expecting to derive great satisfaction from it; nor does loving something necessarily follow from regarding it as especially attractive or desirable, or from judging it to be especially valuable. Rather, love is essentially a somewhat non-voluntary and complex *volitional* structure that bears both upon how a person is disposed to act and upon how he is disposed to manage the motivations and interests by which he is moved. Thus, love not only shapes a person's conduct with respect to whatever it is that he loves. It also guides him in supervising the design and the ordering of his own purposes and priorities.

Disinterested love must be distinguished from the quite different sort of concern for the well-being or flourishing of something that is motivated basically by prudence. An interest in seeing to it that some object is in good shape may not be disinterested at all. On the contrary, it may be grounded in an ulterior expectation that the object will otherwise be incapable of providing various goods or benefits to which the lover aspires. The concern I have in mind is not instrumental in this way. In characterizing it as disinterested, I mean that it is a concern in which the good of the beloved is desired for its own sake rather than for the sake of promoting any other interests.

We commonly assume that it is relationships between people, especially romantic and familial relationships, which provide the most robust and unmistakable instances of love. As I construe love, however, the range of its possible objects is very wide. The beloved object may be a person; but it may also be a concrete individual of another type, such as a country or an institution. It may even be something more abstract, such as a moral or a non-moral ideal to which a person is devoted. Or what is loved may be neither quite like an individual nor quite like an abstraction: for instance, a tradition, or a way of doing things.

Moreover, I believe that it is not a good idea to suppose that romantic relationships provide especially authentic paradigms of love. For one thing, those relationships generally include a number of confusing elements – for instance, various powerful emotions – that do not belong to the essential nature of love but are so vivid and distracting that they make a sharply focused analysis nearly impossible. Furthermore, the attitudes of romantic lovers toward their beloveds are rarely altogether disinterested, and those aspects of their attitudes which are indeed disinterested are generally obscured by more urgent concerns that are conspicuously or covertly self-regarding. Among human relationships, it seems to me that the loving concern of parents for their infants or small children is the mode of caring that comes closest – much closer than romantic or erotically based devotion – to providing pure instances of what I have in mind in speaking of love.

11. Love differs not only from a concern for others that is motivated fundamentally by instrumental or prudential considerations; it also differs from a concern for others that may be unequivocally disinterested, but that is also essentially impersonal or non-specific. Someone who is devoted out of charity to helping the sick or the poor strictly for their own sakes, with no thought of any benefit to anyone or to anything else, may nonetheless be quite indifferent to the identities of those to whom his efforts are addressed. His charitable devotion may perhaps manifest a love of something, but it does not manifest a love of the people whom he endeavors to help. What qualifies them to be beneficiaries of his concern is not their specificity as particular individuals, but merely their membership in a relevant class. For someone who is eager to help the sick or the poor, any sick or poor person will do.

With regard to what we love, on the other hand, that sort of indifference to the identity of the object of concern is out of the question. Substituting some other object for the beloved is not an acceptable and perhaps not even an intelligible option. The significance to the lover of what he loves is not that of an exemplar; its importance to him is not generic, but ineluctably particular. It makes sense for someone who wants to help the sick or the poor to select his beneficiaries randomly from among those sick enough or poor enough to qualify, and to be willing for any good reason to help any one of them rather than any other. Similarly, it makes sense for someone who is proposing to spend time with a friend over a game of chess to consider, as an acceptable alternative, going with his friend for a brisk walk in the country instead; and vice versa. These are acceptable substitutes for each other because the person does not really care about either of them as such. The interest by which he is motivated as he considers them is not an irreducible interest in either of them. It is a more general interest in – let us say – spending an hour or two with his friend in some pursuit that both regard as intrinsically enjoyable.

The situation of a lover is fundamentally different from that of a person who believes that he could satisfy all of his pertinent interests by substituting beneficence to one person for beneficence to another, or by substituting the pleasure of an invigorating walk in the country for the enjoyment of a game of chess. It might really be all the same to the latter person whether he helps this needy person or that one, or whether he spends his time in one recreational way or in another. In contrast, it cannot possibly be all the same to the lover whether he is disinterestedly devoted to what he actually does love or to something else instead. It is only the well-being of his beloved, and not that of anything else, that can possibly satisfy his concern. The needs to which his love gives rise are not disjunctive or generic but rigorously specific and particular.

II. THE NECESSITIES OF LOVE

1. In my first lecture, I spoke of love as a disinterested concern for the well-being or flourishing of a beloved object. My use of the term "disinterested" may perhaps have struck you as somewhat discordant and out of place. After all, the term tends to suggest an austere self-control; the attitude to which it refers seems essentially colorless and lacking in personal warmth. Of course, I did caution against equating love with romance. In fact, I suggested that the objects of love might not be people at all but only abstractions of one sort or another. Still, even if love is not necessarily headlong, hot-blooded, and desperate, there must surely be room in it for a kind of passion and urgency that *disinterestedness* appears to preclude.

Actually, the term "disinterested" was not my first choice. My initial thought was to characterize the concern of the lover for his beloved not as "disinterested" but as "selfless." The phrase "selfless devotion" comes rather naturally, and it gets closer to the subjective intensity and quality of personal involvement that we commonly associate with love. To speak of "disinterested devotion" is suspiciously awkward, and the more natural phrase "disinterested concern" evokes the image of an objectivity and detachment that may well seem antiseptic and too deliberately cool.

There are two reasons, however, why the notion of selflessness will not do. First, its scope is insufficiently inclusive. What is essential to the lover's concern for his beloved is not only that it must be free of any *self*-regarding motive but that it must have no ulterior aim whatsoever. To characterize love as merely *selfless*, then, is not enough. Although the term "disinterested" is – from the point of view of rhetoric – a bit misleading in its tone and associations, it has the virtue of conveying the irrelevance to love not just of considerations that are self-regarding but of *all* considerations that are distinct from the interests of the beloved.

Second, reliance on the term "selfless" to designate an essential characteristic of love makes it very difficult to allow coherently for the possibility that a person may love himself. I suppose that it is fair enough for philosophers to count upon certain terminological peculiarities being more or less tolerantly accepted, but it does seem that tolerance for references to "selfless self-love" is a bit too much to ask. I admit that characterizing self-love as "disinterested" also has a rather fishy sound; but at least it is not blatantly oxymoronic.

The truth is that the notion of self-love as disinterested is really quite straight-forward. To say that a lover is disinterested means simply that he desires the good of his beloved for its own sake rather than for the sake of anything else. Self-love is disinterested in this ordinary sense, then, insofar as a person desires his own well-being for its own sake rather than for the sake of considerations that – as he himself may recognize – are extraneous to his well-being: for instance, that his parents will be pleased if he flourishes, or that it will make him famous or popular or admired by those whose good opinion he desires, or that he expects it to be fun.

In self-love, the lover and his beloved are identical. Therefore, their true interests cannot possibly diverge. This makes it difficult to say that the self-lover is *selfless* in the standard sense in which being selfless entails being unmotivated by any self-regarding concern. On the other hand, it makes it easy to see how his desire for the well-being of his beloved may very well be *disinterested* – that is, unmotivated by any instrumental concern. There is no problem in understanding that a person who desires to flourish may have no ulterior purpose in mind.

From this point of view, love of self may even appear to be in a certain way an exceptionally pure form of love. Not pure in the sense of being especially noble or free of vice, of course, but in the sense of being fully dedicated and unequivocal. For it does seem plausible to suppose that self-love may be the form of love that is least likely to be tainted by motives extraneous to a wholehearted devotion to the interests of the beloved. It also seems to be the variety of love that allows for the most complete and unqualified satisfaction; for it does not leave a place for any distracting conflict between fulfillment of the lover's desire for the well-being of his beloved and fulfillment of his natural concern for his own well-being. Self-love is the only variety of love – except perhaps love of God – that by its very nature cannot possibly require the lover to jeopardize or sacrifice his own true interests.

2. Lovers are not merely concerned for the interests of their beloveds. In a sense that I shall not attempt to define but that I suppose is sufficiently familiar and intelligible, they *identify* those interests as their own. Self-love, in which the interests of the lover and the beloved are *literally* identical, is an unequivocally robust paradigm of this. Self-love is paradigmatic of love in another respect as well.

As I emphasized at the end of my first lecture, the interest of a lover in his beloved is not generic. He does not love his beloved because to do so fulfills certain independently specifiable conditions that qualify it as a member of a certain class. If that were so, then his love would be satisfied by any other objects that might also belong to that class. In fact, however, love of a beloved object cannot be satisfied by anything except that very object itself.

This particularity is saliently unmistakable in the case of self-love. It would be outrageously implausible to take the fact that a person loves himself as a basis for supposing that he will love any other person who is sufficiently similar to him. My love of myself plainly cannot be satisfied by the well-being of someone else who happens to resemble me very closely. The point holds generally for love of any kind. The bond between a lover and his beloved is not transferable. A person cannot coherently accept a substitute for his beloved, even if he is certain that he would find himself loving the substitute just as much as he loves the beloved that it replaces.

The situation of a lover is fundamentally different, then, from that of a person who believes that he could satisfy all of his pertinent interests by substituting the pleasure of an invigorating walk in the country for the enjoyment of a game of chess. It might really be all the same to this person whether he spends his time in one of these recreational ways or in the other. It cannot possibly be all the same to the lover whether he is devoted to what he actually does love or to something else instead.

Now it must not be supposed that this is because loving something entails presuming that it is qualitatively unique. There is a surprisingly widespread tendency to attribute an exaggerated importance to uniqueness. We are accustomed to being told that no two people are exactly alike, that this uniqueness makes every individual especially precious, and that it therefore has a significant bearing upon how people are properly to be treated. It is probably true that if people did not differ from one another they would be less interesting, at least in the sense that there would be less reason for getting to know more of them. It seems to me, however, that the moral value and the moral entitlements of individuals – as distinct from their value as specimens – would not be diminished or altered in the slightest even if they were all exactly alike. In any case, the reason it makes no sense to consider replacing what we love with a substitute is not that loving something entails supposing that it is one of a kind.

Imagine that one day a young woman turns up of whom I discover that she is, and always has been, indistinguishable in every discernible physical, psychical, and behavioral respect from one of my beloved daughters. I would find that bewildering; and it would certainly distress and inhibit me in various ways. But however confusing and disruptive the circumstances might be, they would surely not lead me to conclude that I had all along been somehow wrong to love my daughter because I had erroneously supposed that there was no one quite like her.

169

The reason it makes no sense for a person to consider accepting a substitute for his beloved is not that what he loves happens to be qualitatively distinctive. The reason is that he loves it in its essentially irreproducible *concreteness*. The focus of a person's love is not those general and hence repeatable characteristics that make his beloved *describable*. Rather, it is the specific particularity that makes his beloved *nameable* – something that is more mysterious than describability, and that is in any case manifestly impossible to define.

3. In virtue of this particularity, which cannot conceivably be duplicated or shared and therefore cannot possibly be available elsewhere, the well-being of what a person loves is for him an irreplaceable *necessity*. In other words, the fact that a person has come to love something entails that the satisfaction of his concern for the flourishing of that particular thing is something that he has come to *need*. If he comes to believe that his beloved is not flourishing, then it is unavoidable that this causes him harm. Thus, the well-being of his beloved is important to him; and because it is important to him, it is necessarily in his interest both to regard it as important to him and to desire it. Loving something imposes upon us, then, a kind of necessity. This helps to account, I believe, for an important aspect of love that is often misunderstood.

It is characteristic of our experience of loving that when we love something, there are certain things that we feel we *must* do. Love demands of us that we support and advance the well-being of our beloved, as circumstances make it possible and appropriate for us to do so; and it forbids us to injure our beloved, or to neglect its interests. If we disregard these demands and prohibitions, we feel that we are behaving badly – that we are betraying our love. Now the grip and forcefulness of the requirements that love imposes upon us resemble the forcefulness and grip of moral obligation. In cases of both sorts – those involving love and those involving duty – it seems to us that we are not free simply to do as we please or as we wish; love and duty alike generate in us a sense that we have no choice but to do what they require. In a case of either kind, dereliction on our part both makes us feel that we are somehow at fault and is generally acknowledged to warrant an adverse estimate of our personal character.

The similarity between the ways in which we experience and respond to the requirements of moral obligation and to those of love tends to support a rather common presumption that these requirements are essentially of a single kind. However, this presumption is incorrect. The authority that stands behind the imperatives of love is not at all the same, in fact, as the authority with which moral imperatives are imbued. Betraying what one loves is frequently taken to be fundamentally a moral offense; but it is not. The commands of love are not moral imperatives. The necessities that grip us in the one sort of case have grounds different from the necessities that grip us in the other.

4. Much is often made of the "special" moral obligations that are allegedly entailed by love for another person, and by variants of love such as friendship. I doubt that there are any such special obligations. I do not by any means doubt, of course, that people do ordinarily have important moral responsibilities to those whom they love. Our relationships with those we love are frequently intimate, and intimate relationships lead inevitably to the formation of expectations and modes of dependency by which unusually weighty obligations are engendered. Because of the peculiarly intense and relatively unguarded character of the relationships within which they arise, these obligations tend to be more serious than those that are normally generated within relationships of lesser consequence. Nevertheless, it seems to me that they are of the very same kind. In my judgment, there is no distinctive type or category of moral responsibility that is particularly grounded in or derivative from love.

For one thing, love may make no difference to the beloved. I may love a woman from a distance, with no opportunity to affect her in any way; and she may have no inkling even that I exist. Then my love has no direct or indirect consequences for her at all; and, more to the point, it generates in her no dependencies or expectations. Surely the mere fact that I love her would not, in such a case, make me in any way obligated to her. This leaves open the possibility that my love does nonetheless morally obligate me in certain ways, though it does not obligate me *to her.* Instead of examining this possibility, which does not seem to me to be especially promising, I wish to suggest that there is a better explanation of the unquestionable truth that loving someone or something does generally – even in cases of distant and, so to speak, immaculate love – entail that there are certain things that we *must* and that we *must not do.* A more authentic and illuminating account of the necessities of love can be given, I believe, without resorting to the notion of moral obligation.

The account I have in mind is grounded in two of the ways in which love is important to us. First of all, what we love is important to us by virtue of the fact that we identify the interests of our beloved as our own, and that we therefore encounter psychic obstacles to allowing or causing our beloved to be harmed that are similar in feeling and power to the obstacles that we encounter against harming ourselves or allowing ourselves to be harmed. When we believe that the interests of our beloved are at stake, we find that there are certain things we must do and that there are certain things we cannot bring ourselves to do. These are special cases of the powerful volitional constraint that we naturally experience in matters concerning the advancement or protection of what we take to be our own interests.

Besides the fact that the well-being of what we love is so important to us, because of our identification of it with our own well-being, there is the separate and perhaps even deeper fact that *loving itself* is important to us. Quite apart from our need for the well-being of our beloved, we need to love. In order to satisfy this need, we must do whatever loving requires. It is with this second ground of the necessities of love that I shall be, from now on, mainly concerned. I shall begin by considering another pertinent aspect of love – namely, that the importance that loving has for us does not derive (at least, not exclusively) from any appreciation on our part of the value of what we love.

5. There are many instances in which something that would not otherwise have much (or even any) value to us *becomes* valuable to us (or becomes more valuable to us) from the very circumstance that we love it. No doubt love may sometimes be aroused as a response to the perceived value of its object. But loving may also be itself a creator of value. I think this is true with respect to the value to us of life – that is, of our own lives. Living is so important to us, not because it has some great value inherent in it, but just because – thanks to natural selection – we love living. We may choose to reject and destroy our lives, of course, if they become too hateful or too harsh. Even in such cases, however, our love of living is shown by the fact that we would greatly prefer that our lives be more tolerable rather than give them up.

If we did not love living, we would need another reason to live. Such a reason might perhaps be provided by some compelling "project" to which we were devoted that served to propel us into the future and without which there would be no force motivating us to go on at all. In that case, the value to us of living would be merely instrumental. For a person who loves living, on the other hand, life is valuable for its own sake. Suspending his eagerness to live while wondering whether he has any other reason to go on would strike him as a clear case of having one thought too many.[1]

Life is not the only thing, of course, that we *make* important to ourselves, or more important to us than it would otherwise be, simply by caring about it. The value to me of certain human beings would also be considerably less than it is if those individuals were not my beloved children. My children are immeasurably more important to me, just in virtue of my love for them, than they would be if I did not in fact love them as I do.

Now I want to emphasize that, besides the fact that *my children* are important to me, there is also the quite different and no less significant fact that *loving my children* is important to me. My love for them is an element of my life that I greatly value. My life improved in a variety of ways, and life itself became more important to me, when I began to love my children. Moreover, it would surely be a mistake to suppose that the value to me of loving my children is a response to their being independently valuable to me. There may be some truth in that supposition, but not much. It is not fundamentally because I recognize how valuable or important

1 I suppose it is obvious that I am alluding to some well-known observations made by Bernard Williams in "Persons, Character, and Morality": cf. his *Moral Luck* (Cambridge University Press, 1981), passim.

to me my children are that I love them. My love for them is not derivative from their value or their importance to me. On the contrary, the relationship goes essentially the other way. My children are so valuable and important to me just because I do in fact love them. The point is that loving is valuable *inherently* and for its own sake. It does not enhance our lives simply by connecting us to other valuable things, or by fulfilling some presumed responsibility to care about whatever things have value on their own. Loving is valuable in itself, and not only in virtue of the value of its objects. Other things being equal, our lives would be worse without it.

Needless to say, the other things are generally not equal. Loving is therefore not only inherently valuable; it is also risky. Lovers are vulnerable to profoundly distressing anxieties and sorrows when, in one way or another, things do not go well for their love. So they have to be careful. For an infinite being, secure in its omnipotence, even the most indiscriminate promiscuity would be safe. God need not, out of prudence, cautiously forgo certain opportunities for enjoying the goodness of loving. On some accounts, God's creative activity is aroused and guided by an entirely uninhibited and inexhaustible love that desires an altogether unconstricted plenitude in which every possible object of love is included. What God loves is simply Being of any kind. This divinely uninhibited creative love of Being is entirely indiscriminate, and hence it is incompatible with any goal other than limitless expansion of the varieties of existence. To the extent that God's love is indiscriminate, His creation can have no motive or purpose beyond an utterly promiscuous urge to love without boundary or constraint. Curiously, it would seem that, insofar as God is love, the universe has no point other than simply to be.

In any event, it is clear that finite creatures like ourselves cannot afford to be so heedlessly extravagant. When we permit ourselves from time to time to incur the vulnerabilities that loving entails, we need to exercise a defensive selectivity and restraint. It is important that we be careful to whom and to what we give our love. If we were omnipotent agents, we would be free of all passivity, and so nothing could happen to us. Then we would have nothing to fear. As it is, however, we cannot afford to love *everything*. In view of the harms to which loving exposes us, we cannot be – as God may be – recklessly indiscriminate in what we love.

6. It remains true nonetheless, of course, that loving is valuable to the lover for its own sake, regardless of the character of its object, and regardless also of the fact that its value to the lover may be outweighed by the burdens and injuries that it imposes upon him. I would like to be able to explain just why it is that loving has this intrinsic value. We need to understand just what it is about loving that accounts for its importance in our lives. Presumably, the explanation has something to do with the complex fact that loving entails both volitional constraint and disinterested identification with the well-being of the beloved. But it is not clear

to me why – except perhaps in the case of self-love – either of these features, or the two combined, should be so precious to us.

In any case, as I shall simply stipulate, without loving in one or more of its several modes life for us would be intolerably unshaped and empty. For our own sakes, we *need* to love; otherwise, our lives will be miserably deprived. This means that we need for our own sakes to conduct ourselves in those ways that constitute loving. Suppose that someone fails to obey the commands of love by neglecting or refusing to behave in some way as love requires. In that case, his behavior lacks an element that is essentially constitutive of loving. Therefore he is not actually loving at all. In other words, insofar as a person is untrue to what he loves he is not truly loving it. And to the extent that he fails to do what love requires, and hence fails to love, he necessarily loses from his life the immeasurable value of loving.

This has nothing to do with the risk of losing the benefits of reciprocity – that is, the benefits of being loved. So far as *those* benefits are concerned, the false lover may in fact continue to enjoy them. What he is inescapably bound to lose are not the benefits that may be provided to him by his beloved, but those which are inherent in his own activity of loving. The specific and distinctive reason against betraying what we love has no more to do with the risks of retaliation than it does with the penalties for violating the moral law. The reason we must not betray what we love is that we must not betray ourselves.

7. It may perhaps seem that there is a certain inconsistency between my claim that the authority of love derives from the irreplaceable value to us of loving and the notion that it is essential to the nature of loving that it be disinterested or, in cases other than those of self-love, selfless. After all, how can the attitudes and actions of a person be disinterested or selfless if they are motivated by considerations of such profound self-interest? But suppose a man tells a woman that his love for her is the only thing that makes his life worthwhile. She is surely unlikely to feel – if she actually believes this – that what the man tells her means that he is exploiting her and that he cares about her only because it makes him feel better to do so. She will not think that the selflessness of his love for her is contradicted by the fact that loving her satisfies a deep need of his life. The fact that loving her is so important to him will not strike her as implying that he does not actually love her at all or that his love for her is tainted by self-regarding concerns. The apparent conflict between selflessness and self-interest disappears once it is understood that what serves the self-interest of the lover is, precisely, his selflessness. The benefit of loving accrues to him only if he is genuinely selfless. He fulfills his own need only because in loving he forgets himself.

8. Although the requirements of love and those of duty do not have the same source, there are many situations in which they coincide. For example, under normal circumstances parents are obligated by impersonal principles of morality

to provide for the welfare of their children. Parents who love their children generally acknowledge that they have that duty. However, their readiness to accept the moral obligation to care for their children may have nothing to do with what actually motivates them as they deal with their children. Loving parents do not ordinarily look after their children out of duty, but out of love. They treat their children responsibly because they love them, not because they are morally obligated to do so.

There is a significant formal difference between instances of acting out of duty and instances of acting out of love. This difference pertains to the distinctive structures of the exercises in practical reasoning by which actions of the two sorts are characteristically justified or explained. Consider two situations in which someone gives money to a needy person. Suppose that in both situations the money is given just because the recipient needs it; and suppose also that it is given with the sole intention of helping him. The action and the reason for performing it are in both cases, then, the same: money is given, and it is given to help someone who needs it. But now suppose that the two situations differ in that the donor in one case gives the money out of duty whereas in the other the donor gives it out of love. What is the difference, in circumstances like these, between acting out of duty and acting out of love?

Let us begin inquiring into the difference by considering why the supposition that money will be helpful to the needy person *counts* with each donor as a reason for him to make his gift. In the case of the donor who is motivated by duty, it counts as a reason for him to do what he does because he considers himself morally obliged to help the needy person. For the donor who acts out of love, the fact that the money will help the needy person counts as a reason to give it because the needy person is someone whom he loves. Up to this point, the practical reasoning in the one case parallels that in the other. Both donors give money to the needy person for the same reason: namely, that the money will be helpful to him. This counts as a reason for the one donor because he believes it is his duty to help the needy person. It counts as a reason for the other donor to help the needy person because the donor loves him.

Now there is an important difference between these two explanations of why the dutiful and the loving donors regard the fact that the money will help the needy person as a reason for giving it to him. In the deliberations of the donor who acts out of duty, his belief that he has a duty to help the needy person functions for him as a reason only because he is inclined or desires to do whatever he considers himself morally obligated to do. This inclination may derive from a determination on his part to lead a virtuous life, or it may be simply an expression of his natural respect for the moral law. Regardless of its source, it is distinct from his belief that it is his duty to help the needy person; and it is only when the fact that he wants to do his duty combines with this belief that the belief grounds his decision to act as he does. In other words, unless he is actively interested in fulfilling his moral obligations – at least in situations like the current one – the fact that he believes he has a duty to help the needy person will not lead him to decide to help that person.

The deliberations of the donor who acts out of love, on the other hand, involve no third element beyond his belief that the money will help the needy person and the fact that he loves that person. For both donors, the fact that the money will help the needy person serves as a reason for giving it. The explanation of *why* this serves as a reason when the moving force is love, however, is nothing more than the fact that the needy person is someone whom the donor loves. No additional element is needed to mediate between his love for the needy person on the one hand and, on the other, his recognition that he is provided with a reason for giving money to the needy person by the fact that the money will help to meet that person's need.

The immediacy of the linkage between loving and what counts as a reason for doing things that help the beloved is part of what *essentially constitutes* loving. A person will not take the fact that a certain action would fulfill a duty as a reason for performing that action unless the person has a desire to do what duty demands. On the other hand, it is merely a tautology that a lover takes the fact that a certain action would be helpful to his beloved as a reason for performing the action. His taking it as a reason for performing the action is not the outcome of an inference. That it provides him with this reason is not a conclusion that the lover reaches by reasoning from the premise that he loves his beloved. His taking it as a reason is a constitutive aspect of his loving: to love a person *is* essentially (in part) to take the fact that a certain action would be helpful to that person as a reason for performing it.

It is no more than an elementary redundancy, then, to say that the donor who acts out of love takes the fact that the money will help the needy person as a reason for giving it to him. His love of the needy person in part explains why he helps him, but it does not serve him as a reason for helping. In this respect he differs from the dutiful donor, for whom the fact that helping the needy person is his duty does serve as a reason by virtue of his desire to do what duty demands of him.

9. I want to turn now to consider certain aspects of the relationship between love and its object. Love requires, of course, an object that is loved. By virtue of the fact that love cannot be satisfied by anything other than its object, the beloved object is needed by the person who loves it. Because the person needs it, the object of his love is necessarily important and valuable to him. In addition to making what he loves valuable to him, his loving is valuable to him for its own sake. As I have been maintaining, loving has an intrinsic value that does not derive from the value of its object. Needless to say, however, loving has this intrinsic value only because it has an object. Indeed, loving is inherently valuable precisely on account of the fact that it is focused upon its object.

My point here is not a merely logical or conceptual one. To be sure, it is logically or conceptually impossible to love without loving something; so it can certainly be said that the value of loving depends upon the beloved object in the rather uninteresting sense that without the object there would be no loving at all, and hence no intrinsically valuable loving. What I am suggesting, however, is that the beloved object is an essential and indispensable condition of the specific kind of value that loving possesses.

The beloved object is not only a logically or conceptually indispensable condition of the possibility of loving at all. The value of loving is not the value of a pleasurable activity, which might be experienced and appreciated without attending to anything beyond the activity itself. It is the value of being in a certain kind of relationship. The fact that the lover is in just this sort of relationship to the beloved object does not merely satisfy an element of the definition of love. It is what provides loving with its distinctive value. Thus, although loving is indeed valuable intrinsically, regardless of the value of its object, at the same time it depends upon its object for the value that is inherent in it.

The relationships of independence and interdependence between the value of loving and the value of its object are curiously entangled. They strike me as analogous to certain peculiar and rather neglected features of the relationships between means and ends. Just as the value to us of loving is not straightforwardly derivative from or determined by the value to us of what we love, so the value to us of using means is not wholly derivative from or determined by the value to us of the ends that using effective means enables us to attain. Just as loving has a value that is inherent in it as such and regardless of the character or value of its object, so it is important to us for its own sake to engage in the use of effective means regardless of the specific character or value of the outcomes at which we are aiming.

10. As we need to love, so do we need to engage in productive activity – that is, work. It makes a great difference, of course, whether what we love or produce is worthy of our love or of our effort. It also makes a great difference, needless to say, whether the contingent consequences of our loving and working are on the whole beneficial or injurious to us and to others. Quite apart from considerations of these kinds, however, it is important to us for its own sake that there be something that we love. And it is similarly important to us for its own sake that we have some kind of work to do.

In my view, the importance to us of having means is not simply tantamount to the importance to us of attaining our ends. It is a mistake to presume that the value of a means is exhausted by the value of the ends to which the means lead. What I am urging here must not be confused with the commonplace that an activity possessing instrumental value may independently possess intrinsic value as well – in the way, for instance, that vigorous exercise may be enjoyable for its own sake quite apart from the fact that it is also conducive to good health, or in the way that food may be tasty as well as nourishing. The point I am making is that certain kinds of activity – such as productive work – are inherently valuable not simply *in addition to* being instrumentally valuable but *precisely because of* their instrumental value.

Vigorous workouts and tasty meals are valuable to us for their own sakes alone simply because the exercise or the food is enjoyable, without taking at all into account whether they are also valuable because they conduce to good health. On the other hand, work is valuable to us for its own sake regardless of whether we enjoy the activity in which it consists. The value that working possesses inherently or as such is not independent of the fact that the activity is instrumentally valuable. Quite to the contrary, it is inherently valuable only in virtue of the fact that it is useful.

Without the goal-directed activity that is the locus of instrumental value, we would lack the indispensably foundational sense that we have of ourselves as rational agents. Our lives would be insupportably devoid of the cohesion and meaning that are generated by solving problems, by making decisions, and by carrying out plans. The activity in which we engage can serve these foundational needs only insofar as it is guided by purposes or aims at products, but it is valuable to us not only for the sake of its products or goals. It is also valuable to us in itself, because it is inherently important to us to have something useful to do.

The fact that there is intrinsic value in having something useful to do suggests another rather surprising thought – namely, that even what we regard as our most final and unconditioned ends may also appropriately be considered to be means. If we had no ends, after all, there would be no such thing as useful activity. Our ends are necessary conditions, therefore, of there being something useful for us to do. It is a familiar saying that "all action is for the sake of some end." It may also be said that all ends are for the sake of action.

We need ends in order to be able to engage in purposeful activity. From this point of view, a goal or end is an indispensable means to something – namely, useful activity – that is inherently valuable. The fact that something possesses the terminal value that is characteristic of an end necessarily provides it, accordingly, with instrumental value too. Thus, paradoxical as it may seem, final ends necessarily possess instrumental value just by virtue of their terminal value as ends, and means are inherently important to us as final ends just by virtue of the instrumental value that they possess as means.

11. The fact that we have a variety of needs, and that we are therefore vulnerable to numerous kinds of harm, requires us to be more or less circumspect with regard to both love and work. We cannot permit ourselves to be altogether thoughtless or impulsive in selecting their objects. This suggests a consideration that must be acknowledged to have a certain degree of justificatory force when we are considering what to love or what work to do. The consideration I have in mind has less to

do with evaluating the merits of possible objects of love or work than it has to do with a judgment about ourselves. This judgment concerns what we are in fact *able* to love or what kind of work we are in fact *capable* of doing.

Love and work are important to us for their own sakes, whatever their objects may be. It follows from this that one good reason in favor of a certain prospective object of love is simply that it is *possible* for us to love it; and it follows similarly that one good reason in favor of undertaking a prospective type or task of productive activity is simply that it is *possible* for us to engage in it. Whatever it is we love, and whatever the work that we do, we will benefit at least from the inherent value of loving or working.

It is therefore always a good reason for loving something that we find it lovable, meaning by this not that we regard it as especially worthy of love but just that we are capable of loving it. Of course, the reason may not be good enough; it may be outweighed by other considerations. However, the possibility of loving something is in every instance a reason that tends, at least minimally, to justify doing so. The same thing holds for work. The fact that a person is capable of doing a certain kind or piece of work is always a good reason, though of course not a decisive one, for him to do it.

12. I will conclude with a few observations concerning Thomas Hobbes's idea that happiness consists entirely in getting what one wants. His account of happiness is actually nuanced by a complexity that Hobbes himself introduces. The truth of the matter, he says, is that simply getting whatever a person happens from time to time to want does not really suffice to make the person happy. Someone who always manages to get what he wants may nonetheless be occasionally, or even chronically, uncertain that he *will* get it. Hobbes appreciates that this anxiety concerning whether one *will* prosper, even if it turns out that one *does* prosper, is incompatible with felicity. Thus he insists that our happiness requires, not only that we satisfy our desires, but also that we be steadily confident that we will do so.

In addition to a succession of particular desires for one thing or another, we have, then, a more generic higher-order desire to feel assured that our particular desires will be satisfied. As Hobbes puts it: "the object of a man's desire is . . . to assure forever the way of his future desire; and therefore the voluntary actions and inclinations of all men tend, not only to the procuring, but also to the assuring of a contented life." Every person has at all times a standing desire to be capable of satisfying any and every one of the more specific desires that he may during his lifetime come to have. "So," Hobbes declares, "I put for a general inclination of all mankind, a perpetual and restless desire of power after power, that ceaseth only in death." This endless desire for power is not at all, as Hobbes construes it, megalomaniacal or perverse. It is a natural and more or less reasonable desire to be confident that we will be able to attain the endlessly successive and unpredictable goals to which we will in the course of our lives aspire.

The relationship between the value of confidence and the values of the various goals that we are confident of being able to attain parallels the relationships between the values to us of love and work and the values to us of what we love and of what we work to achieve. Confidence is a matter of feeling that one has sufficient power – in other words, the necessary means – for getting what one wants. It goes without saying that power is useful. However, as Hobbes makes clear, the value of power is not only instrumental. Because the possession of power is an indispensable constituent of happiness, it is itself an end that is valuable in its own right and for its own sake. Now what makes the possession of power an essential constituent of happiness is simply, of course, the fact that power is instrumentally valuable. The only reason we require it in order to be happy, and accordingly value it as an end in itself, is that it is valuable to us as a means. Like loving and like working, the possession of power derives inherent value from the fact that it is instrumental for the attainment of outcomes that are valued for their own sakes.

Printed in the United States
81570LV00002B/112-120